LEISURE ARTS
PRESENTS

# THE SPIRIT OF CHRISTMAS

CREATIVE
HOLIDAY IDEAS

BOOK TWELVE

*For generations, the holidays have been a time for singing joyous carols and wishing glad tidings to one and all. We wrap and adorn presents to give as tokens of love and good cheer, and pause to remember the true meaning of the season with those we hold dear. In this enchanting volume, we bring you a medley of ways to spread the merriment of the season throughout your home. Turn the page and discover festive trimmings to complement a variety of decors, unique gifts wrapped up in style, and delicious recipes to tempt the taste buds of those who join in your celebrations. May these Yuletide visions inspire your holiday and bring Christmas blessings in abundance!*

LEISURE ARTS, INC.
Little Rock, Arkansas

# THE SPIRIT OF CHRISTMAS®
## BOOK TWELVE

*"...and it was always said of him, that he knew how to keep Christmas well, if any man alive possessed the knowledge. May that be truly said of us, and all of us!"*

— From *A Christmas Carol* by Charles Dickens

## EDITORIAL STAFF

**Vice President and Editor-in-Chief:** Anne Van Wagner Childs
**Executive Director:** Sandra Graham Case
**Design Director:** Patricia Wallenfang Sowers
**Test Kitchen Director/Foods Editor:** Celia Fahr Harkey, R.D.
**Editorial Director:** Susan Frantz Wiles
**Publications Director:** Kristine Anderson Mertes
**Creative Art Director:** Gloria Bearden
**Senior Graphics Art Director:** Melinda Stout

### PRODUCTION
#### DESIGN
**Designers:** Katherine Prince Horton, Sandra Spotts Ritchie, Anne Pulliam Stocks, Linda Diehl Tiano, and Rebecca Sunwall Werle
**Executive Assistants:** Debra Smith and Billie Steward
**Craft Assistant:** Melanie Vaughan

#### FOODS
**Assistant Foods Editor:** Jane Kenner Prather
**Test Kitchen Home Economist:** Rose Glass Klein
**Test Kitchen Coordinator:** Nora Faye Taylor
**Test Kitchen Assistants:** Camille T. Alstadt and Tanya Harris

#### TECHNICAL
**Managing Editor:** Charlotte Loftin
**Senior Technical Writer:** Susan McManus Johnson
**Technical Writers:** Sherry Ford, Jennifer L. Hobbs, Briget Laskowski, Laura Lee Powell, and Barbara McClintock Vechik
**Technical Associates:** Tammy Kreimeyer and Christopher McCarty
**Production Assistant:** Sharon Gillam

### EDITORIAL
**Managing Editor:** Linda L. Trimble
**Senior Associate Editor:** Janice Teipen Wojcik
**Associate Editor:** Stacey Robertson Marshall
**Assistant Editor:** Terri Leming Davidson

### ART
**Book/Magazine Graphics Art Director:** Diane M. Hugo
**Senior Graphics Artist:** Michael A. Spigner
**Photography Stylists:** Pam Choate, Sondra Daniel, Laura Reed, Karen Smart Hall, Aurora Huston, Courtney Jones, and Christina Myers

### PROMOTIONS
**Managing Editors:** Alan Caudle and Marjorie Ann Lacy
**Associate Editors:** Steven M. Cooper, Dixie L. Morris, Jennifer Ertl Wobser, Ellen J. Clifton, and Marie Trotter
**Designer:** Dale Rowett
**Art Director:** Linda Lovette Smart
**Production Artist:** Leslie Loring Krebs
**Publishing Systems Administrator:** Cynthia M. Lumpkin
**Publishing Systems Assistant:** Susan Mary Gray and Robert Walker

## BUSINESS STAFF

**Publisher:** Bruce Akin
**Vice President and General Manager:** Thomas L. Carlisle
**Retail Sales Director:** Richard Tignor
**Vice President, Retail Marketing:** Pam Stebbins
**Retail Marketing Director:** Margaret Sweetin

**Retail Customer Services Manager:** Carolyn Pruss
**General Merchandise Manager:** Cathy Laird
**Vice President, Finance:** Tom Siebenmorgen
**Distribution Director:** Rob Thieme

Library of Congress Catalog Card Number 98-65188
International Standard Book Number 1-57486-119-0

# TABLE OF CONTENTS

THE SIGHTS OF CHRISTMAS

*Page 6*

# TABLE OF CONTENTS
## (Continued)

# THE SHARING OF CHRISTMAS

*Page 94*

# THE TASTES OF CHRISTMAS

*Page 114*

# THE SIGHTS OF CHRISTMAS

*The magical sights of Christmas enchant and excite us with their dazzling display while reminding us of holiday joys gone by. From elegant bows and shimmering organza to rustic spices and playful snow people, our imaginative offerings will inspire you to energize your decor with sparkling finery. Or you can explore the richness of our holiday heritage with novel interpretations of nostalgic themes. Our captivating collections contain creative Yuletide ornaments for the tree, along with a colorful collage of stockings, garlands, wreaths, centerpieces, and more for your home's holiday attire. Add to the marvelous magic of this joyous season with inspiration from our irresistible designs!*

# COUNTRY SPICE

Coated in seasonings and spice and everything nice, our Country Spice collection
is chock-full of charming items to wrap your home — from foyer to family room — with inviting
holiday spirit. Warm, friendly evergreens create a serene Christmas scene, complemented
by a handsome wreath, a homespun stocking, and a savory assortment of candles in exciting
shapes, textures, and containers. You'll also find one-of-a-kind accents, like our winsome
spice angel with delicate dried fruit wings and cinnamon heart and stocking
ornaments dotted with sweet-smelling spices. Instructions for the projects
shown here and on the following pages begin on page 14.

Create an entrance with aromatic appeal by adding our cinnamon heart ornaments and spice angel to a boxwood
**Country Spice Wreath** *(page 14)*. Bright canella berries, fragrant cinnamon sticks, dried orange slices, and torn-fabric
bows are also nestled in the sprigs of greenery.

8

Seasoned with a comfortable, down-home ambience, our **Country Spice Tree** *(page 14)* is brimming with original ornaments such as cranberry-haired **Spice Angels** *(page 14)*, charming **Cinnamon Stocking and Heart Ornaments** *(page 16)*, rustic **Spice-Covered Apples** *(page 15)*, and golden **Wax Star Ornaments** *(page 15)*. The lively tree has a sprinkling of metal gelatin molds, **Spiced Spoon Ornaments** *(page 15)*, and **Orange Peel Spirals** *(page 14)*. Clever **Spice Buckets** *(page 14)* are laden with spices and bows, and a **Spicy Fruit Garland** *(page 17)* holds dried fruit and spices. The tree is capped with our large **Apple-Cinnamon Star Tree Topper** *(page 16)*, which features a star-shaped gelatin mold *(shown on page 9)*.

10

Our **Patchwork Cuff Stocking** *(page 17)* has an easy-to-stitch piecework cuff and coordinating welting. Set off the stocking's appealing country look with one of our spice angels, decorated with imaginative orange-slice wings, a fragrant spice-filled bag, and cinnamon stick legs.

Bring the simple serenity of holidays past into your home with **Spiced Candles** *(page 16)*. Glowing with hospitality and sentiment, this mood-setting arrangement is enhanced with clever containers and accents — a verse-trimmed wooden box, pewter holders with wax star ornaments, and gelatin-mold or jar-lid bases.

Crowned with our small apple-cinnamon star, this **Scented Tabletop Tree** *(page 15)* is embellished with a cornucopia of treasures, including wooden beads, torn-fabric bows, our orange peel spirals, and spice bags decorated with holly leaves, cinnamon, and fruit. *(Opposite, top)* Fill a cozy corner with **Spice Candles** *(page 16)* by arranging votive candles in jars filled with dried fruit, spices, and grains. *(Opposite, bottom)* Stuff appliquéd fabric pockets with rice and cloves to make **Spicy Mug Mats** *(page 15)*, and glue sweet-smelling spices to faux fruit for **Spice-Covered Apples and Oranges** *(page 15)*.

# COUNTRY SPICE TREE

(Shown on page 9)

Those scrumptious smells aren't just coming from the kitchen! Our seven-foot-tall Country Spice Tree is laden with heavenly aromas befitting the holiday season.

Spice Angels with dried orange-slice wings silently keep watch over Christmas proceedings while sitting among limbs draped with Spicy Fruit Garland (page 17). Spice-Covered Apples clothed in cinnamon hang upon the tree. Following the country theme, gelatin tins serve as ornaments while Wax Star Ornaments add golden warmth.

We used our own special recipes to whip up Cinnamon Stocking and Heart Ornaments (page 16), Spiced Spoon Ornaments, Orange Peel Spirals, and little Spice Buckets to hang all over the tree. The scent from our large Apple-Cinnamon Star Tree Topper (page 16) will lead many well-wishers to the hub of the Yuletide festivities.

For bows to tuck among the aromatic branches, we used pinking shears to cut 4" x 6" pieces from cotton fabric and tied a piece of twine around the center of each fabric piece. To complete the ensemble, we wrapped a country print fabric around the base of our spicy evergreen.

## COUNTRY SPICE WREATH

(Shown on page 8)

**You will need** 22" lengths of $^3/_4$"w to 1$^1/_4$"w torn fabric strips, hot glue gun, dried orange slices, cinnamon sticks, dried canella berries, cedar sprigs, Cinnamon Heart Ornaments without wire hangers (page 16), Spice Angel, and a 24" dia. boxwood wreath.

1. Tie fabric strips into bows.
2. Arrange and glue cedar sprigs, orange slices, cinnamon sticks, canella berries, bows, heart ornaments, and angel to wreath.

# SPICE BUCKETS

(Shown on page 10)

**For each bucket,** you will need silver spray paint, hammer and nail, 12" of heavy-gauge floral wire, pliers, hot glue gun, cedar sprigs, dried canella berries, cinnamon sticks, small pinecones, and dried star anise.

**For each wide bucket,** you will **also** need a wide, clean can (we used 3"h x 2$^1/_2$" dia. cans), bay leaves, fabric to wrap around can, raffia, and a $^7/_8$" dia. button.

**For each narrow bucket,** you will **also** need a narrow, clean can (we used 3$^1/_2$"h x 2$^1/_8$" dia. cans), 16" length of 1"w torn fabric strip, and a $^1/_2$" dia. button.

1. Spray paint wire silver; allow to dry. Use hammer and nail to punch a hole near rim on each side of can. Insert wire ends through holes in can. Use pliers to bend back wire ends.
2. For each wide bucket, measure height of can; subtract 1". Measure around can; add 1". Tear a fabric strip the determined measurements. Wrap strip around can; glue to secure. Tie raffia into a bow around can. Glue button to knot of bow. Glue cedar sprigs, bay leaves, canella berries, and cinnamon sticks in bucket. Glue one pinecone to base of bucket handle and a star anise to cedar sprig.
3. For each narrow bucket, tie fabric strip into a bow. Glue bow to bucket near rim. Glue button to knot of bow. Glue cedar sprigs, canella berries, and cinnamon sticks in bucket. Glue one pinecone to base of bucket handle.

# ORANGE PEEL SPIRALS

(Shown on page 10)

**You will need** large citrus zester, oranges, $^3/_8$" dia. wooden dowel, and a cookie sheet.

1. Use zester to peel long strips of orange rind. Curl strips around dowel and place on cookie sheet. Bake at 150° for six to eight hours.
2. Remove cookie sheet from oven. Allow rinds to completely cool before removing from dowel.

# SPICE ANGELS

(Shown on page 10)

**For each angel,** you will need tracing paper, muslin for head, print fabric for arms and body, polyester fiberfill, linen scraps for bag, fabric marking pen, cedar sprig, one 3" and two 7" cinnamon sticks, floral wire, wire cutters, 14" of $^1/_2$"w fusible web tape, hot glue gun, dried cranberries, dried orange slice, 10" of natural raffia, black permanent fine-point marker, and a red colored pencil.

**Note:** Use a $^1/_4$" seam allowance for all sewing unless otherwise indicated.

1. Trace head and body patterns onto tracing paper; cut out. Use patterns and follow **Sewing Shapes**, page 158, to make head and body. Stuff body and head with fiberfill. Sew head opening closed.
2. Cut two 2$^1/_2$" squares from linen for bag. With right sides together and edges even, sew three sides together. Turn bag right side out. Fringe top edge. Place cedar sprig and 3" long cinnamon stick in bag. Wrap a length of floral wire around top of bag; twist ends to secure.
3. Cut a 1" x 14" strip from body fabric. Fuse web tape along one long edge on wrong side of strip. Matching wrong sides, fold strip in half lengthwise; fuse together. Tie a knot 1" from each end of strip.
4. Glue cranberries to head for hair. Glue head and bag to front of body. Glue center of fabric strip to back of body and knotted ends to front of bag for arms. Cut orange slice in half; glue to back of body for wings. Glue ends of 7" long cinnamon sticks into body opening for legs. Tie raffia into a bow; glue bow to neck.
5. Use marker to draw face. Use red pencil to add color to cheeks.

HEAD

BODY

leave open

## SPICY MUG MATS
(Shown on page 12)

**For each mug mat,** you will need paper-backed fusible web, fabrics for binding and appliqués, two 5½" squares of linen, red embroidery floss, ½ cup uncooked rice, and one tablespoon whole cloves.

**Note:** Match right sides and raw edges and use a ¼" seam allowance for all sewing.

1. Using patterns, follow **Making Appliqués**, page 158, to make leaves and berries appliqués. Arrange appliqués on right side of one linen square; fuse in place. Use three strands of floss to work one **French Knot**, page 157, in center of each berry.
2. Cut four 1" x 6" fabric strips. Press all edges of each strip ¼" to wrong side.
3. Place wrong sides of linen squares together. Center and pin one strip along one side edge of mat front. Center and pin a second strip along opposite edge. Stitch strips to mat through all thicknesses.
4. Fold pressed edges of strips over to back of mat, covering seam allowances; hand sew in place.
5. Center and pin one strip along bottom edge of mat front. Stitch through all thicknesses. Fold pressed edge to back of mat, covering seam allowance; hand sew in place.
6. Fill mat with rice and cloves. Centering and pinning strip along top edge, repeat Step 5 to finish top edge of mat.

## SCENTED TABLETOP TREE
(Shown on page 13)

**You will need** a galvanized metal bucket, spray primer, burgundy and black acrylic paint, paintbrush, natural sponge, wood tone spray, three-foot-tall artificial tree, floral foam, Spanish moss, 8" lengths of ¾"w to 1¼"w torn fabric strips, small artificial apples, dried star anise, floral wire, wire cutters, burgundy wooden bead garland, Orange Peel Spirals, Aromatic Spice Bags (page 17), small Apple-Cinnamon Star Tree Topper (page 16), and a hot glue gun.

**Note:** Allow primer, paint, and wood tone spray to dry between applications.

1. Spray bucket with primer. Painting in a horizontal direction only, use paintbrush to paint outside of bucket burgundy. Use dampened sponge to lightly stamp black paint around bucket. Spray bucket with wood tone spray.
2. Place tree in bucket. Fill bucket with floral foam around tree to secure. Cover foam with Spanish moss.
3. For each apple ornament, tie a torn fabric strip into a bow around stem; glue to secure. Glue one star anise to knot of bow. Cut a 6" length of wire; twist ends together to form loop for hanger. Glue hanger to apple stem.
4. Drape bead garland on tree. Hang apples, Orange Peel Spirals, and Aromatic Spice Bags on tree. Use wire at back of tree topper to attach small Apple-Cinnamon Star Tree Topper to tree.

## SPICE-COVERED APPLES AND ORANGES
(Shown on page 12)

**You will need** ground cinnamon, shallow pan, craft glue, artificial apples and oranges, and ground cloves.

1. For each spice-covered apple, sprinkle cinnamon in pan. Leaving some areas bare, spread a thin layer of glue over fruit. Roll fruit in cinnamon; allow to dry.
2. For each spice-covered orange, repeat Step 1, using cloves in place of cinnamon.

## WAX STAR ORNAMENTS
(Shown on page 10)

**For each ornament,** you will need a 3½" star-shaped gelatin mold, candle release, saucepan, a can for melting wax, yellow wax chips, 10" of jute twine, and wood tone spray.

**Caution:** Do not hang ornaments near hot lights or other heat sources.

1. Spray mold with candle release. Follow **Melting Wax**, page 159, to melt wax chips. Pour wax into mold.
2. Fold twine in half. Place ends of twine into wax. Allow wax to harden.
3. Remove star from mold. Lightly spray star with wood tone spray; allow to dry.

## SPICED SPOON ORNAMENTS
(Shown on page 10)

**For each ornament,** you will need craft glue, silver spoon, 16" length of 1"w torn fabric strip, assorted spices (we used whole cloves, crushed quince, and dried cranberries), and dried star anise.

1. Pour a small amount of glue into bowl of spoon. Press desired spices lightly into glue. Allow to dry.
2. With knot on back of spoon, tie fabric strip around handle. Knot strip ends together to form hanger. Glue star anise to fabric on front of spoon.

LEAVES AND BERRIES

## SPICED CANDLES (Shown on pages 11 and 12)

**Note:** Follow **Working With Wax**, page 159, when making and decorating candles.

**Caution:** Do not leave burning candles unattended.

Let our Spiced Candles carry the appealing aroma of the holidays to every room of your home. With little effort, you can transform unadorned votive, taper, and pillar candles into a symphony of fragrance.

We dipped tapers in melted wax crystals and then rolled them in spices such as cinnamon, allspice, and cloves. For variation in color and texture, we added spices to red or green melted wax crystals, dabbed the wax mixture onto the candle, and then used a light stamping motion on the soft wax with a stiff-bristled brush, creating a craggy surface. For a romantic flair, we used a foam brush to drizzle the wax mixture on the top and down the sides of the candle.

Other aromatic gifts from nature complement our candles. We used wild rice, star anise, rose hips, peppercorns, lemon peel, orange slices, dried cranberries, quince, nutmeg, and poppy seeds. You will enjoy formulating your own special blend of "scentsations."

For a rustic touch, tie a torn fabric strip around a bundle of tapers, or place tapers in homey candlesticks. A Wax Star Ornament (page 15) lends the pewter candlesticks an extra touch of "starlight."

Containers for our scented candles abound with heartwarming finishes. The painted galvanized containers match the bucket holding our Scented Tabletop Tree (page 15). Spices, grains, and dried fruits fill bowls, gelatin molds, and glass jars with votive candles nestled in their earthy beds. Inverted jar lids and small gelatin molds are each topped with a

dried orange slice to serve as a resting place for small candles. For an easy accent, tie a simple torn fabric strip around the rim of a jar or center of a large pillar candle.

A variety of fragrant candles are displayed in a humble box that heralds a comforting message. In a flash, you can make our decorated verse! Simply make a photocopy of the tag design and decorate it with colored pencils. Glue the tag to a piece of fabric-covered poster board and trim, leaving a $1/2$" border encasing the Christmas candle verse.

The glow and aromas radiating from our spice candles will fill your heart with cherished memories of Christmases past and the hope of Christmases to come.

## APPLE-CINNAMON STAR TREE TOPPER
(Shown on pages 9 and 13)

**For each large and small tree topper,** you will need three 12" long cinnamon sticks, floral wire, wire cutters, hot glue gun, one dried star anise, and seven dried apple slices.
**For large tree topper,** you will **also** need a 9" star-shaped metal gelatin mold.

**1.** Overlapping center of cinnamon sticks, arrange sticks in a star shape. Wrap wire around center of star. Twist wire to secure. Glue star anise to center of star, covering wire.
**2.** Overlapping edges, arrange and glue apple slices in a circle on star.
**3.** For small tree topper, use wire at back of star to attach tree topper to tree. For large tree topper, center and glue completed star to rim of gelatin mold. Cut a 10" length of wire. Glue center of wire to back of gelatin mold. Use wire to attach large tree topper to top of tree.

## CINNAMON STOCKING AND HEART ORNAMENTS
(Shown on page 10)

**For each ornament,** you will need tracing paper, yellow foam food tray, craft knife, paintbrush, craft glue, hot glue gun, ground cinnamon, silver spray paint, 12" of heavy-gauge floral wire, red raffia, 10" length of 1"w torn fabric strip, and dried canella berries.
**For stocking ornament,** you will **also** need sugar, whole cloves, and dried star anise.
**For heart ornament,** you will **also** need whole allspice.

### STOCKING
**1.** Trace stocking pattern onto tracing paper; cut out. Draw around pattern on foam tray. Use knife to cut out stocking.
**2.** Place pattern on stocking. Use a pencil to draw over detail lines, scoring foam.
**3.** Leaving toe and heel areas dry, use paintbrush to apply a thin layer of craft glue over front and sides of stocking. Sprinkle cinnamon over glue; allow to dry. Shake off excess cinnamon.
**4.** Mix eight parts sugar to one part cinnamon. Apply craft glue to toe and heel areas of stocking. Sprinkle cinnamon-sugar mixture over glue; allow to dry. Shake off excess cinnamon-sugar. Push cloves into foam along inside toe and heel lines. Use hot glue to attach star anise along top of stocking.
**5.** For hanger, bend wire into a U-shape. Spray paint wire silver; allow to dry. Glue wire ends to back of ornament. Wrap wire with raffia; glue raffia ends on back of ornament. Tie fabric strip into a bow around hanger. Glue canella berries to knot of bow.

### HEART
**1.** Trace heart pattern onto tracing paper; cut out. Draw around pattern on foam tray. Use knife to cut out heart.
**2.** Follow Step 3 of stocking to cover entire front and sides of heart with cinnamon. Use hot glue to attach allspice around side edges.
**3.** Follow Step 5 of stocking to make a hanger for heart.

**TAG**

Christmas candle, Oh so bright. Keep us company, Through the night.

## AROMATIC SPICE BAGS

(Shown on page 13)

**For each bag,** you will need 4" x 11" piece of fabric, pinking shears, whole cloves, uncooked rice, raffia, 6" cinnamon stick, hot glue gun, 5" pine stem cut from artificial pine garland, artificial holly leaves with berries, dried apple or orange slices, and dried cranberries.

**1.** Matching right sides and short edges, fold fabric in half. Using a 1/4" seam allowance, sew sides of bag together. Use pinking shears to trim top of bag. Turn bag right side out.
**2.** Fill bag with cloves and rice. Tie raffia into a bow around top of bag. Insert cinnamon stick between bow and bag.
**3.** Glue pine stem and holly leaves to bow. Glue dried fruit to holly leaves.

## SPICY FRUIT GARLAND

(Shown on page 10)

**For each length of garland,** you will need 2 yds. of natural rope, cinnamon sticks cut in 2" and 3 1/2" lengths, 6" lengths of 3/4"w green and 1 1/4"w gold torn fabric strips, hot glue gun, two small artificial apples, red artificial berries with leaves, dried apple and orange slices, dried cranberries, rose hips, star anise, and assorted spices (we used crushed quince and whole cloves).

**1.** Knot rope 5" from each end.
**2.** For each cinnamon stick bundle, tie a 1 1/4"w fabric strip around two 3 1/2" cinnamon sticks.
**3.** For each fruit cluster, glue two apple or orange slices together. Glue dried cranberries, quince, and cloves to clusters.
**4.** For each spice cluster, glue three rose hips together. Glue quince and cloves to cluster.
**5.** Tie a 3/4"w fabric strip around stem of each artificial apple.
**6.** Arrange and glue cinnamon stick bundles, fruit clusters, artificial apples and berries, 2" cinnamon sticks, and star anise along rope.

## PATCHWORK CUFF STOCKING (Shown on page 11)

**You will need** two 12" x 20" fabric pieces for stocking, two 12" x 20" fabric pieces for lining, 1 3/4 yds. each of 2"w bias fabric strip (pieced as necessary) and 1/4" dia. cord for welting, 2" x 8" fabric piece for hanger, assorted fabrics for cuff, 1/2"w paper-backed fusible web tape, thread to match fabrics, fabric marking pen, tracing paper, one Spice Angel (page 14), and a hot glue gun.

**Note:** Match right sides and raw edges and use a 1/2" seam allowance for all sewing unless otherwise indicated.

**1.** Aligning arrows and dotted lines, trace stocking top and stocking bottom patterns, page 72, onto tracing paper. Draw a second line 1/2" outside traced line along sides and bottom of stocking. Cut out pattern along top and outer lines.
**2.** Matching right sides, place stocking fabrics together. Cutting through both layers of fabric, use pattern to cut out stocking front and back. Repeat for lining pieces.
**3.** For cuff, cut thirteen 1 3/4" x 2 3/4" pieces from assorted fabrics. Sew short ends of five fabric pieces together end to end to make long strip. Using four fabric pieces each, repeat to make two short strips. Sewing along long edges, center and sew one short strip to long strip. Repeat to sew remaining short strip along remaining raw edge of long strip. Trim ends of long strip even with short strips (**Fig. 1**).

**Fig. 1**

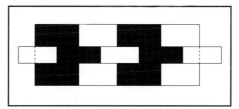

**4.** Fuse web tape along one long edge on right side of cuff. Do not remove paper backing. Press fused edge 1/2" to wrong side; remove paper backing. Place cuff right side up on right side of stocking front, matching unpressed long edge of cuff and top raw edge of stocking; baste edges together. Fuse pressed edge in place.
**5.** For welting, press one end of bias fabric strip 1/2" to wrong side. Beginning 1/2" from folded edge, center cord on wrong side of strip. Fold strip over cord. Beginning 1/2" from folded end, use a zipper foot to baste close to cord along length of strip. Trim seam allowance to 1/2".
**6.** Beginning with unpressed end, matching raw edges, and placing welting on right side of stocking front, baste welting along side and bottom edges of stocking front. Trim excess welting and set aside. At each end of welting on stocking, open bias strip and trim 1/2" from cord; rebaste welting. Matching right sides, place stocking front and stocking back together. Using a zipper foot, leaving top edge open, and sewing as close to welting as possible, sew stocking together. Clip curves and turn right side out; press.
**7.** Beginning with pressed end of remaining welting at cuff seam, pin welting along top of stocking. Trimming to fit, insert unfinished end of welting into folded end. Use zipper foot to sew around top of stocking as close to welting as possible. Press seam allowances to inside of stocking.
**8.** For hanger, press long edges of fabric piece 1/2" to wrong side. Matching wrong sides and long edges, press in half; stitch together close to pressed edges. Fold hanger in half to form a loop. Matching raw edges, tack ends of loop inside stocking at heel seam.
**9.** Matching right sides and leaving top edge open, sew lining pieces together; do not turn. Press top raw edge of lining 1/2" to wrong side. Matching wrong sides, insert lining in stocking. Hand sew pressed edge of lining to seam allowance of welting.
**10.** Glue Spice Angel to stocking front.

# TOYLAND EXPRESS

*D*ecked out in a rainbow of treasures from Santa's workshop, our Toyland Express collection
is brimming with amusement for all ages! Imaginative ornaments, frolicking on a playful
evergreen, are teamed with a "countdown to Christmas" banner, heartwarming Santa bears,
a cheerful chimney stocking, and a crafty ceramic picture frame and cookie plate. Turn your
home into a wonderland of toys as you celebrate Christmas with mirth and merriment
using ideas from this fun-filled medley of designs! Instructions for the projects
shown here and on the following pages begin on page 22.

Santa will delight in treats presented on his own special **Gingerbread Cookie Plate** *(page 27)* accompanied by a matching
**Ceramic Photo Frame** *(page 26)* showing one of his favorite fans! Charming painted snowflake and gingerbread designs
add jolly accents to this one-of-a-kind set.

The countdown is on! This **No-Sew Advent Banner** *(page 23)* offers 24 peppermint treats as a sweet way to mark the days until Santa's heralded arrival. Embellished with fused fabric hearts, bright red bows, and a jingle bell, this clever calendar sends an urgent message to our beloved Christmas gent.

Crown your tree with a **Cuddly Santa Bear** *(page 24)* popping out of our **Snowcapped Chimney Tree Topper** *(page 24)*. Red brick-print fabric covers a boutique tissue box with a "snowy" collar created by painting white felt with artificial snow.

Holding lots of joy for girls and boys, our simple-to-stitch **Cheery Chimney Stocking** *(page 25)* has a felt cuff and is lined with muslin. Nestled with the stocking and his bear buddies is a **Cuddly Santa Bear** *(page 24)*, capped with a child's brightly colored sock and bearded with acrylic fur.

Jam-packed with playful delights, our **Toyland Express Tree** *(page 22)* features **Santa's Mailbag Ornaments** *(page 22)*, **"I Love Santa" Banners** *(page 26)*, **Cuddly Santa Bears** *(page 24)*, **Bright Gum Ball Wreaths** *(page 22)*, and a **Hearts and Candy Garland** *(page 22)*. The tree also has a generous assortment of jump rope garlands, colorful foam balls, children's books, plastic toy trains and tools, and skate ornaments scattered among its branches.

## TOYLAND EXPRESS TREE
(Shown on page 19)

Santa has received tons of mail requesting toys for girls and boys! His list grows longer as his elves work away those final hours and he readies his sleigh for special deliveries. Our elves have been busy too, loading the Toyland Express Tree with plastic trains, foam balls of every color, plastic tools, ice-skate ornaments, and children's books!

We draped jump ropes around this seven-foot-tall pine tree, as well as Hearts and Candy Garland made by stringing hard candies with center holes, wrapped candies, and gum balls between fabric-covered heart shapes. We used more multicolor gum balls to make Bright Gum Ball Wreaths. Cuddly Santa Bears (page 24), dressed in red felt finery, play hide-and-seek among branches brimming with Santa's Mailbag Ornaments and "I Love Santa" Banners (page 26). At the top of the tree, a precocious Santa bear pops from our Snowcapped Chimney Tree Topper (page 24).

To complete this fun-filled fantasy, we spread four yards of white print fabric over five yards of red print fabric to encircle the base of the tree. You'll have hours of fun with our Toyland Express this Christmas!

## BRIGHT GUM BALL WREATHS
(Shown on page 21)

**For each ornament,** you will need 12" of floral wire, T-pin, fourteen gum balls, and one 10" length each of $1/2$"w red and green satin ribbon.

**1.** Bend wire into a 3" dia. circle. Use pin to make a hole through center of each gum ball. Thread gum balls onto wire. Twist wire ends together.
**2.** Tie ribbons into a bow around wire ends.

## SANTA'S MAILBAG ORNAMENTS
(Shown on page 21)

**For each ornament,** you will need a 6" x 15" piece of print fabric; polyester fiberfill; tracing paper; transfer paper; white, red, and green cardstock; black medium-point marker; craft glue; hole punch; and a 15" length of jute twine.

**Note:** Allow glue to dry after each application.

**1.** Matching right sides and short edges, fold fabric in half; press. Using a $1/2$" seam allowance, sew long edges together. For each bottom corner, match side seam to bottom fold and sew across corner $1/2$" from point (**Fig. 1**).

**Fig. 1**

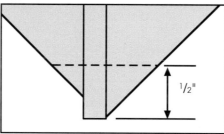

**2.** Turn bag right side out and stuff with fiberfill to $2^1/2$" from top edge.
**3.** Trace label and tag patterns onto tracing paper. Use patterns to cut label from white cardstock and tag from green cardstock. Use transfer paper to transfer words to label and tag. Use marker to draw over transferred words. Glue label to red cardstock. Leaving a $1/4$" red border, cut out label. Glue label to green cardstock. Leaving a $1/4$" green border, cut out label. Glue tag to white cardstock. Leaving a $1/8$" white border, cut out tag. Punch a hole in point of tag.
**4.** Glue label to front of bag. Thread tag onto twine and tie twine into a bow around top of bag.

## HEARTS AND CANDY GARLAND
(Shown on page 21)

**For each length of garland,** you will need red print fabric scraps, paper-backed fusible web, poster board, T-pin, gum balls, a hot glue gun, 12 ft. of white heavy-duty thread, #20 sharp needle, hard candies with center holes, and wrapped candies.

**1.** Using heart pattern, page 26, follow **Making Appliqués**, page 158, to make 14 heart appliqués from red print fabric. Fuse hearts to poster board; cut out hearts.
**2.** Use pin to make a hole through each gum ball. Thread needle and knot thread ends together. Matching wrong sides, glue two hearts together over knot. Add 9" of gum balls and candies to thread. Glue two more hearts together over thread. Continue adding gum balls, candies, and hearts until thread is full. Tie remaining thread end into a knot. Glue two hearts over knot to secure.

LABEL

TAG

22

# NO-SEW ADVENT BANNER (Shown on page 20)

**You will need** 18" of 1" dia. wooden dowel, white spray paint, 17" x 27" piece of white canvas, 1"w fusible web tape, 1"w green grosgrain ribbon, tailor's chalk, 2 yds. of $1\frac{1}{2}$"w red satin ribbon, tracing paper, transfer paper, red plaid fabric, paper-backed fusible web, red fabric marker, black permanent medium-point marker, 7 yds. of $\frac{1}{8}$"w red satin ribbon, large embroidery needle, 24 wrapped disk candies, 2" dia. jingle bell, hot glue gun, and assorted buttons.

**1.** Spray paint dowel white; allow to dry.
**2.** Working on wrong side of banner, fuse web tape along one short edge of canvas (top edge). Fold edge to wrong side and fuse in place. Repeat for side edges. Mark each side of banner $19\frac{1}{2}$" from top edge. Mark bottom edge at center. Using marks as a guide, fold bottom of banner to a point; press. Unfold and mark each edge of point 1" outside fold. Cut along drawn lines. Fuse web tape to one edge of point. Refold edge and fuse in place. Repeat for remaining edge.

**3.** Fuse web tape to wrong side of 1"w ribbon. Use chalk to lightly draw a horizontal line across banner $9\frac{3}{4}$" from top edge; center and fuse a 14" length of 1"w ribbon over drawn line. Overlapping and trimming ends to fit, fuse 1"w ribbon $\frac{1}{4}$" inside bottom, side, and top edges of banner.
**4.** For each hanging loop, cut a 10" length of $1\frac{1}{2}$" ribbon. Fuse web tape across one end of ribbon. Fuse ends together. With 2" of loop extending above top edge of banner and placing loop 2" from side edge, glue loop to wrong side of banner.
**5.** Trace "Hurry Santa!" design onto tracing paper. Use transfer paper to transfer design onto banner. Using heart patterns, follow **Making Appliqués**, page 158, to make one large and two small heart appliqués from plaid fabric. Arrange and fuse on banner.

**6.** Use red fabric marker to fill in letters. Use black marker to outline letters, draw "stitches" along inside edges of each banner section, and draw "stitches" on hearts.
**7.** To mark positions for candy placement, begin $1\frac{1}{4}$" from side ribbon and 1" below center ribbon. Mark six points 2" apart. Working 2" below previous marks, repeat for three more rows. Use needle to thread a 10" length of $\frac{1}{8}$"w ribbon through banner at each mark. Attach a piece of candy at each ribbon by tying ribbon into a bow around one end of candy wrapper.
**8.** Cut a 42" length of $1\frac{1}{2}$"w ribbon. Thread bell to center of ribbon and tie ribbon into a bow. Glue knot of bow to point of banner.
**9.** Glue buttons to banner as desired. Insert dowel through loops.

SMALL HEART

LARGE HEART

# CUDDLY SANTA BEARS (Shown on page 21)

**For each bear,** you will need tracing paper, 10" square of red felt, hot glue gun, white medium-width rickrack, 10" teddy bear, 10" of ⁵⁄₈"w black satin ribbon, 1" dia. wooden button, white acrylic fur, child-size sock for hat, 1" dia. white pom-pom.

1. Trace coat and beard patterns onto tracing paper.
2. Fold felt in half. Aligning shoulders of pattern with fold of felt, cut out coat. Using a thin line of glue, glue side and sleeve seams together. Cut coat open down center front. Glue a length of rickrack along each edge of coat opening and around each sleeve.

3. Place coat on bear. Overlapping and gluing ribbon ends at front of coat, wrap ribbon around waist of coat. Glue button over ribbon ends.
4. Draw around beard pattern on wrong side of acrylic fur. Being careful not to cut fur, cut out beard along drawn lines. Glue beard under bear's chin.
5. For hat, turn sock inside out. Cut 5½" from cuff of sock; discard bottom of sock. Baste around hat ¼" from cut edge. Pull basting threads to gather tightly; knot threads. Turn hat right side out. Glue pom-pom to top of hat. Place hat on bear's head. Cut slits in hat for ears; stretch hat over ears. Glue a piece of acrylic fur to underside of hat front for hair.

COAT

BEARD

# SNOWCAPPED CHIMNEY TREE TOPPER
(Shown on page 20)

**You will need** an empty boutique tissue box; white, red, tan, and black felt; red brick-print fabric; spray adhesive; hot glue gun; ¼" thick foam core; craft knife; brush-on artificial snow; paintbrush; and one Cuddly Santa Bear.

**Note:** Use hot glue for all gluing unless otherwise indicated.

1. Draw around bottom of box on red and black felt. Cut out each piece along drawn lines. Remove plastic from box opening.
2. Measure height of box; add ½". Measure around box; add ½". Cut a piece from brick fabric the determined measurements. Apply spray adhesive to wrong side of fabric. Overlapping ends at back and matching one long edge with top of box, glue fabric around box. Fold and glue excess fabric to bottom of box.
3. Glue red felt piece over bottom of box and black felt piece over top of box. Carefully cut felt from box opening.
4. Measure width of one side of box. Use knife to cut two pieces of foam core 2"w by the determined measurement. With foam pieces extending 1" above top of box, glue foam pieces to opposite sides of box.
5. Repeat Step 4, cutting foam pieces ½" longer than the determined measurement.
6. Measure around foam core; add ½". Cut a strip of tan felt 3½"w by the determined measurement and a strip of white felt 2½"w by the determined measurement.
7. Apply spray adhesive to one side of tan strip. With ¼" extending past bottom of foam core and overlapping ends at back, glue strip around chimney. Fold and glue excess fabric to bottom of foam core and over top edge of chimney.
8. Trace cuff pattern onto tracing paper. Use pattern to trim one long edge of white strip. Apply spray adhesive to one side of strip. With 1" of straight edge extending past top of chimney and overlapping ends at back, glue strip around chimney. Fold and glue excess fabric over top edge of chimney. Follow manufacturer's instructions to paint white felt with artificial snow.
9. For treetop placement, use craft knife to cut a small hole in bottom of box. Place bear in opening at top of chimney.

# CHEERY CHIMNEY STOCKING (Shown on page 21)

**You will need** tracing paper, ruler, ¹/₂ yard of red brick-print fabric for stocking, ¹/₂ yd. of muslin for lining, 4" x 11¹/₂" rectangle each of white and tan felt, and a ³/₄" x 5¹/₂" strip of white felt for hanger.

**Note:** Use a ¹/₄" seam allowance for all sewing.

**1.** Aligning arrows and dotted lines, trace stocking top and stocking bottom patterns onto tracing paper. Use ruler to extend top of stocking pattern 9¹/₂". For seam allowance, draw a second line ¹/₄" outside first line around sides and bottom of stocking. Cut out pattern along outer line. Fold stocking fabric piece in half with right sides together. Use pattern to cut stocking from fabric. Repeat using muslin for stocking lining.

**2.** Leaving top edge open, sew stocking pieces together. Clip curves and turn stocking right side out. Repeat to sew lining pieces together; do not turn.

**3.** For cuff, follow **Making Patterns**, page 158, to make snow pattern. Use pattern to cut snow cuff from white felt rectangle. Matching long straight edges, stack white felt on tan felt. Matching white sides and short edges, fold cuff in half. Sew short edges together; press seam open. Turn right side out.

**4.** Matching top edges and cuff seam to heel seam of stocking, place cuff in stocking. Sew along top of stocking through all layers; turn cuff out over stocking.

**5.** For hanging loop, fold white felt strip in half. Tack ends inside stocking at heel seam. Fold top edge of lining ¹/₄" to wrong side; press. Place lining in stocking. Covering seam allowance, hand sew pressed edge of lining to top of stocking.

STOCKING TOP

STOCKING BOTTOM

For **Santa's Stocking Cake** pattern, page 153, align arrows and dotted lines to trace stocking top and stocking bottom patterns onto white paper; cut out.

CUFF

## "I LOVE SANTA" BANNERS (Shown on page 21)

**For each banner,** you will need tracing paper, white and green cardstock, red fabric scraps, paper-backed fusible web, transfer paper, black medium-point marker, red colored pencil, glue stick, 24" of ½"w red ribbon, hot glue gun, ⅝" dia. jingle bell, three buttons, and a wrapped peppermint stick.

**Note:** Use hot glue gun for all gluing unless otherwise indicated.

1. Trace banner design onto tracing paper. Following grey line of design, cut banner from white cardstock.
2. Using heart pattern, follow **Making Appliqués**, page 158, to make heart appliqué from red fabric. Fuse heart to banner.
3. Use transfer paper to transfer letters to banner. Use marker to draw over transferred lines and to draw "stitches" along edges of banner and on heart. Use red pencil to color letters.
4. Use glue stick to glue banner to green cardstock. Leaving a ⅛" green border, cut out banner.
5. For each hanging loop, cut a 2" length of ribbon. Trim ends to a point. Glue ends to front and back of banner ½" from edge. For streamer, notch ends of remaining ribbon length. Thread bell onto center of ribbon. Glue buttons and bell to banner. Insert peppermint stick into hanging loops.

**BANNER**

## CERAMIC PHOTO FRAME
(Shown on page 18)

**Note:** Greenware, underglaze, peel-off masking product, glaze, ceramic tools, paintbrushes, and kiln firing should be available at local ceramic studios or craft stores.

**You will need** a cleaning tool, greenware photo frame (we used a 7½"h frame), sponge, peel-off masking product, green and black opaque underglaze, soft paintbrushes, and clear glaze.

1. Use cleaning tool to clean and smooth frame. Wipe with slightly damp sponge to remove dust.
2. Follow manufacturer's instructions to apply masking product to areas for snowflakes.
3. Follow manufacturer's instructions to apply green underglaze over front of frame; allow to dry. Remove masking product. Using black underglaze, freehand paint snowflakes and inner border on frame.
4. Fire frame. Follow manufacturer's instructions to apply clear glaze to frame. Fire frame again.

# GINGERBREAD COOKIE PLATE (Shown on page 18)

**Note:** Greenware, underglaze, peel-off masking product, glaze, ceramic tools, paintbrushes, and kiln firing should be available at local ceramic studios or craft stores.

**You will need** a cleaning tool; greenware plate (we used an 8" dia. plate); sponge; tracing paper; removable tape; carbon paper; peel-off masking product; red, green, dark green, brown, and black opaque underglaze; soft paintbrushes; and food-safe clear glaze.

1. Use cleaning tool to clean and smooth plate. Wipe with slightly damp sponge to remove dust.
2. Trace cookie plate pattern onto tracing paper. Center pattern on plate and tape in place. Place carbon paper under pattern. Lightly transfer design to plate.
3. Follow manufacturer's instructions to apply masking product to areas for snowflakes and over hair, eyes, nose, mouth, and arm and leg bands. Follow manufacturer's instructions to apply green underglaze around edge of plate and

brown underglaze over gingerbread man; allow to dry. Remove masking product. Use red underglaze to paint cheeks, swirls on gingerbread man, and dots on plate; allow to dry. Using black underglaze, paint outlines and details on gingerbread man, lettering, and freehand snowflakes; allow to dry. Using dark green underglaze, paint marks around inner rim of plate.
4. Fire plate. Follow manufacturer's instructions to apply clear glaze to plate. Fire plate again.

# BERIBBONED ELEGANCE

**E**xquisitely shaded in regal red and gold, our collection of beautiful bows and kindhearted Santas spreads a sense of excitement and anticipation throughout the house. Gilded bows, sashes, and garlands are artfully woven through a magnificent evergreen laden with cross-stitched Christmas gentlemen, brilliant poinsettias, and tasseled ornaments. Eye-catching packages and a plaid skirt complete the majestic mood. This grand elegance is extended from room to room with a festive wreath, posh pillows, graceful garlands, and a needlecrafted St. Nicholas. You won't believe how easy it is to create the impressive projects shown here and on the following pages with our step-by-step instructions, which begin on page 34.

Our heartwarming cross-stitched **Father Christmas Shelf Sitter** *(page 36)* and **Bow-Tied Book Bundle** *(page 35)* make a spirited arrangement.

28

Crowned with a gilded multi-loop bow, our **Beribboned Elegance Tree** *(page 34)* glitters with festive finery. Graceful streamers from the beautiful bows entwine through its branches. The tree is also dotted with crimson **Ribbon Poinsettias** *(page 35)* crafted from velvet and gold mesh wired ribbons, cross-stitched **Jolly Old Gent Ornaments** *(page 36)* edged in twisted gold cord, ornate **Painted Glass Ornaments** *(page 35)*, and **Tasseled Glass Ornaments** *(page 35)*. Sprigs of variegated holly and glittering garlands of rope and beads enhance the regal effect.

Our dramatic **Beribboned Elegance Wreath** (*page 34*) is beautifully decked with ribbon poinsettias, cross-stitched Santa ornaments, and a golden bow. Natural pinecones and a string of glittery beads add finishing touches.

A swath of festive plaid fabric is the backdrop for an eye-catching collection of **Regal Packages** (*page 34*). Trimmed in assorted wrapping papers, ribbon, and gold netting, these treasures have delightful accents — a tasseled velvet bow, sprigs of holly, a painted glass ornament, and our ribbon poinsettia.

**Pretty Pillows** *(page 34)* in elegant fabrics are trimmed with regal ribbons and a singular jeweled button for perfect accents.

Our **Beribboned Elegance Garland** *(page 35)* graces a magnificent setting with an impressive arrangement of ribbon poinsettias, golden bows, painted glass ornaments, and a beaded garland on evergreen boughs.

A genteel **Father Christmas Framed Piece** *(page 38)*, flanked by elegant tapers, tops our handsome **Beribboned Elegance Mantel** *(page 34)*. The trimmings include evergreen and bead garlands, our ribbon poinsettias, and red glass ornaments.

## BERIBBONED ELEGANCE TREE
(Shown on page 29)

Putting a bow on something is sure to make it pretty. Well, just look what bows have done for our tree! You can do it too with just a little help from our Beribboned Elegance selections.

Five yards of plaid Christmas fabric tucked around the base and stand of the tree set a lovely foundation for dazzling designs. Beaded and gold cord garlands, woven through branches abloom with Ribbon Poinsettias and purchased holly picks, paint a festive background for hanging Painted Glass Ornaments and Tasseled Glass Ornaments. Three poses of a welcome Christmas guest are cross stitched, framed, and prominently displayed as our Jolly Old Gent Ornaments (page 36).

Atop this spectacular display is a classic bow fashioned from eleven yards of 2¹/₂"w gold mesh wired ribbon, as instructed in **Making a Bow** (page 159). This bow has eight 13" loops and two 4-foot streamers. Simple bows tied from 28" lengths of the same gold ribbon are tucked into the tree for added fullness. This crowning glory ties it all up in a Christmas of Beribboned Elegance.

## BERIBBONED ELEGANCE WREATH
(Shown on page 31)

**You will need** 2¹/₂"w gold mesh wired ribbon, beaded garland, 24" dia. fresh evergreen wreath, floral wire, wire cutters, pinecones, five Ribbon Poinsettias, and three Jolly Old Gent Ornaments (page 36).

**1.** Follow **Making a Bow**, page 159, to make a bow with eight 8" loops and two streamers.
**2.** Arrange garland on wreath. Wire garland in place. Wire pinecones to wreath.
**3.** Use wire to secure Ribbon Poinsettias, Jolly Old Gent Ornaments, and bow to wreath.

## REGAL PACKAGES
(Shown on page 31)

**You will need** wrapped packages and 2¹/₂"w wired ribbon (we used satin, organza, and gold mesh ribbons)
**You may also need** gold netting, 2"w wired velvet ribbon, Painted Glass Ornament, Ribbon Poinsettias, artificial holly leaves with gold berries, gold tassel, two red faceted beads, one gold pony bead, floral wire, wire cutters, and a hot glue gun.

### BASIC BOW PACKAGE
**1.** Follow **Making a Bow**, page 159, to make a bow with six to ten loops to fit top of package and streamers to fit around package.
**2.** Overlapping ends, glue streamers to bottom of package.

### ORNAMENT PACKAGE
**1.** Follow **Making a Bow**, page 159, to make a bow with six 6" loops and streamers to fit around package.
**2.** Use wire to secure Painted Glass Ornament to center of bow. Overlapping ends, glue streamers to bottom of package.

### GOLD NETTING PACKAGE
**1.** Place package in center of gold netting. Gather netting at top of package.
**2.** Tie ribbon into a bow around gathers.

### POINSETTIA PACKAGE
**1.** Cut lengths of ribbon to fit around package. Wrap ribbons around package. Overlap and glue ribbon ends to bottom of package.
**2.** Wire Ribbon Poinsettia to center of ribbons on top of package. Glue holly leaves around poinsettia as desired.

### TASSELED PACKAGE
**1.** Knotting ribbon on front of package, tie 2¹/₂"w wired ribbon around package. Tie a 20" length of velvet ribbon into a bow.
**2.** Thread beads onto hanger of tassel. Glue hanger end to back of velvet bow. Glue bow to knot of wired ribbon.

## BERIBBONED ELEGANCE MANTEL
(Shown on page 33)

**You will need** 2¹/₂"w gold mesh wired ribbon, fresh evergreen garland, beaded garland, five Ribbon Poinsettias, red glass ornaments, floral wire, and wire cutters.

**1.** Follow **Making a Bow**, page 159, to make two bows with six 10" loops and two streamers.
**2.** Use wire to secure beaded garland, Ribbon Poinsettias, bows, and ornaments to garland.

## PRETTY PILLOWS
(Shown on page 32)

**You will need** purchased pillows and wired ribbons in desired widths.
**You may also need** a jeweled button and a hot glue gun.

### RED PILLOW
**1.** Measure around center of pillow from side to side in both directions. Cut a length of ribbon five feet longer than determined measurement.
**2.** Beginning with center of ribbon on front of pillow, wrap ribbon to back of pillow. Twist ribbon ¹/₄ turn and bring ribbon ends back to front of pillow.
**3.** Tie ribbon into a bow and notch ends.

### GOLD PILLOW
**1.** Measure across top of pillow diagonally; double measurement and add five feet. Cut a length of ribbon the determined measurement.
**2.** Beginning with center of ribbon on front of pillow, wrap ribbon around opposite corners of pillow and tie into a bow. Notch ribbon ends.

### GREEN PILLOW
**1.** Measure around widest part of pillow; add 1". Cut a length of wide ribbon the determined measurement. Overlap and glue ribbon ends at back of pillow.
**2.** Cut one each 14" length and 12" length from narrow ribbon. Tie ribbon lengths into bows. Glue button to small bow, small bow to large bow, and large bow to wide ribbon on front of pillow.

## BOW-TIED BOOK BUNDLE
(Shown on page 28)

**You will need** three hardcover books in assorted sizes, three coordinating Christmas fabrics to cover books, 2"w red velvet wired ribbon, ³/₈"w gold mesh wired ribbon, measuring tape, and a hot glue gun.

**1.** To cover each book, place open book on wrong side of fabric. Cut fabric 1¹/₂" wider on all sides than book; cut notches in fabric at top and bottom of book spine (**Fig. 1**). Fold corners of fabric diagonally over corners of cover; glue to secure. Fold edges of fabric over edges of cover; glue to secure.

**Fig. 1**

**2.** Stack covered books. Measure around stack of books; add 2". Cut a length of velvet ribbon the determined measurement. Wrap ribbon around books. Overlap and glue ribbon ends to center top of book.
**3.** Cut a 24" length of velvet ribbon. Cut two 18" lengths of mesh ribbon. Tie ribbon lengths into bows. Notch ribbon ends. Glue velvet bow to ribbon on book stack. Glue mesh bows to center of velvet bow.

## RIBBON POINSETTIAS
(Shown on page 30)

**For each Poinsettia,** you will need 48" of 2¹/₂" wired velvet ribbon in red or dark red, two 12" lengths of ³/₈"w gold mesh wired ribbon, 24 gauge floral wire, wire cutters, scissors, ruler or yardstick, and a hot glue gun.

**1.** Use velvet ribbon and follow **Making a Bow**, page 159, to make a bow with three 10" loops and two 5" streamers. Cut loops open at fold. Trim each ribbon end to a point. Arrange ribbon ends to resemble a poinsettia.
**2.** Tie each mesh ribbon length into a bow. Glue bows to center of poinsettia.
**3.** Use wire to secure poinsettia to tree.

## PAINTED GLASS ORNAMENTS
(Shown on page 30)

**For each ornament,** you will need a red glass ornament, pencil, gold paint pen, gold glitter dimensional paint, and 12" of ³/₈" dia. gold cord.

**1.** Use pencil to draw desired designs on ornament.
**2.** Use paint pen to draw over designs; allow to dry.
**3.** Use dimensional paint to add detail to designs; allow to dry.
**4.** Tie cord into a bow through ornament hanger.

## TASSELED GLASS ORNAMENTS
(Shown on page 30)

**For each ornament,** you will need a red glass ornament, 6" of ³/₈" dia. red satin cord, desired gold braid and trim, gold tassel, and household cement.

**1.** Beginning and ending at back of ornament and trimming to fit, glue braids and trims around ornaments as desired.
**2.** Glue tassel to bottom of ornament. Thread cord though ornament hanger; knot ends together.

## BERIBBONED ELEGANCE GARLAND
(Shown on page 32)

**You will need** 2¹/₂"w gold mesh wired ribbon, fresh evergreen garland, beaded garland, Ribbon Poinsettias, Painted Glass Ornaments, red glass ornaments, floral wire, and wire cutters.

**1.** Follow **Making a Bow**, page 159, to make desired number of bows with six 10" loops and two streamers. If desired, make a larger bow with ten 12" loops and two streamers.
**2.** Use wire to secure beaded garland, Ribbon Poinsettias, bows, and ornaments to natural garland.

## FATHER CHRISTMAS SHELF SITTER (Shown on page 28)

**You will need** two 10" x 12" pieces and one 4" x 6" piece of Cream Quaker Cloth (24 ct), embroidery floss (see color key, pages 38 and 39), #24 tapestry needle, embroidery hoop (optional), polyester fiberfill, tracing paper, plastic filler pellets, a sewing needle and thread to match fabric.

**1.** Follow **Cross Stitch**, page 156, to work Santa portion only of Father Christmas design (no background stitches), pages 38 and 39, on one 10" x 12" piece of Quaker Cloth. Use three strands of floss for Cross Stitch, Three-Quarter Stitch, and Quarter Stitch. Use one strand of floss for Backstitch and French Knots.
**2.** Matching right sides, place remaining 10" x 12" Quaker Cloth piece over

stitched piece. Leaving bottom edge open, sew pieces together ¹/₂" outside design. Trim bottom edge 1" below lowest section of design area. Trim remaining edges ¹/₄" outside stitched line. Clip seam allowances at curves; turn figure right side out and carefully push curves outward. Stuff with fiberfill to 1¹/₂" from opening.
**3.** Trace small oval pattern onto tracing paper. Use pattern to cut base from 4" x 6" piece of Quaker cloth. Baste around base ¹/₂" from raw edge. Press raw edges to wrong side along basting line.
**4.** Fill opening with plastic pellets. Pin wrong side of base over opening. Stitch in place, adding pellets as necessary to fill bottom of figure. Remove basting stitches.

## JOLLY OLD GENT ORNAMENTS
(Shown on page 30)

**For each ornament,** you will need two 8" x 10" pieces of Cream Belfast Linen (32 ct), embroidery floss (see color key page 37), #26 tapestry needle, embroidery hoop (optional), tracing paper, poster board for backing, lightweight batting, a hot glue gun, 18" of ¹/₄"w gold twisted cording with flange, 18" of ⁵/₈"w gold mesh wired ribbon, and clear thread (optional).

**1.** Follow **Cross Stitch**, page 156, to work desired Santa design on one linen piece. Use two strands of floss for Cross Stitch and Quarter Stitch. Use one strand of floss for Backstitch and French Knots.
**2.** Trace large oval pattern onto tracing paper; cut out. Draw around pattern on poster board, batting, and remaining linen piece; cut out shapes. Center pattern over design on back of stitched piece; draw around pattern. Cut out ¹/₂" outside drawn line. Clip curves to ¹/₄" outside drawn line.
**3.** Center batting, then poster board on back of stitched piece. Fold and glue edges of fabric to back of poster board. Gluing flange to back and overlapping ends at top of ornament, glue cording around ornament. Glue linen oval over back of ornament.
**4.** Tie ribbon into a bow. Notch ribbon ends. Glue bow to top of ornament.
**5.** If desired, follow **Making a Hanger**, page 159, to add hanger to ornament.

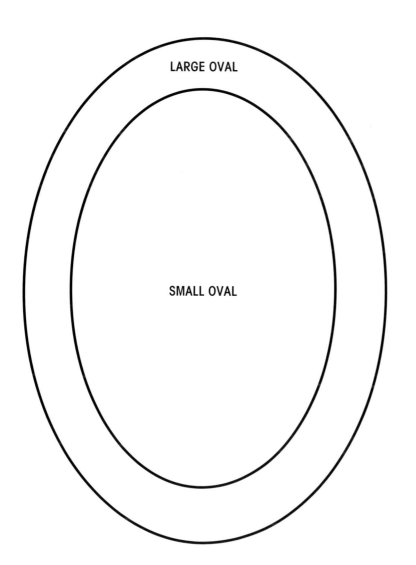

LARGE OVAL

SMALL OVAL

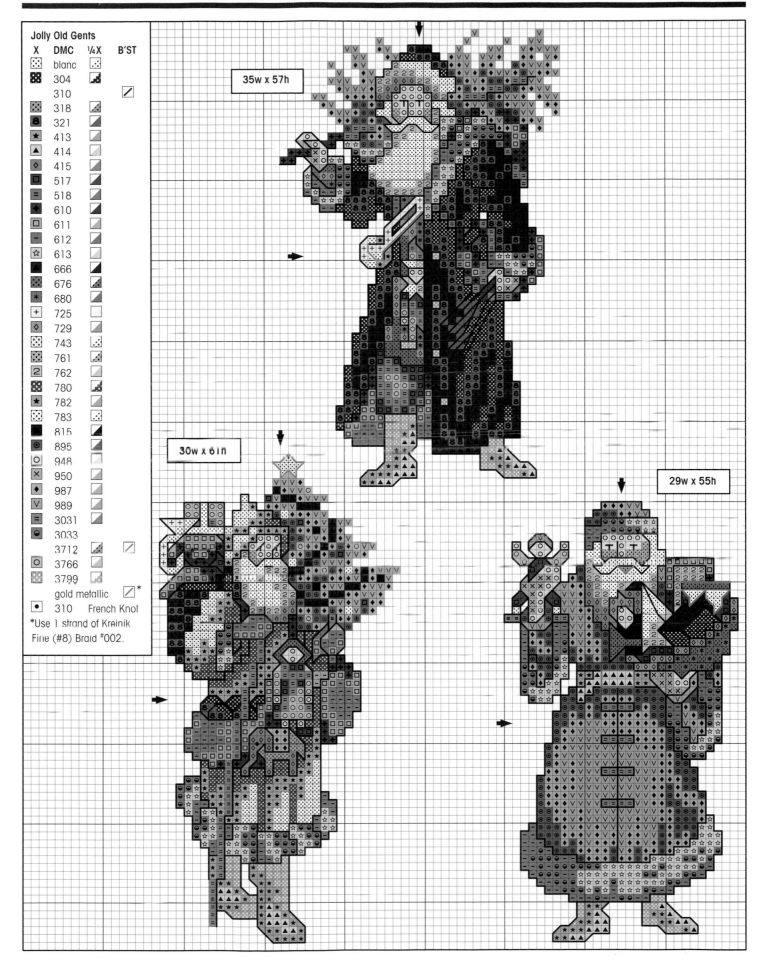

Jolly Old Gents

| X | DMC | ¼X | B'ST |
|---|---|---|---|
| | blanc | | |
| | 304 | | |
| | 310 | | ✓ |
| | 318 | | |
| 8 | 321 | | |
| ★ | 413 | | |
| ▲ | 414 | | |
| ◇ | 415 | | |
| □ | 517 | | |
| = | 518 | | |
| ✦ | 610 | | |
| ◻ | 611 | | |
| - | 612 | | |
| ☆ | 613 | | |
| ■ | 666 | | |
| ◫ | 676 | | |
| * | 680 | | |
| + | 725 | | |
| ◇ | 729 | | |
| | 743 | | |
| | 761 | | |
| 2 | 762 | | |
| | 780 | | |
| ★ | 782 | | |
| | 783 | | |
| ■ | 815 | | |
| ◉ | 895 | | |
| ○ | 948 | | |
| ✕ | 950 | | |
| ◆ | 987 | | |
| V | 989 | | |
| = | 3031 | | |
| ◓ | 3033 | | |
| | 3712 | | ✓ |
| ○ | 3766 | | |
| | 3799 | | |
| | gold metallic | | ✓* |
| ● | 310 | French Knot | |

*Use 1 strand of Kreinik
Fine (#8) Braid #002.

35w x 57h

30w x 61h

29w x 55h

# FATHER CHRISTMAS FRAMED PIECE (Shown on page 33)

**You will need** one 20" x 26" piece of cream Aida (14 ct), embroidery floss (refer to color key), embroidery hoop (optional), frame and mats (we used a custom frame), and #20 tapestry needle.

**1.** Follow **Cross Stitch**, page 156, to work Father Christmas design on Aida over two squares. Use six strands of floss for Cross Stitch, Three-Quarter Stitch, and Quarter Stitch. Use three strands of floss for Half Cross Stitch. Use three strands of each color floss for blended stitches. Unless otherwise noted, use two strands of floss for Backstitch. Use four strands of floss for French Knots.

**2.** Frame stitched piece as desired.

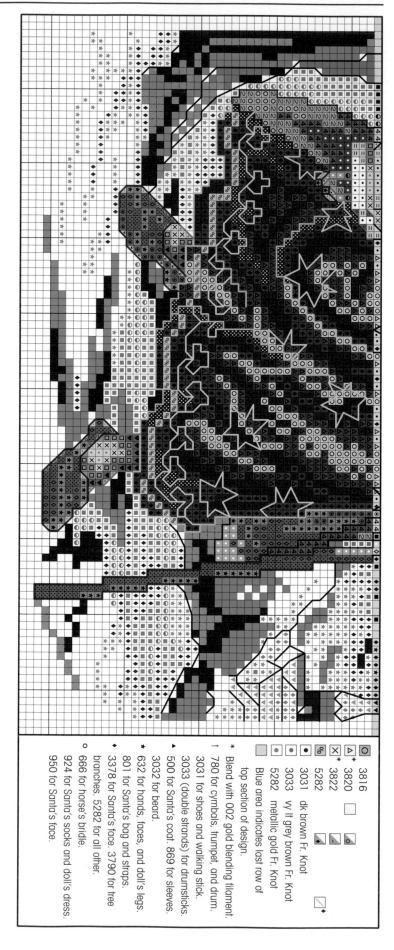

○ 950 for Santa's face.
924 for Santa's socks and doll's dress.
666 for horse's bridle.
branches. 5282 for all other.
3378 for Santa's face. 3790 for tree
★ 801 for Santa's bag and straps.
632 for hands, faces, and doll's legs.
3032 for beard.
▶ 500 for Santa's coat. 869 for sleeves.
3033 (double strands) for drumsticks.
3031 for shoes and walking stick.
↑ 780 for cymbals, trumpet, and drum.
* Blend with 002 gold blending filament.
top section of design.
Blue area indicates last row of
5282 metallic gold Fr. Knot
3033 vy lt grey brown Fr. Knot
3031 dk brown Fr. Knot
5282
3822
3820
3816

38

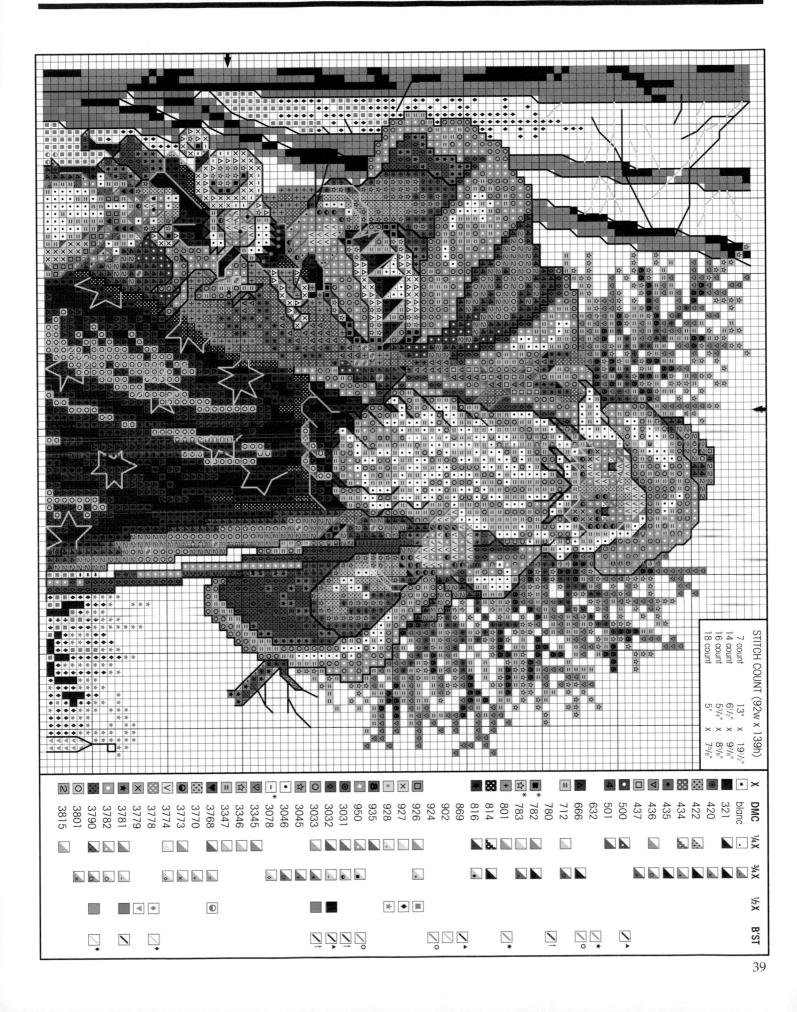

STITCH COUNT (92w x 139h)

| | | |
|---|---|---|
| 7 count | 13" | x 19½" |
| 14 count | 6½" | x 9⅞" |
| 16 count | 5¾" | x 8⅝" |
| 18 count | 5" | x 7⅝" |

| X | DMC | ¼X | ¾X | ½X | B'ST |
|---|---|---|---|---|---|
| • | blanc | | | | |
| | 321 | | | | |
| | 420 | | | | |
| | 422 | | | | |
| | 434 | | | | |
| | 435 | | | | |
| | 436 | | | | |
| | 437 | | | | |
| | 500 | | | | |
| | 501 | | | | |
| | 632 | | | | |
| | 666 | | | | |
| | 712 | | | | |
| | 780 | | | | |
| | 782 | | | | |
| | 783 | | | | |
| | 801 | | | | |
| | 814 | | | | |
| | 816 | | | | |
| | 869 | | | | |
| | 902 | | | | |
| | 924 | | | | |
| | 926 | | | | |
| | 927 | | | | |
| | 928 | | | | |
| | 935 | | | | |
| | 950 | | | | |
| | 3031 | | | | |
| | 3032 | | | | |
| | 3033 | | | | |
| | 3045 | | | | |
| | 3046 | | | | |
| | 3078 | | | | |
| | 3345 | | | | |
| | 3346 | | | | |
| | 3347 | | | | |
| | 3768 | | | | |
| | 3770 | | | | |
| | 3773 | | | | |
| | 3774 | | | | |
| | 3778 | | | | |
| | 3779 | | | | |
| | 3781 | | | | |
| | 3782 | | | | |
| | 3790 | | | | |
| | 3801 | | | | |
| | 3815 | | | | |

# HUMBLE HOLY FAMILY

Our Savior's humble birth in a lowly manger is the focal point of this festive season. For reverent adornments that keep the intent of the holy day firmly in mind, add a small standing crèche and a devout wall decoration to prominent spots in your home. With these ready reminders of Christmas's purpose, it will be easy to keep the reason for the season close to your heart. Instructions for these projects begin on page 42.

Perfect for the pure at heart, the **Balsa Wood Nativity** (*page 42*) features a prayerful Holy Family with a joyful fabric-embellished wooden star overhead. (*Opposite*) These simple, inspiring figures make a poignant decoration on the muslin **Nativity Wall Hanging** (*page 42*).

## NATIVITY WALL HANGING (Shown on page 41)

**For an 18" square wall hanging,** you will need a 20" square of muslin for background; 17¹/₂" square of fusible interfacing; paper-backed fusible web; pencil; ruler; tracing paper; transfer paper; brown permanent fine-point marker; red, blue, and brown colored pencils; 4" square of fabric for star; pressing cloth; two 1¹/₂" x 15³/₄" and two 1¹/₂" x 12³/₄" strips of fabric for border; four 1" dia. wooden buttons; 28" of 1"w ecru grosgrain ribbon; 19" of ³/₄" dia. wooden dowel; and thick craft glue.

**1.** Cut four ³/₄" x 19" strips from fusible web. Fuse one web strip along each edge on wrong side of muslin square. Fold edges 1" to wrong side over web; fuse in place. Center and fuse interfacing square on wrong side of muslin square.
**2.** For checkerboard border, measure 3" inside each pressed edge to draw a 12" square on muslin. Draw a parallel line 1" inside each line of square. Draw lines to divide border into 1" squares. Trace square pattern onto tracing paper. Use transfer paper to transfer detail lines onto alternating squares of border.
**3.** Omitting arches, trace Joseph, Mary, Baby Jesus, and large star patterns onto tracing paper. Arranging as desired, transfer designs inside checkerboard border. Use marker to draw over all lines

and color sawtooth border on star.
**4.** Trace small star pattern onto paper side of fusible web. Fuse web to wrong side of star fabric. Cut out star along drawn lines. Using pressing cloth, fuse fabric star to center of large star on muslin.
**5.** For fabric border, cut two 1¹/₂" x 15³/₄" and two 1¹/₂" x 12³/₄" strips from fusible web. Aligning edges, fuse matching web strip to wrong side of each fabric strip. Arranging short strips on top and bottom, long strips on sides, and using pressing cloth, center and fuse strips around checkerboard border.
**6.** Use marker to draw "stitches" ¹/₄" inside edges of wall hanging. Use blue pencil to color headdress and alternating stripes of robe on Joseph, blanket on Baby Jesus, and shawl on Mary. Use red pencil to color cheeks of each figure. Use brown pencil to add shading to Joseph, Mary, Baby Jesus, and manger.
**7.** For hanging loops, cut ribbon into four 7" lengths. Fold each ribbon length in half to form loop; glue ribbon ends together. Spacing evenly with loops extending 2" above top edge, glue ends of loops to back of wall hanging. Glue buttons to corners of fabric border. Insert dowel through hanging loops.

## BALSA WOOD NATIVITY
(Shown on page 40)

**You will need** 4" x 36" strip of ¹/₈" thick balsa wood, tracing paper, transfer paper, craft knife, sandpaper, ruler, brown permanent fine-point marker, red and blue colored pencils, one 4" square each of paper-backed fusible web and fabric for star, flat wooden toothpick, and thick craft glue.

**1.** For base, cut a 3" x 10" piece from wood; sand edges smooth. Use pencil and ruler to draw three rows of 1" squares on base. Trace square pattern onto tracing paper. Use transfer paper to transfer detail lines onto alternating squares.
**2.** Trace Joseph, Mary, Baby Jesus, and large star patterns onto tracing paper. Use transfer paper to transfer designs onto balsa wood.
**3.** Use craft knife to cut out each design along outside lines; sand edges smooth. Use marker to draw over all transferred lines. Use blue pencil to color headdress and alternating stripes of robe on Joseph, blanket on Baby Jesus, and shawl and shading of dress on Mary. Use red pencil to color cheeks on each figure.
**4.** Trace small star pattern onto paper side of fusible web. Fuse web to wrong side of star fabric. Cut out star along drawn lines. Center and fuse fabric star on wooden star.
**5.** Cut three ¹/₂" x 3" strips from wood; sand edges smooth. Glue one long edge of strip to wrong side of figure along bottom edge. Arrange figures on base as desired; glue in place. Glue star between Joseph and Mary; reinforce on wrong side by gluing toothpick across point of star and Joseph.

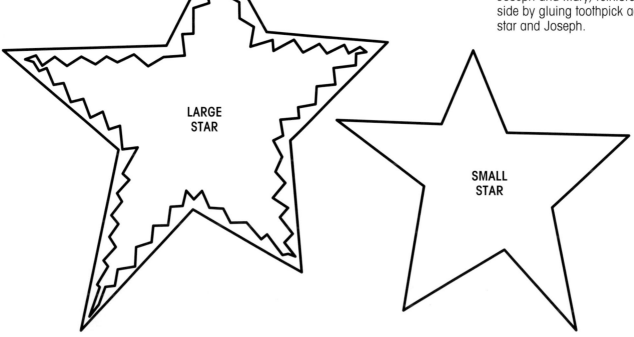

LARGE STAR

SMALL STAR

SQUARE

BABY JESUS

JOSEPH

MARY

# SNOWMAN FROLIC

*Blanket your home with the lighthearted charm of these lovable snow fellows! Covered with a blizzard of tube-sock snowmen, wintry white mitten ornaments, and miniature buckets of 5-cent "snowballs," our captivating evergreen gives a carefree, cuddly appeal to your holiday decor. Fun-loving snow people decked out with top hats, ice skates, and other fanciful flourishes add to the mischievous mood. Carry the fun outdoors with a one-of-a-kind snowman tree (complete with galoshes!) and a measuring stick friend to gauge snowfall. Indoors or out, our easy-to-make snow folk will make sure your holidays are full of merriment! Instructions for the projects shown here and on the following pages begin on page 50.*

No matter what the weather, our cheerful **Snow Buddy Pillow** *(page 53)* will melt your heart and warm your spirit. This happy-faced threesome sports cozy stocking hats on their stuffed tube-sock bodies. Buttons, jingle bells, and a pom-pom add clever accents.

From **Mini Snowball Buckets** *(page 50)* to **Cozy Mitten Ornaments** *(page 50)*, our **Snowman Frolic Tree** *(page 50)* is a frosty delight! Clever **Nordic Sock Ornaments** *(page 50)*, hand-painted **Heartwarming Ornaments** *(page 50)*, lovable **Snow Buddy Ornaments** *(page 53)*, and whimsical **Juggling Snowmen** *(page 51)* and **Top-Hat Snowmen** ornaments *(page 53)* add to the merriment. Nestled among the branches are purchased icicles, snowflakes, white ball fringe, and garlands of wooden beads and ice crystals. We also placed a glistening snowflake atop the tree.

Display festive treats, favors, or cards in a sprightly basket escorted by a pair of jolly snow characters. This **Snow Buddy Basket** *(page 53)* makes a useful and eye-catching centerpiece.

Our quick-and-easy **Snowball Tree Skirt** *(page 50)*, featuring white ball fringe and pom-pom "snowballs" in assorted sizes, echoes the tree's spirit of wintry fun.

Let your favorite people know how much you care with our **Heartwarming Ornaments** *(page 50)*. These painted iridescent glass balls are terrific as package accents, great little gifts, or glistening touches on your own evergreen.

Put smiles on the faces of all your holiday visitors with our **Whimsical Snow Buddy Tree** *(page 52)*. Decked out in wintry garb, from top hat and scarf to galoshes, this "tree-man" has irresistible appeal!

Show your love for wintertime fun by planting our **Snowfall Gauge** *(page 52)* in your yard. This measuring stick is an outdoor decoration with a purpose — youngsters can keep track of the local snowfall while declaring a love for snowy days.

Although they're dressed for frosty weather, our snow characters are quite comfortable indoors on your mantel, table, or bookshelf! Our **Skating Snow Lady** *(page 51)* is ready to take a twirl on the ice with darling "skates" — doll shoes fitted with craft steel "blades." The **Juggling Snowman** *(page 51)* and **Top-Hat Snowman** *(page 53)* are her cuddly companions. For a cute accent that's a snap to make, whip up some **Mini Snowball Buckets** *(page 50)* filled with stuffed felt "snowballs."

## SNOWMAN FROLIC TREE

(Shown on page 45)

"Let it snow! Let it snow! Let it snow!" Our frolicsome snowmen bring merriment and joy to our seven-foot-tall fir tree. Their mission is to keep you in good spirits through the Christmas season.

For whimsical fancies, we draped white ball fringe, red and green wooden bead garland, and acrylic ice crystal garland on the branches of our Snowman Frolic Tree. We purchased a majestic snowflake tree topper, acrylic icicles, and a blizzard of frosted snowflakes.

Mini Snowball Buckets are suspended from the evergreen boughs, while Heartwarming Ornaments carry a message for a special someone.

Can you believe the Nordic Sock Ornaments, Cozy Mitten Ornaments, and Snow Buddy Ornaments (page 53) began as ordinary socks? Clad in red and green, our Juggling Snowmen and Top-Hat Snowmen (page 53) are bursting with personality and ready to bring your holiday festivities to life.

To complete the effect, we used bright red felt, white pom-poms, and white ball fringe for a Snowball Tree Skirt to catch any snowballs that might fall from our flurry of fun.

## COZY MITTEN ORNAMENTS

(Shown on page 46)

**For each mitten,** you will need tracing paper, one adult-size white tube sock, stencil plastic, craft knife, cutting mat, red acrylic paint, stencil brush, child-size striped sock, white and red yarn, hot glue gun, and a 1/2" dia. button.

**1.** Trace mitten pattern, page 64, onto tracing paper. Using pattern and leaving wrist open, follow **Sewing Shapes,** page 158, to make mitten from sock.
**2.** Trace snowflake pattern onto stencil plastic. Use craft knife to cut out stencil. Place stencil on mitten and use stencil brush to paint snowflake red. Remove stencil and allow to dry.
**3.** For cuff, cut a 2 1/2" tube from child-size sock. Matching wrong sides and raw edges, fold tube in half. Matching raw edges, insert cuff in mitten; pin in place. Use a 1/4" seam allowance to sew cuff to mitten. Fold cuff out over mitten.
**4.** For yarn bow, cut several 3" lengths of white and red yarn. Knot a 10" length of yarn around center of 3" lengths, then knot ends together. Glue bow and button to mitten.

50

## SNOWBALL TREE SKIRT

(Shown on page 47)

**You will need** string, thumbtack, pencil, 60" square of red felt, 5 yds. of white ball fringe, white pom-poms in assorted sizes, and fabric glue.

**1.** Using a 2" measurement for inside cutting line and a 28" measurement for outside cutting line, follow **Cutting a Fabric Circle,** page 157, to cut skirt from red felt square.
**2.** For opening, match edges and fold skirt in half. Cut along one fold from center to outer edge.
**3.** Unfold tree skirt. With 1/2" of fringe end extending beyond one opening edge, glue fringe along outer edge of skirt. Trim remaining fringe end 1/2" past edge. Fold fringe ends to wrong side of skirt and glue in place. Glue pom-poms randomly to tree skirt. Allow to dry.

## HEARTWARMING ORNAMENTS

HEART

(Shown on page 48)

**For each ornament,** you will need an iridescent white glass ornament; red, green, and black paint pens; tracing paper; and transfer paper.

**1.** Use green paint pen to write "You melt my" on ornament.
**2.** Trace heart pattern onto tracing paper.
**3.** Use transfer paper to transfer heart to ornament.
**4.** Use red paint pen to paint heart. Use black paint pen to outline heart and freehand paint snowflakes and heart rays as desired.

SNOWFLAKE

## MINI SNOWBALL BUCKETS

(Shown on page 46)

**For each bucket,** you will need a 9-oz. red plastic cup, craft knife, hot glue gun, 2 1/2" dia. plastic foam ball, 2 1/4" x 3 1/2" piece of tan paper, black permanent fine-point marker, 5" twig, white felt, drawing compass, white thread, polyester fiberfill, 1/8" dia. hole punch, green chenille stem, craft glue, paintbrush, and artificial snow.

**Note:** Use hot glue for all gluing unless otherwise indicated.

**1.** Draw around cup 1 1/4" from bottom. Cut away bottom just above drawn line. Glue foam ball in bucket.
**2.** Use marker to write "Snowballs 5¢" and draw border on tan paper. Glue sign to one end of twig and insert opposite end into foam ball.
**3.** For snowballs, use compass to draw five 3" circles on felt; cut out. Baste 1/8" from edge around each felt circle. Stuff circles with fiberfill while gathering basting threads. Tie basting threads to secure.
**4.** Punch a hole on each side of cup for handle. Thread one end of chenille stem through each hole; bend stem ends to secure. Glue snowballs in bucket. Lightly brush craft glue on snowballs; sprinkle with snow and allow to dry.

## NORDIC SOCK ORNAMENTS

(Shown on page 46)

**For two ornaments,** you will need one ladies' knee-high red and white patterned sock, sewing needle and thread, two 4" dia. plastic foam balls, rubber band, two 18" lengths of 3/8"w green satin ribbon, hot glue gun, two 1" dia. jingle bells, and clear thread.

**1.** Cut toe from sock. Matching ends, fold sock in half; cut sock along fold. Turn tubes wrong side out. Use needle and thread to tightly gather one end of each tube. Turn tubes right side out. Place one foam ball inside each tube. Gather sock over top of ball; secure with rubber band.
**2.** Tie one ribbon length into a bow around rubber band on each ornament. Glue one bell to knot of each bow.
**3.** Follow **Making a Hanger,** page 159, to add hanger to ornament.

## SKATING SNOW LADY (Shown on page 49)

**You will need** one adult-size white tube sock; polyester fiberfill; white, brown, and black embroidery floss; white and red thread; 3½" x 11", 11" x 34", and ¼" x 3" pieces of red checked flannel; drawing compass; tracing paper; 1½" x 14" red felt strip for muffler; red and black felt; pinking shears; 2" x 3" piece of white felt; hot glue gun, orange bugle bead; small artificial holly sprig; 1" twig; ultra-thin craft steel; removable tape; sandpaper; and a pair of 2" doll shoes.

**Note:** Use a ¼" seam allowance for all sewing. Refer to **Embroidery Stitches**, page 157, and use three strands of floss for all embroidery stitches.

1. Stuff toe section of tube sock with fiberfill up to beginning of ribbed cuff. Tightly knot a length of floss 2" below toe of sock for neck. For legs, cut cuff in half from opening edge to stuffing. Use sewing thread to stitch long edges together, forming legs. Stuff each leg with fiberfill and sew ends closed.
2. For arms, match right sides and long edges of 3½" x 11" flannel piece. Sew long edges together. Turn arms right side out and stuff with fiberfill. Tack center of arms to back of body.
3. Use compass to draw a 2¾" dia. and a 9" dia. circle on tracing paper for hand and hat patterns. For each hand, use pattern to cut one 2¾" dia. circle from red felt. Baste ½" inside edge of circle. Stuff with fiberfill while pulling thread ends to gather; knot thread ends to secure. Insert gathered end into arms; sew arm to hand.
4. For dress, match right sides and short edges of 11" x 34" flannel piece. Sew short edges together and turn right side out. Baste around top of dress ¼" from edge. For armholes, position seam at center back and cut a ¾" vertical slit 1" below top edge on each side of dress.

Place dress on doll. Pull thread ends to gather dress around neck; knot thread ends. For fringe on muffler, make ½" cuts ⅛" apart on each end of red felt strip.
5. Follow **Making Patterns**, page 158, to trace jacket, eye, and blade patterns onto tracing paper. Fold black felt square in half. Aligning shoulders of jacket pattern with fold of felt, use pinking shears to cut out jacket. Sew along side seams. Use pinking shears to cut jacket open down center front; turn right side out.
6. For snowman on jacket, trace snowman pattern onto tracing paper. Use pattern to cut snowman from white felt. Using black floss, stitch French Knots for eyes. Sew bead to face for nose. Wrap ¼" x 3" strip of flannel around neck. Glue snowman to jacket front. Using brown floss, work Straight Stitch for twig arms.
7. Using white floss, stitch a ¾" and a ⅜" Cross Stitch for each large snowflake on opposite side of jacket front. Work a French Knot at each end of ¾" cross stitch. Work additional French Knots on jacket front as desired.
8. Using 9" dia. circle pattern and pinking shears, cut one circle from black felt. Using black floss, baste around circle 1" inside edge. Stuff with fiberfill while pulling thread ends to loosely gather; knot thread ends to secure. Glue hat to head. Glue holly to hat.
9. Use patterns to cut two eyes from black felt. Glue eyes to face. Make a small clip in sock for nose. Apply glue to one end of twig and insert ¼" of glued end into hole. Using black floss and Running Stitch, stitch mouth. Work a French Knot at each end of mouth.
10. For each skate, tape blade pattern on craft steel; cut out. Sand edges smooth. Fold blade posts to a 90° angle as indicated by dashed lines on pattern. Glue blade to bottom of shoe. Glue leg in skate.

## JUGGLING SNOWMEN
(Shown on page 49)

**For each ornament,** you will need 2¼" wooden heart, black acrylic paint, paintbrush, white child-size tube sock, polyester fiberfill, rubber band, white thread, two 10" lengths of white thread-covered floral wire, hot glue gun, orange and black felt, black embroidery floss, red colored pencil, one striped child-size crew sock, 4" twigs for arms, four ½" dia. pom-poms, and one green child-size crew sock.

1. Paint heart black; allow to dry.
2. Stuff toe section of tube sock with fiberfill up to beginning of ribbed cuff. Gather sock over fiberfill; secure with rubber band. Roll cuff over rubber band.
3. Divide body into three equal sections by knotting a length of thread around body in two places.
4. Fold one length of wire in half. Push wire into body for support. Glue wooden heart to cuff for feet.
5. Cut two circles from black felt for eyes and one triangle from orange felt for nose; glue to face. Use three strands of black floss and **Running Stitch**, page 157, to stitch mouth. Use red pencil to color cheeks.
6. Cut a 2½" tube from striped sock. Use thread to baste around one edge of tube. Place tube over snowman; gather and tie thread ends around neck. Stuff front of tube with fiberfill; turn cut edge under.
7. For each arm, cut a 1½" x 3" piece from striped sock. Wrap and glue sock piece around one end of one twig end. Glue sock-covered end of twig to body.
8. Thread three pom-poms onto remaining wire; bend wire into a semicircle. Wrap one end of wire around each arm; glue to secure. Arrange and glue pom-poms as desired.
9. For hat, roll cuff of green sock ½" to right side two or three times. Glue hat to head. Glue remaining pom-pom to hat.

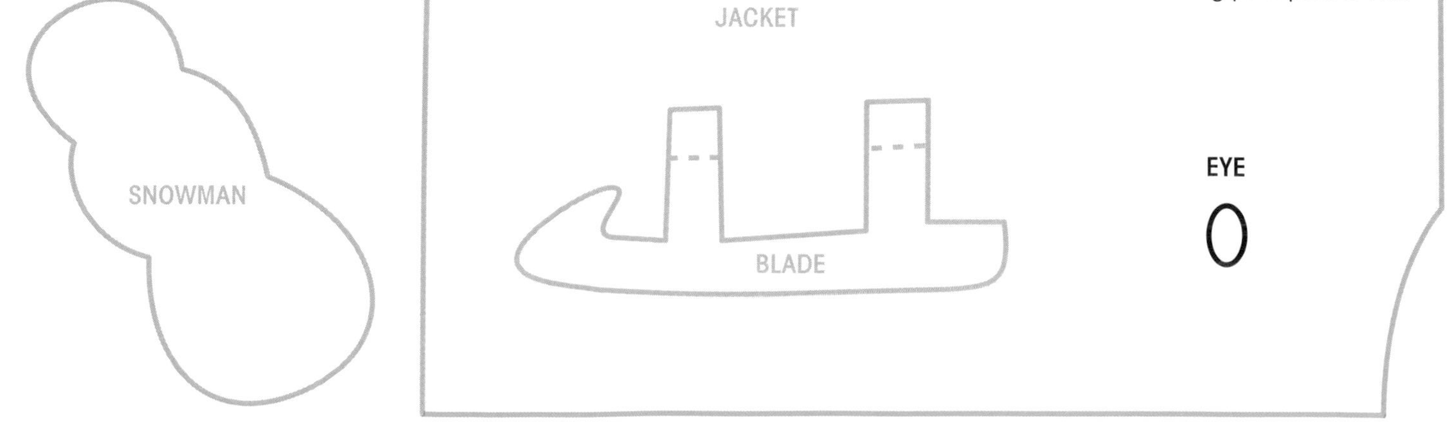

SNOWMAN

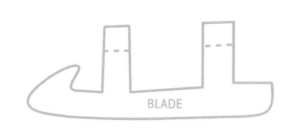

JACKET

BLADE

EYE

0

## WHIMSICAL SNOW BUDDY TREE (Shown on page 48)

**You will need** tracing paper; string; thumbtack; pencil; white corrugated plastic; white, orange, pink, red, green, and black craft foam; craft knife; low-temperature hot glue gun; orange, pink, and black markers; two white chenille stems; drawing compass; a pair of galoshes; a 5-foot-tall artificial tree; 2$\frac{1}{2}$" dia. and 4" dia. plastic foam balls for snowballs; batting; artificial snow; craft glue; and a 10" x 48" piece of red fleece for muffler.

**Note:** Use glue gun for all gluing unless otherwise indicated.

**1.** Using a 6$\frac{1}{2}$" measurement for cutting line, follow **Cutting a Fabric Circle**, page 157, to cut head pattern from a 14" square of tracing paper. Use pattern to cut head from corrugated plastic.
**2.** For hat pattern, cut a 2" x 18" rectangle and a 6" x 10$\frac{1}{2}$" rectangle from tracing paper. Center 10$\frac{1}{2}$" edge of wide rectangle on one 18" edge of narrow rectangle. Use pattern to cut hat from black foam. For hatband, cut a 2$\frac{1}{2}$" x 10$\frac{1}{2}$" piece from red foam.
**3.** Trace star, eye, nose, highlight, and heart patterns onto tracing paper; cut out. Use patterns to cut one nose from orange foam, two eyes from black foam, two highlights from white foam, two hearts from pink foam, and three stars from green foam. Use markers to add shading to nose and hearts.
**4.** Glue stars to hatband, hatband to hat, and highlights to eyes. Glue eyes, nose, and hearts to face. Use black marker to draw mouth on face.
**5.** Glue one end of each chenille stem to center back of head. Use chenille stems to fasten head to top of tree.
**6.** For buttons, use drawing compass to draw three 4" dia. circles on green craft foam and three 5" dia. circles on red craft foam; cut out. Center and glue one green circle on each red circle. Use black marker to draw an "X" in the center of each green circle. Draw dots at outer points of each "X."
**7.** Place galoshes under tree for feet. For snowballs, cover foam balls with batting; glue in place. Lightly spread craft glue over ball and roll in artificial snow. Tuck 6"w strips of batting into tree branches and sprinkle with artificial snow. Place snowballs in tree limbs. Glue buttons to front of tree.
**8.** For fringe on muffler, make 4" cuts $\frac{1}{2}$" apart on each end of fleece. Loosely tie muffler around tree.

## SNOWFALL GAUGE
(Shown on page 49)

**You will need** tracing paper; string; thumbtack; pencil; white corrugated plastic; craft knife; white, orange, pink, red, green, and black craft foam; orange, pink, and black permanent markers; 1$\frac{1}{2}$"w yardstick; 24" square of kraft paper; 17" length of $\frac{1}{4}$" x 1" wooden stick; and a low-temperature hot glue gun.

**1.** Follow Steps 1 - 4 of Whimsical Snow Buddy Tree to make head.
**2.** For sign, cut a 7" x 10" piece of corrugated plastic. Cut two each 1" x 7" and 1" x 10" strips from black foam for border. Trace border pattern onto tracing paper. Use pattern to cut notches along one long edge of each border strip. Use heart pattern to cut one heart from red foam. Glue heart and border strips to sign. Use black marker to write "I" and "Snow" on sign. Glue sign to wooden stick.
**3.** Aligning arrows and dotted lines, trace upper arm and hand patterns onto tracing paper; cut out. For full arm pattern, fold kraft paper in half. Matching blue line of pattern to fold of paper, draw around pattern; cut out and unfold. Use full arm pattern to cut arms from corrugated plastic.
**4.** Glue head to 36-inch end of yardstick. Glue arms to back of yardstick. Glue sign to hand.

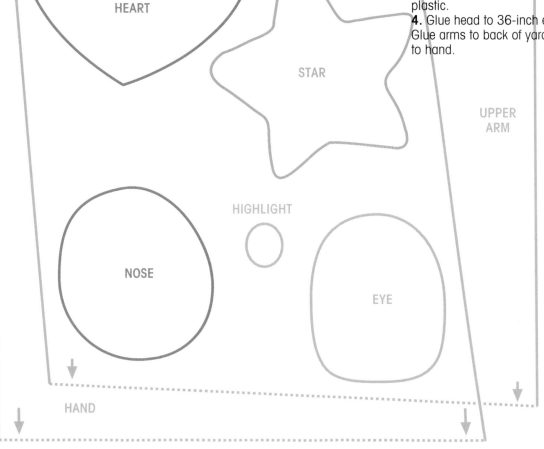

BORDER

HEART

STAR

UPPER ARM

HIGHLIGHT

NOSE

EYE

HAND

## SNOW BUDDY ORNAMENTS (Shown on page 46)

**For each ornament,** you will need one youth-size white tube sock, polyester fiberfill, rubber band, fabric scraps, fabric glue, two 1/4" dia. black shank buttons for eyes, red and green embroidery floss, assorted buttons for front of body, 3/8" dia. jingle bell, tracing paper, one pair of infant-size crew socks for arms, white thread, and clear thread.

**For white hat buddy,** you will **also** need a 1/4" dia. red shank button for nose and a 1" dia. green pom-pom for hat.

**For green or red hat buddy,** you will **also** need a child-size green or red crew sock and a 1/4" dia. red shank button for nose.

**For striped hat buddy,** you will **also** need a child-size striped crew sock, orange and green felt, and red worsted weight yarn.

**Note:** Large snow buddies can be made from adult-size tube socks using 1/2" dia. jingle bells, 1/2" dia. shank button for nose, and 11/2" dia. pom-poms. Allow glue to dry after each application.

### WHITE HAT BUDDY
1. Stuff toe section of tube sock with fiberfill up to beginning of ribbed cuff. Gather sock over fiberfill; secure with rubber band.
2. For hat, fold cuff down over stuffed sock. Fold edge of hat 1/2" to right side two or three times.
3. Tear 1" squares of fabric for patches. Glue patches and pom-pom to hat.
4. Sew buttons to face for eyes and nose. Use three strands of red floss to work **Stem Stitch**, page 157, for mouth. Use floss to sew buttons and jingle bell to snowman.
5. For muffler, tear a 3" x 12" fabric strip. Tie muffler around neck.
6. Trace heart pattern, page 50, onto tracing paper. Use pattern to cut one heart from fabric; glue to hat.
7. For each arm, cut foot from infant-size sock; stuff toe section with fiberfill. Sew opening closed. Use thread to gather a small amount of sock to form thumb. Sew arms to body.
8. Follow **Making a Hanger**, page 159, to add hanger to ornament.

### GREEN OR RED HAT BUDDY
1. Follow Step 1 of White Hat Buddy to make body. Cut off cuff above rubber band.

2. For hat, cut ribbed cuff from red or green sock. Fold finished edge of hat 1/2" to right side two or three times. Place hat on head. Tie floss into a bow around top of hat.
3. Follow Steps 4 - 8 of White Hat Buddy to finish ornament.

### STRIPED HAT BUDDY
1. Follow Step 1 of White Hat Buddy to make body. Cut off cuff above rubber band.
2. For hat, fold cuff of striped sock 1" to right side two or three times. Place hat on head. Glue tip of hat to cuff. Glue bell to tip of hat.
3. Trace nose pattern onto tracing paper. Use pattern to cut nose from orange felt. Roll nose into a cone shape; glue to secure. Glue nose to face. Use three strands of red floss to work **Stem Stitches**, page 157, for mouth. Sew buttons to face for eyes. Use floss to sew buttons to front of snowman.
4. Follow Step 7 of White Hat Buddy to add arms to snowman.
5. Trace mitten pattern onto tracing paper. Use pattern to cut four mittens from green felt. Glue two mittens together over each end of yarn. Knot mittens around body.
6. Trace heart pattern onto tracing paper. Use pattern to cut two hearts from fabric; glue one heart to each mitten.
7. Follow **Making a Hanger**, page 159, to add hanger to ornament.

## SNOW BUDDY BASKET
(Shown on page 47)

Make a large White Hat Buddy and a large Green or Red Hat Buddy. Glue one buddy to each side of a handled basket.

## SNOW BUDDY PILLOW
(Shown on page 44)

Make one large White Hat Buddy with right arm, one large Green or Red Hat Buddy with left arm, and one large Striped Hat Buddy with no arms. Sew buddies together along sides.

## TOP-HAT SNOWMEN
(Shown on page 49)

**For one ornament,** you will need a 21/4" wooden heart; white, green, and black acrylic paint; paintbrush; child-size white tube sock; polyester fiberfill; rubber band; white, red, and black thread; 10" of floral wire; a hot glue gun; tracing paper; orange, red, green, and black felt; white and black embroidery floss; red colored pencil; 4" twigs for arms; drawing compass; three 3/8" dia. black buttons; red berry pick; and a 2" wooden tree.

1. Follow steps 1 - 5 of Juggling Snowman, page 51, to make body. For arms, glue one twig to each side of body.
2. Follow **Making Patterns**, page 158, to trace coat pattern onto tracing paper. Use pattern to cut coat from red felt. Beginning between curved edges, cut coat open along center front.
3. Use two strands of white floss to work **Blanket Stitch**, page 157, along front and neck edges of coat. Place coat on snowman. Use red thread to stitch side and sleeve edges together. Fold up sleeves.
4. Use compass to draw a 31/2" dia. and a 5" dia. circle on tracing paper for hat patterns. Use patterns to cut one of each circle from black felt.
5. Use thread to baste 1/8" inside edge of 5" dia. circle; stuff with fiberfill while pulling thread ends to gather. Fold gathered edges under. Center and glue folds on 31/2" dia. circle.
6. For muffler, cut a 11/2" x 10" piece of green felt. For fringe, make 1/2" clips in short ends.
7. Glue hat, muffler, and buttons to snowman. Glue holly to hat.
8. Paint tree green; allow to dry. Dot white paint on tree; allow to dry. Glue tree to one arm.

COAT

MITTEN

NOSE

# YULETIDE MEMORIES

*The coming together of family and friends at Christmastime creates memories that last a lifetime. This festive collection is full of ways to capture those cherished moments so they may be enjoyed again and again. For decorating the tree, you'll find creative photograph ornaments and hand-painted baubles, as well as a merry memento tin. For truly timeless reminders of your loved ones, there are precious keepsakes such as a memory album and a personalized Christmas quilt. Instructions for the projects shown here and on the following pages begin on page 58.*

A charming quilt square and cheery bow adorn our fabric-covered **Yuletide Memories Album** *(page 62)*. The **Memory Album Pages** *(page 62)* are decorated with jolly motifs to accent your favorite photographs. *(Opposite)* Wrap someone special in holiday spirit with a **Yuletide Memories Quilt** *(page 58)*. Each block contains a loved one's signature that is stitched over with embroidery floss.

*(Top left)* Remember the holidays with our charming dated **Quilt-Block Ornament** *(page 62)* made from remnants of holiday fabric or show off a picture of someone sweet in this **Candy Cane Heart Ornament** *(page 65)*. **Starry Glass Ornaments** *(page 63)* are easy to decorate using paint pens. *(Top right)* Leave lasting impressions of a child's touch on these **Handprint Ornaments** *(page 64)*. They're created from fabric-covered poster board shapes stamped with handprints. *(Above)* These **Stocking Photo Ornaments** *(page 61)*, fashioned from painted canvas and "stuffed" with photographs, make fun and festive decorations for the mantel or tree.

Store your precious remembrances in a colorful **Holiday Keepsake Tin** *(page 60)*. We accented a spray-painted can with simple Christmas designs and topped it with a fabric-covered lid.

These decorations are even more festive when they're sporting the faces of your favorite folks! To make our adorable **Star Photo Ornaments** *(page 61)*, **Snow Folk Ornaments** *(page 63)*, **Bearded Santa Ornaments** *(page 65)*, and **Gingerbread Photo Ornaments** *(page 64)*, simple holiday shapes are cut from felt.

# YULETIDE MEMORIES QUILT (Shown on page 55)

**Block size:** 14¼" x 14¼"
**Quilt size:** 75" x 91"

**Note:** Fabric yardage is based on 45"w fabric. All fabrics should be washed, dried, and pressed before beginning project.

**You will need** 3⅝ yds. of green print fabric, 3¾ yds. of white print fabric, 2⅜ yds. of red print fabric, rotary cutter, rotary cutting ruler, cutting mat, sewing thread, quilter's silver pencil, embroidery floss, embroidery needle, embroidery hoop (optional), stencil plastic, craft knife, 81" x 96" fabric (pieced as necessary) for quilt backing, masking tape, 81" x 96" batting, quilting hoop or frame, quilting needle, quilting thread, thimble, and 1 yd. of fabric for binding.

## CUTTING OUT THE PIECES

**Note:** All measurements include a ¼" seam allowance. Strips are cut from selvage to selvage across the width of the fabric. To cut strips, fold fabric, matching selvages. Aligning ruler at a right angle to fold of fabric, cut one edge to even fabric. Continue cutting strips from evened edge. Use rotary cutter, rotary cutting ruler, and cutting mat for all cutting.

**1.** From green print:
• Cut 12 **strips** 2⅞"w.
• Cut 2 lengthwise **side borders** 4" x 83¾".
• Cut 2 lengthwise **top/bottom borders** 4" x 74½".
**2.** From white print:
• Cut 12 **strips** 2⅞"w.
• Cut 3 strips 14¾"w. From these strips, cut 49 **sashing strips** 2½" x 14¾".
• Cut 6 strips 5¼"w. From these strips, cut 80 **rectangles** 2⅞" x 5¼".
• Cut 3 strips 5¼"w. From these strips, cut 20 **large squares** 5¼" x 5¼".
**3.** From red print:
• Cut 6 strips 5¼"w. From these strips, cut 80 **rectangles** 2⅞" x 5¼".
• Cut 12 strips 2⅞"w. From these strips, cut 160 **squares** 2⅞" x 2⅞".
• Cut 2 strips 2½"w. From these strips, cut 30 **sashing squares** 2½" x 2½".

## ASSEMBLING THE QUILT TOP

**Note:** Unless otherwise indicated, match right sides and raw edges and use a ¼" seam allowance and sewing thread for all sewing. Press seam allowances to one side (toward darker fabric when possible).

**1.** Sew 1 white and 1 green **strip** together to make **Strip Set**. Make 12 **Strip Sets**. Cut across **Strip Sets** at 2⅞" intervals to make 160 **Unit 1's**.

**Strip Set** (make 12)       **Unit 1** (make 160)

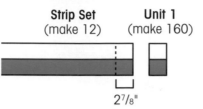
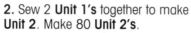

2⅞"

**2.** Sew 2 **Unit 1's** together to make **Unit 2**. Make 80 **Unit 2's**.

**Unit 2** (make 80)

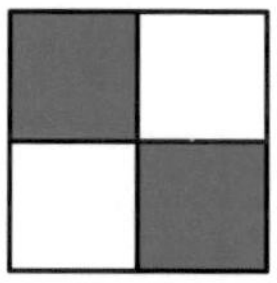

**3.** Place 1 red **square** on 1 white **rectangle** and stitch diagonally as shown in **Fig. 1**. Trim ¼" from stitching line as shown in **Fig. 2**. Press open, pressing seam allowance toward darker fabric.

**Fig. 1**          **Fig. 2**

**4.** Place 1 red **square** on opposite end of **rectangle**. Stitch diagonally, as shown in **Fig. 3**. Trim ¼" from stitching line as shown in **Fig. 4**. Press open, pressing seam allowance toward darker fabric, to make **Unit 3**.

**Fig. 3**          **Fig. 4**

**Unit 3**

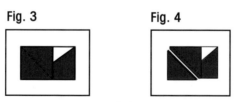

**5.** Using remaining red **squares** and white **rectangles**, repeat Steps 3 and 4 to make a total of 80 **Unit 3's**.
**6.** Sew 1 **Unit 3** and 1 red **rectangle** together to make **Unit 4**. Make 80 **Unit 4's**.

**Unit 4** (make 80)

**7.** Sew 2 **Unit 2's** and 1 **Unit 4** together to make **Unit 5**. Make 40 **Unit 5's**.

**Unit 5** (make 40)

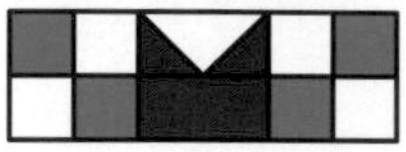

**8.** Sew 2 **Unit 4's** and 1 **large square** together to make **Unit 6**. Make 20 **Unit 6's**.

**Unit 6** (make 20)

**9.** Sew 2 **Unit 5's** and 1 **Unit 6** together to make **Block**. Make 20 **Blocks**.

**Block** (make 20)

**10.** Sew 5 **sashing squares** and 4 **sashing strips** together to make **Sashing Row**. Make 6 **Sashing Rows**.

**Sashing Row** (make 6)

**11.** Sew 5 **sashing strips** and 4 **Blocks** together to make **Block Row**. Make 5 **Block Rows**.

**Block Row** (make 5)

**12.** Referring to **Quilt Top Diagram**, sew **Sashing Rows** and **Block Rows** together to make center section of quilt top.
**13.** Sew **side**, then **top** and **bottom borders** to center section of quilt top.

## COMPLETING THE QUILT

**14.** For embellishment, have family members use silver pencil to write names and messages on center squares of quilt blocks. Use embroidery floss to work **Stem Stitch**, page 157, over penciled messages.

**15.** Using quilting patterns, this page and page 60, follow **Making Patterns**, page 158, to trace patterns onto stencil plastic. Use craft knife to cut narrow segments along traced lines. Referring to **Quilting Diagram**, use stencils and silver pencil to mark quilting lines on quilt top.

**16.** To layer quilt, place quilt backing wrong side up on a large, flat surface. Use masking tape to tape edges in place. Center batting on backing. Center quilt top right side up on batting. Beginning at center of quilt and smoothing fullness toward outer edges, baste quilt layers together (use long stitches and place basting lines 3" to 4" apart).

**17.** Secure quilt in a quilting hoop or frame. Thread quilting needle with an 18" to 20" length of quilting thread; knot one end. Using a thimble, insert needle into quilt top 1/2" from where you wish to begin quilting. Bring needle back up at desired beginning point. When knot catches on quilt top, give thread a quick, short pull to "pop" knot through fabric into batting. Using a short **Running Stitch**, page 157, through all fabric layers, quilt along all marked lines. At end of each thread length, knot thread close to fabric and "pop" knot into batting. Clip thread close to fabric.

**18.** Cutting binding strips 2 1/2"w, follow **Binding**, page 158, to bind quilt.

**QUILT TOP DIAGRAM**

**QUILTING DIAGRAM**

# HOLIDAY KEEPSAKE TIN (Shown on page 57)

**You will need** a large tin (we used a 10" dia. x 11"h tin); white spray primer; white spray paint; medium-weight batting; white solid, red and green print, and red striped fabrics; paper-backed fusible web; 3/8"w red print and 3/4"w green grosgrain ribbon; 3/4" iron-on letters; green and red felt; tracing paper; pinking shears; fabric glue; and a hot glue gun.

**Note:** Use hot glue for all gluing unless otherwise indicated.

**1.** Remove lid from tin. Allowing to dry between applications, paint outside of tin with primer, then white paint.

**2.** Trace around lid on batting, white fabric, and wrong side of red print fabric. Cut out batting along drawn line. Cut out print fabric 3/4" outside drawn line. Use pinking shears to cut out white fabric 1 1/2" inside drawn line.

**3.** Glue batting to top of lid. Center and glue print fabric circle over batting. Make 1/2" clips in fabric around lid. Glue edges of fabric to side of lid. Trim fabric even with bottom edge of lid if necessary.

**4.** Measure around lid; add 1/2". Cut a length of each ribbon the determined measurement. Overlapping ends at back, glue 3/4", then 3/8" ribbons around lid. Repeat to add ribbon around bottom of tin.

**5.** Use fabric glue to glue white circle to green felt. Using pinking shears and leaving a 1/8" felt border, cut out circle. Follow manufacturer's instructions to fuse letters to circle. Using fabric glue, center and glue circle to lid.

**6.** Using patterns, pages 106 and 107, follow **Making Appliqués**, page 158, to make one each tree, gingerbread boy, large star, and heart appliqués from desired fabrics.

**7.** Cut four 5" x 7 1/4" rectangles each from white fabric and web. Cut one 4" x 7 1/4" rectangle each from striped fabric and web. Cut one 4" x 5" rectangle each from striped fabric and web. Fuse web to wrong side of each fabric piece. Cut 4" x 7 1/4" rectangle into eight 1/2" x 7 1/4" strips. Cut 4" x 5" rectangle into eight 1/2" x 5" strips.

**8.** Use pinking shears to cut two 5 1/2" x 7 3/4" rectangles each from red and green felt. Center and fuse one white rectangle to each felt rectangle. Center and fuse one appliqué to each rectangle. Fuse long, then short strips along edges of each white rectangle.

**9.** Spacing evenly, glue rectangles to side of tin.

QUILTING PATTERN

## STOCKING PHOTO ORNAMENTS (Shown on page 56)

**For each ornament,** you will need tracing paper; canvas fabric; gesso; transfer paper; white, red, and green acrylic paint; paintbrushes; black permanent medium-point marker; white paper; craft glue; photograph; poster board; craft stick; hot glue gun; 4" of grosgrain ribbon; and a button.

**Note:** Use hot glue for all gluing unless otherwise indicated. Allow gesso, paint, and glue to dry after each application.

1. Trace stocking pattern, including detail lines, onto tracing paper. Use pattern to cut two stocking shapes from canvas.
2. Matching edges and leaving top edge open, use a ¹/₄" seam allowance to sew stocking pieces together. Trim seam allowance to ¹/₈".

3. Paint stocking with gesso. Use transfer paper to transfer cuff, toe, and heel lines onto stocking. Use acrylic paints to paint cuff white and stocking, heel, and toe desired colors. If desired, transfer small star and "stitches" to stocking. Paint details on stocking. Use marker to write desired message on white paper; cut out. Use craft glue to glue message on cuff.
4. Use craft glue to glue photograph on poster board; cut out as desired. Glue craft stick to back of poster board. Insert craft stick in stocking; glue to secure.
5. For hanging loop, glue ends of ribbon inside stocking. Glue button to front of stocking below hanger.

## STAR PHOTO ORNAMENTS
(Shown on page 57)

**For each ornament,** you will need one 6" square each of white felt and poster board, craft glue, green print fabric scrap, red print fabric scrap, paper-backed fusible web, green felt, pinking shears, tracing paper, photograph, hot glue gun, 12" of ¹/₈"w gold braid, black permanent fine-point marker, five 5mm gold jingle bells, and clear thread.

**Note:** Use craft glue for all gluing unless otherwise indicated. Allow glue to dry after each application.

1. Glue white felt to poster board.
2. Using heart and large star patterns, follow **Making Appliqués**, page 158, to make heart appliqué from green fabric and star appliqué from red fabric. Fuse star to felt-covered poster board. Leaving a ¹/₄" white border, cut out star. Glue star to green felt. Using pinking shears and leaving a ¹/₄" green border, cut out star. Fuse heart to center of red star.
3. Trace star photo pattern onto tracing paper. Use pattern to cut face from photograph. Glue photograph to center of heart. Beginning at top, hot glue braid around photograph. Tie remaining braid into a bow. Hot glue bow above photograph.
4. Use marker to draw "stitches" around heart and along edges of red star. Hot glue a jingle bell to each point of red star.
5. Follow **Making a Hanger**, page 159, to add hanger to ornament.

LARGE
STAR

STOCKING

SMALL
STAR

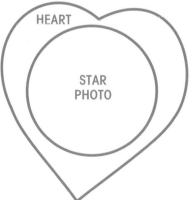

HEART

STAR
PHOTO

# YULETIDE MEMORIES ALBUM
(Shown on page 54)

**You will need** a photo album with acid-free pages and aluminum post-and-screw binders; batting; red striped fabric to cover album; red, green, and white print fabrics; paper-backed fusible web; hot glue gun, 8" of 60"w green felt; decorative-edge craft scissors; poster board; one Quilt-Block Ornament without buttons, bow, and hanger; 16" length of 1"w satin ribbon; and a 1" dia. button.

**1.** Draw around closed album twice on poster board and batting. Cut out batting pieces along drawn lines and poster board pieces 1/4" inside drawn lines. Glue one batting piece each to front and back covers. Remove covers from album. With stripes positioned vertically on album, draw around entire front cover on wrong side of fabric. Cut out 4" outside drawn lines. Repeat for back cover.
**2.** Center album front batting side down on wrong side of one fabric piece. Fold corners of fabric piece diagonally over corners of cover; glue in place. Fold edges of fabric over edges of cover; glue in place. Make clips in fabric at holes for posts. Repeat for back cover. Replace covers on album.
**3.** Measure height of album; add 3". Cut one piece 7"w by the determined measurement each from red fabric and web. Fuse web to wrong side of fabric. Fuse fabric to green felt. Using craft scissors and leaving a 3/8" felt edge, trim edges of fabric piece. Centering fabric piece on front cover, wrap and glue short ends to inside of cover.
**4.** With stripes positioned vertically on poster board piece, draw around poster board piece on wrong side of fabric. Cut out 2" outside drawn lines. Center poster board on wrong side of fabric. Fold corners of fabric piece diagonally over corners of poster board; glue in place. Fold edges of fabric over edges of poster board; glue in place. Center and glue fabric-covered poster board inside front cover. Repeat for back cover.
**5.** Center and glue ornament on front of album.
**6.** Tie ribbon into a bow. Glue button and bow at top of quilt square.

# MEMORY ALBUM PAGES
(Shown on page 54)

**You will need** tracing paper; 8 1/2" x 11" sheets of acid-free paper in solids and prints; colored pencils; green, brown, and black permanent medium-point markers; photographs; glue stick; decorative-edge craft scissors; and acid-free album pages.

## GINGERBREAD BOY PAGE
**1.** Trace gingerbread boy pattern, page 106, onto tracing paper; cut out. For each gingerbread boy, use brown marker to draw around pattern on right side of acid-free paper; cut out just outside drawn lines. Use black marker to add face and buttons to gingerbread boy. Use brown pencil to shade edges of gingerbread boy. Use white pencil to draw zigzags across arms and legs.
**2.** For each photo, glue photo to desired paper for border. Using craft scissors and leaving a 1/4" border, cut out photo. Arrange photos and gingerbread boys on desired paper for background; glue in place. Use markers and colored pencils to freehand greenery and berry details on page as desired. Glue photo page to album page.

## TREE PAGE
**1.** Trace tree and trunk patterns, page 106, onto tracing paper; cut out. Draw around patterns on wrong side of acid-free paper; cut out.
**2.** For each photo, glue photo to desired paper for border. Using craft scissors and leaving a 1/4" border, cut out photo. Use green pencil to add line and dot details along edges of border. Arrange photos, trunk, and tree on desired background paper; glue in place. Use white pencil to add snowflakes and dots to background paper. Glue photo page to album page.

# QUILT-BLOCK ORNAMENTS
(Shown on page 56)

**For each ornament,** you will need one 4 1/2" square each of white print fabric, poster board, and paper-backed fusible web; red and green print fabric scraps; paper-backed fusible web; craft glue; green felt; pinking shears; 12" of 1"w red satin polka-dot ribbon; four 3/8" dia. white buttons; black permanent fine-point marker; and clear thread.

**1.** Fuse web square to white fabric square. Fuse fabric to poster board.
**2.** Using patterns A and B, follow **Making Appliqués**, page 158, to make four A appliqués from red fabric and eight B appliqués from green fabric.
**3.** Arrange appliqués on fabric-covered poster board and fuse in place.
**4.** Glue quilt block to green felt. Using pinking shears and leaving a 1/4" green border, cut out quilt block.
**5.** Tie ribbon into a bow; glue bow and buttons to ornament.
**6.** Use marker to write date across center of ornament.
**7.** Follow **Making a Hanger**, page 159, to add hanger to ornament.

A

B

## SNOW FOLK ORNAMENTS (Shown on page 57)

**For each ornament,** you will need one 4" x 6" piece each of white felt and poster board, craft glue, tracing paper, assorted colors of felt scraps, photograph for face, buttons, small artificial holly with berries, and clear thread.

**Note:** Allow glue to dry after each application.

**1.** Glue white felt to poster board.
**2.** Trace snowman photo, body, hat or bonnet, and shawl or scarf patterns onto tracing paper; cut out.

**3.** Use body pattern to cut body from felt-covered poster board. Use snowman photo pattern to cut face from photograph. Cut remaining pieces from desired colors of felt scraps.
**4.** Glue photograph, felt pieces, and buttons to body. Glue holly to hat.
**5.** Follow **Making a Hanger**, page 159, to add hanger to ornament.

## STARRY GLASS ORNAMENTS
(Shown on page 56)

**For each ornament,** you will need a red frosted glass ornament, pencil, and white and green paint pens.

**1.** Use pencil to draw desired designs on ornament.
**2.** Use paint pens to draw over designs; allow to dry.

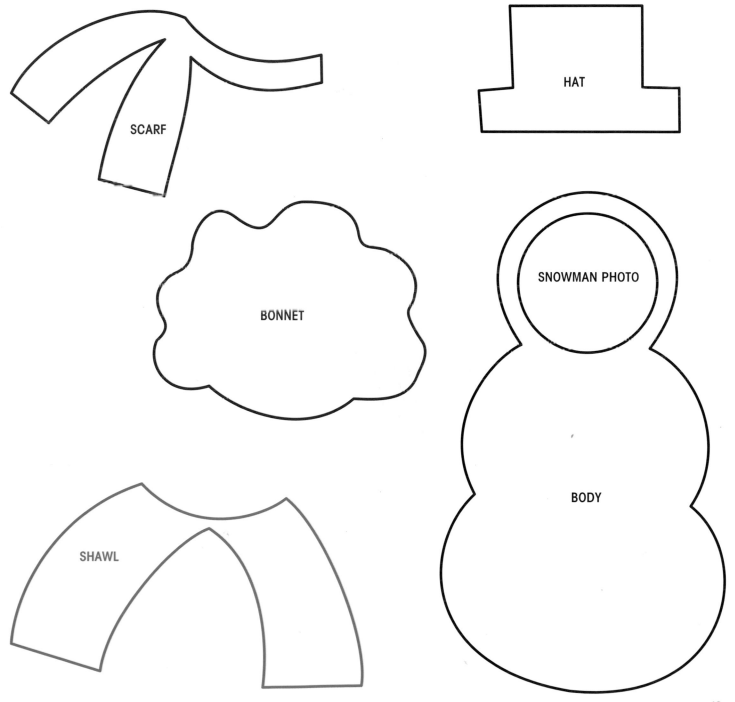

SCARF

HAT

BONNET

SNOWMAN PHOTO

BODY

SHAWL

# HANDPRINT ORNAMENTS (Shown on page 56)

**For each ornament,** you will need paper-backed fusible web, green gingham fabric, poster board, red acrylic paint, foam plate, tracing paper, white fabric, transfer paper, black permanent fine-point marker, red and green dimensional paint, $1/8$"w red braided trim, 8" length of $1/8$"w red satin ribbon, and a hot glue gun.

1. Fuse web to wrong side of fabrics. Fuse gingham fabric to poster board.
2. Pour acrylic paint onto plate. Place child's hand palm down in paint. Stamp handprint on gingham.
3. Follow **Making Patterns**, page 158, to make mitten and cuff patterns; cut out.
4. Centering palm prints on mitten, draw around pattern. Cut out mitten.
5. Use cuff pattern to cut cuff from white fabric. Use transfer paper to transfer holly design to cuff. Fuse cuff to mitten. Use marker to write year on cuff. Use dimensional paint to add name and paint holly leaves and berries.
6. Wrapping ends to wrong side, glue trim along lower edge of cuff. Forming a 1" loop at center of ribbon, knot ends together. Glue knot of loop to corner of cuff.

# GINGERBREAD PHOTO ORNAMENTS
(Shown on page 57)

**For each ornament,** you will need one 7" square each of tan felt and poster board, tracing paper, photograph for face, craft glue, white baby rickrack, 8" of $1/8$"w red satin polka-dot ribbon, three buttons, and clear thread.

**Note:** Allow glue to dry after each application.

1. Glue felt to poster board.
2. Trace gingerbread man and photo patterns onto tracing paper; cut out.
3. Use gingerbread man pattern to cut body from felt-covered poster board. Use photo pattern to cut face from photograph. Glue face to body.
4. Overlapping ends, glue rickrack along edges of body. Tie ribbon into a bow. Glue bow to neck and buttons to body.
5. Follow **Making a Hanger**, page 159, to add hanger to ornament.

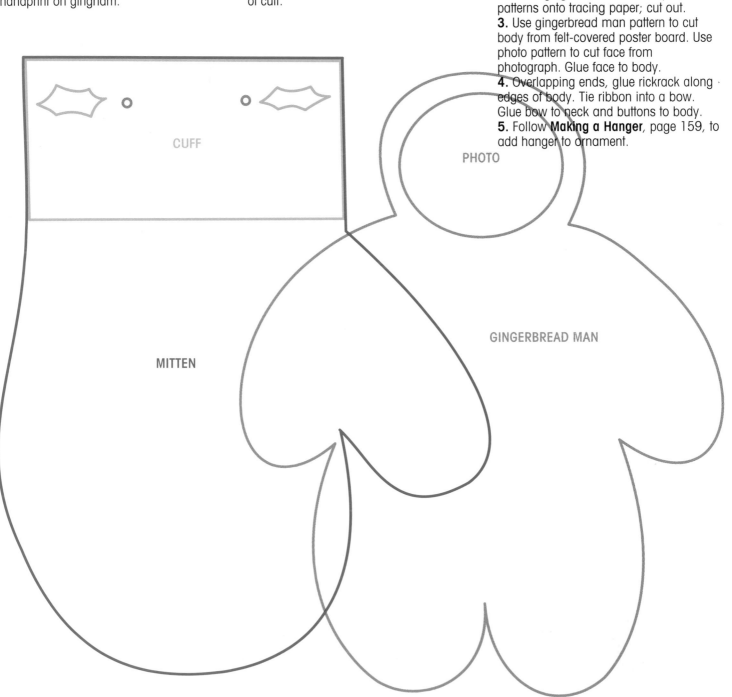

CUFF

PHOTO

MITTEN

GINGERBREAD MAN

## CANDY CANE HEART ORNAMENTS (Shown on page 56)

**For each ornament,** you will need tracing paper, aluminum foil, cookie sheet, white polymer clay, 1" of craft wire, red acrylic paint, paintbrush, 2¼"w wooden heart, black permanent fine-point marker, hot glue gun, spray matte sealer, 9" of ³⁄₈"w green satin ribbon, craft glue, poster board, photograph, 14" of ⅛"w green satin polka-dot ribbon, and a ½" dia. gold jingle bell.

**Note:** Use hot glue for all gluing unless otherwise indicated. Allow paint and sealer to dry after each application.

**1.** Trace heart pattern onto tracing paper. Place a piece of aluminum foil larger than pattern on cookie sheet. Trace over pattern on aluminum foil. Roll an 18" long ¼" dia. piece of clay. Place clay on pattern, trimming ends as necessary. Bend wire and insert ends into point of heart. Follow manufacturer's instructions to bake clay. Allow to cool.

**2.** Use red paint to paint wooden heart and stripes on candy canes. Use marker to write name and date on wooden heart. Glue wooden heart between tops of candy canes. Spray frame with sealer.

**3.** Fold 9" ribbon length in half. Glue ends to back of wooden heart.

**4.** Use craft glue to glue photograph to poster board; allow to dry. Draw around heart frame on tracing paper. Cut out pattern ⅛" inside drawn lines. Use pattern to cut out photograph. Hot glue photo to back of frame.

**5.** Thread remaining ribbon length through bell and wire loop at bottom of heart. Tie ribbon into a bow.

## BEARDED SANTA ORNAMENTS
(Shown on page 57)

**For each ornament,** you will need a 1"w wooden star, yellow acrylic paint, paintbrush, one 4½" x 6" piece each of white felt and poster board, craft glue, tracing paper, red and white fabric scraps, photograph for face, brown and black permanent fine-point markers, and clear thread.

**Note:** Allow paint and glue to dry after each application.

**1.** Paint wooden star yellow. Glue felt to poster board.

**2.** Trace hat, hat trim, mustache, and beard onto tracing paper. Use patterns to cut hat trim, mustache, and beard from white fabric and hat from red fabric.

**3.** Center and glue beard and hat on felt-covered poster board. Leaving a ⅛" felt border, cut out ornament.

**4.** Cut out face from photograph; center and glue on ornament. Glue hat trim and mustache over photograph. Use brown marker to draw "stitches" along edges of hat trim and beard. Use black marker to draw "stitches" along edges of star. Glue star to hat trim.

**5.** Follow **Making a Hanger**, page 159, to add hanger to ornament.

HAT

HAT TRIM

MUSTACHE

BEARD

# RADIANT WHITE CHRISTMAS

Wrap your home in the rare and radiant wonder of a sparkling snowy landscape with inspiration from this frosty collection. The star of our glistening fairyland is a striking evergreen filled with the elegant innocence of icicles and angels. The dreamy scene is accented with pristine packages topped with shimmering bows, a silvery stocking cuffed in white satin, and unforgettable greeting cards dusted with snowflakes. Instructions for the projects shown here and on the following pages begin on page 70.

For unbeatable holiday greetings, acknowledgments, and gift enclosures, send your wishes on **Radiant White Christmas Cards** *(page 70)*, topped with crocheted snowflakes and edged with silvery rickrack.

Our **Radiant White Christmas Tree** *(page 70)* is frosted with one-of-a-kind **Crocheted Snowflake Ornaments** *(page 71)*, captivating **Crocheted Angel Ornaments** *(page 73)*, picture-perfect **Silvery Rose Clusters** *(page 70)*, and crafty **Hand-Painted Jingle Bells** *(page 70)*. The lustrous image is enhanced with silver rope and iridescent bead garlands, snowflake and star ornaments, acrylic icicles, and star burst mini-lights.

A white satin cuff edged with lacy crochet trims our **Silver Jacquard Stocking** *(page 72)*, which is sure to catch Santa's eye.

Puffy bows in organza and brocade crown **Shimmering Packages** *(page 70)*. For an elegant accent, add handmade paper roses or a crocheted angel.

## RADIANT WHITE CHRISTMAS TREE
(Shown on page 67)

Start dreaming of your own White Christmas with an eight-foot-tall flocked spruce tree. We entwined strands of white mini-lights and white mini star burst lights on tree branches. Then we draped silver rope and white iridescent bead garlands around the tree.

We added Silvery Rose Clusters to charm even the crustiest old scrooge and painted glittering holly berries on Hand-Painted Jingle Bells to ring in the holidays.

Lacy Crocheted Snowflake Ornaments and Crocheted Angel Ornaments (page 73) grace the branches with the essence of timeless perfection.

Five yards of frothy white fabric became soft snowdrifts when we strategically placed crinkled tissue paper beneath this downy wrap-around Christmas tree skirt.

We tied simple bows from 28" lengths of 2¹/₂"w white and silver plaid wired ribbon and nestled them in the foliage. We then topped the tree with an ornate bow. To make the bow, we used four yards of ribbon and followed **Making a Bow** instructions (page 159), making a 4" center loop, twelve 9" loops, and two 15" streamers.

To complete the tree, we tucked purchased flocked twig branches, white pearl acorn picks, and crystal stems among tree branches for fullness. Glass snowflakes, porcelain star ornaments, and acrylic icicles lend a frosty elegance to this Radiant White Christmas.

## SHIMMERING PACKAGES
(Shown on page 69)

**You will need** wrapped gifts, desired silver and white ribbons (we used checked, brocade, mesh, and organza wired ribbons), Paper Twist Roses (page 159) or a Crocheted Angel Ornament (page 73), white crochet thread (optional), and a hot glue gun.

**1.** Follow **Making A Bow**, page 159, to make a bow for package.
**2.** If desired, glue roses to bow or use crochet thread to tie angel to bow.

## RADIANT WHITE CHRISTMAS CARDS
(Shown on page 66)

**For each card and envelope,** you will need bristol board, one 7" square each of background fabric and paper-backed fusible web, silver baby rickrack, hot glue gun, and a small Crocheted Snowflake Ornament.

**Note:** If mailing card, envelope should be marked "HAND CANCEL."

### CARD
**1.** Cut a 6¹/₄" x 12¹/₂" piece from bristol board. Matching short edges, fold card in half.
**2.** Fuse web to wrong side of fabric. Cut a 5¹/₂" square from fabric. Fuse fabric square to front of card. Glue rickrack along edges of fabric square. Use a needle and thread to tack snowflake to front of card.

### ENVELOPE
**1.** Cut a 7¹/₂" x 14" piece from bristol board.
**2.** For flap, fold one short edge of board 1" to one side. Clip each corner of flap diagonally.
**3.** For pocket, fold opposite short edge 6¹/₂" toward flap. Glue side edges to secure.
**4.** Place card in envelope. Glue flap to pocket to secure.

## SILVERY ROSE CLUSTERS
(Shown on page 68)

**For each decoration,** you will need a sprig of white holly with berries, silver spray paint, silver glitter paint, paintbrush, two or three white Paper Twist Roses (page 159), silver paint pen, and a hot glue gun.

**1.** Spray paint holly sprig silver; allow to dry. Lightly paint leaves with glitter paint; allow to dry.
**2.** Use paint pen to add accents to rose petals; allow to dry. Glue roses to holly stem.

## HAND-PAINTED JINGLE BELLS
(Shown on page 68)

**For each ornament,** you will need a 3¹/₂" dia. jingle bell with center rim, white spray paint, tracing paper, transfer paper, green paint pen, black permanent medium-point marker, silver glitter dimensional paint, silver glitter, 12" length of 1"w silver ribbon, foam brush, and craft glue.

**Note:** Allow paint to dry after each application.

**1.** Spray paint bell white.
**2.** Trace holly pattern onto tracing paper. Use pattern and transfer paper to transfer pattern to bell.
**3.** Use paint pen to paint leaves green. Use marker to outline leaves and berries and to draw detail lines on leaves. Use glitter paint to paint berries and a thin line around rim of bell. Brush a thin layer of glue over top of bell; sprinkle glitter over glue. Shake off excess glitter and allow to dry.
**4.** Thread ribbon through ring at top of bell. Tie ribbon into a bow.

# CROCHETED SNOWFLAKE ORNAMENTS (Shown on pages 66 and 68)

**For each ornament,** you will need bedspread weight (#10) white cotton thread, steel crochet hook size 7 (1.65), tracing paper, corrugated cardboard or plastic foam sheet, plastic wrap, fabric stiffener, one-pint plastic bag with zipper closure, rustproof straight pins, and tape.

**Note:** Refer to **Crochet**, page 156, for abbreviations and general instructions.

## SIX-POINT SMALL SNOWFLAKE
Ch 6, join with sl st to beginning ch to form a ring.
**Rnd 1** (Right side): Ch 3 (**counts as first dc, now and throughout**), dc in ring, ch 1, (2 dc in ring, ch 1) 5 times; join with sl st to beginning dc: 6 ch-1 sps.
**Rnd 2:** Sl st in next dc, sl st in next ch-1 sp, ch 3, (dc, ch 2, 2 dc) in same sp, ch 1, ★ (2 dc, ch 2, 2 dc) in next ch-1 sp, ch 1; repeat from ★ 4 times **more**; join with sl st to beginning dc: 12 sps.
**Rnd 3:** Sl st in next dc, sl st in next ch-2 sp, ch 3, (dc, ch 2, 2 dc) in same sp, ch 3, skip next ch-1 sp, ★ (2 dc, ch 2, 2 dc) in next ch-2 sp, ch 3, skip next ch-1 sp; repeat from ★ 4 times **more**; join with sl st to beginning dc: 12 sps.
**Rnd 4:** Sl st in next dc, sl st in next ch-2 sp, ch 3, (dc, ch 2, 2 dc) in same sp, ch 7, skip next ch-3 sp, ★ (2 dc, ch 2, 2 dc) in next ch-2 sp, ch 7, skip next ch-3 sp; repeat from ★ 4 times **more**; join with sl st to beginning dc: 12 sps.
**Rnd 5:** Sl st in next dc, sl st in next ch-2 sp, ch 1, in same sp work [sc, ch 3, tr, (ch 6, sl st in third ch from hook) 5 times, ch 3, tr, ch 3, sc], ch 3, in next ch-7 sp work [2 sc, (ch 3, sl st in third ch from hook, 2 sc) 3 times], ch 3, ★ in next ch-2 sp work [sc, ch 3, tr, (ch 6, sl st in third ch from hook) 5 times, ch 3, tr, ch 3, sc], ch 3, in next ch-7 sp work [2 sc, (ch 3, sl st in third ch from hook, 2 sc) 3 times], ch 3; repeat from ★ 4 times **more**; join with sl st to beginning sc; finish off.
Using Blocking Pattern A, follow **Finishing Snowflakes** to stiffen snowflake.

## EIGHT-POINT SMALL SNOWFLAKE
Ch 8, join with sl st to beginning ch to form a ring.
**Rnd 1** (Right side): Ch 1, (sc in ring, ch 8) 8 times; join with sl st to beginning sc: 8 ch-8 sps.
**Rnd 2:** Sl st in next 4 chs, ch 1, sc in same sp, ch 12, ★ sc in next ch-8 sp, ch 12; repeat from ★ 6 times **more**; join with sl st to beginning sc: 8 ch-12 sps.
**Rnd 3:** Sl st in next ch-12 sp, ch 1, in same sp and in each ch-12 sp around work [3 sc, (ch 3, sl st in third ch from hook, sc) 3 times, (ch 5, sl st in third ch from hook) 3 times, ch 8, sl st in eighth ch from hook, ch 3, sl st in third ch from hook (ch 5, sl st in third ch from hook) twice, ch 2, sc, (ch 3, sl st in third ch from hook, sc) twice, ch 3, sl st in third ch from hook, 3 sc]; join with sl st to beginning sc; finish off.
Using Blocking Pattern B, follow **Finishing Snowflakes** to stiffen snowflake.

## EIGHT-POINT LARGE SNOWFLAKE
Ch 6, join with sl st to beginning ch to form a ring.
**Rnd 1** (Right side): Ch 4 (counts as first dc plus ch-1), (dc in ring, ch 1) 7 times; join with sl st to third ch of beginning ch-4: 8 ch-1 sps.
**Rnd 2:** Sl st in next ch-1 sp, ch 1, sc in same sp, ch 8, ★ sc in next ch-1 sp, ch 8; repeat from ★ 6 times **more**; join with sl st to beginning sc: 8 ch-8 sps.
**Rnd 3:** Sl st in next 4 chs, ch 1, sc in same sp, ch 12, ★ sc in next ch-8 sp, ch 12; repeat from ★ 6 times **more**; join with sl st to beginning sc: 8 ch-12 sps.

**Rnd 4:** Sl st in next ch-12 sp, ch 1, in same sp work [sc, 7 hdc, ch 6, sl st in sixth ch from hook, (ch 10, sl st in sixth ch from hook) 3 times, ch 10, sl st in tenth ch from hook, ch 6, sl st in sixth ch from hook, (ch 5, sl st in third ch from hook) 3 times, 7 hdc, sc], ch 6, sl st in sixth ch from hook, ★ in next ch-12 sp work [sc, 7 hdc, ch 6, sl st in sixth ch from hook, (ch 10, sl st in sixth ch from hook) 3 times, ch 10, sl st in tenth ch from hook, ch 6, sl st in sixth ch from hook, (ch 10, sl st in sixth ch from hook) 3 times, 7 hdc, sc], ch 6, sl st in sixth ch from hook; repeat from ★ 6 times **more**; join with sl st to beginning sc; finish off.
Using Blocking Pattern B, follow **Finishing Snowflakes** to stiffen snowflake.

## FINISHING SNOWFLAKES
1. Make one blocking pattern for each snowflake by tracing indicated Blocking Pattern onto tracing paper. Tape traced patterns on cardboard or foam sheet. Cover patterns with plastic wrap.
2. Place one snowflake and a small amount of stiffener in a plastic bag. Squeeze plastic bag and snowflake until snowflake is completely soaked with stiffener. Squeeze excess stiffener from snowflake. Pin snowflake over blocking pattern with right side up, making sure spokes of snowflake are centered over pattern lines and interior sections of snowflake are even and smooth. Repeat for remaining snowflakes. Allow snowflakes to dry completely. Remove pins.

BLOCKING PATTERN A

BLOCKING PATTERN B

71

# SILVER JACQUARD STOCKING (Shown on page 69)

## CROCHETED EDGING

**You will need** bedspread weight silver/white cotton thread and steel crochet hook size 6 (1.80) **or** size needed for gauge.

**Note:** Refer to **Crochet**, page 156, for abbreviations and general instructions.

**Gauge Swatch:** 1⁵⁄₈"w x 2¹⁄₂"h
Work same as edging for five rows.

Ch 11, place marker in last ch made for st placement, ch 4: 15 chs.
**Row 1** (Right side): Working in back ridges of beginning ch (**Fig. 1**), dc in sixth ch from hook, ch 2, skip next 2 chs, sc in next ch, ch 2, skip next 2 chs, (dc, ch 2, dc) in next ch, skip next 2 chs, dc in last ch: 5 sts and 4 sps.

**Fig. 1**

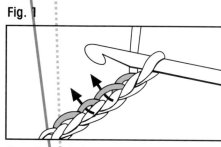

**Row 2:** Ch 3 **(counts as first dc, now and throughout)**, turn; (dc, ch 2, dc) in next ch-2 sp, ch 5, skip next 2 ch-2 sps, (dc, ch 2, dc) in next sp: 5 dc and 3 sps.
**Row 3:** Ch 5, turn; (dc, ch 2, dc) in next ch-2 sp, ch 2, sc in next ch-5 sp, ch 2, (dc, ch 2, dc) in next ch-2 sp, skip next dc, dc in last dc: 6 sts and 5 sps.

**Row 4:** Ch 3, turn; (dc, ch 2, dc) in next ch-2 sp, ch 5, skip next 2 ch-2 sps, (dc, ch 2, dc) in next ch-2 sp, place marker around last dc made for st placement, ch 1; working in end of rows, dc in next ch-5 sp, (ch 2, dc in same sp) 4 times, ch 1, sl st in marked st, remove marker: 10 dc and 9 sps.
**Row 5:** Turn; sc in first ch-1 sp (sc in next dc, 2 sc in next ch-2 sp) 3 times, ch 7, **turn**; skip first 5 sc, sl st in next sc, **turn**, 8 sc in next ch-7 sp, ch 5, **turn**; skip first 3 sc, sl st in next sc, **turn**; (4 sc, ch 3, 4 sc) in next ch-5 sp, 5 sc in remaining sp of ch-7 sp, sc in next dc, 2 sc in next ch-2 sp, sc in next dc and in next ch-1 sp, sl st in next dc and in next ch-2 sp, place marker in last sl st made for st placement, ch 5, dc in same sp, ch 2, sc in next ch-5 sp, ch 2, (dc, ch 2, dc) in next ch-2 sp, skip next dc, dc in last dc.
**Row 6:** Ch 3, turn; (dc, ch 2, dc) in next ch-2 sp, ch 5, skip next 2 ch-2 sps, (dc, ch 2, dc) in next sp, leave remaining sts unworked: 5 dc and 3 sps.
Repeat Rows 3-6 for 16", ending by working Row 4.
**Last Row:** Turn; sc in first ch-1 sp, (sc in next dc, 2 sc in next ch-2 sp) 3 times, ch 7, **turn**; skip first 5 sc, sl st in next sc, **turn**; 8 sc in next ch-7 sp, ch 5, **turn**; skip first 3 sc, sl st in next sc, **turn**; (4 sc, ch 3, 4 sc) in next ch-5 sp, 5 sc in remaining sp of ch-7 sp, sc in next dc, 2 sc in next ch-2 sp, sc in next dc and in next ch-1 sp, sl st in next dc; finish off.

## STOCKING

**You will need** ²⁄₃ yd. of white satin for cuff and lining, tracing paper, ¹⁄₂ yd. of 45"w silver jacquard fabric for stocking, 20" of ³⁄₁₆" dia. cord, and 7¹⁄₂" of 1"w white satin ribbon.

1. From satin, cut a 2" x 22" strip for welting and a 7¹⁄₂" x 15" piece for cuff.
2. Aligning arrows and dotted lines, trace stocking top and stocking bottom patterns onto tracing paper. For seam allowance, draw a second line ¹⁄₄" outside first line around sides and bottom of stocking. Cut out pattern along outer line. Fold stocking fabric piece in half with right sides together. Use pattern to cut stocking from fabric. Repeat using satin fabric for stocking lining.
3. (**Note:** Use a ¹⁄₄" seam allowance for all sewing.) Leaving top edge open, sew stocking pieces together. Clip curves and turn stocking right side out. Repeat to sew lining pieces together; do not turn.
4. For welting, press one end of satin strip ¹⁄₂" to wrong side. Beginning ¹⁄₂" from folded end, center cord on wrong side of strip. Fold strip over cord. Beginning ¹⁄₂" from folded end, use a zipper foot to baste close to cord along length of strip. Trim seam allowance to ¹⁄₄".
5. For cuff, match right sides and stitch short edges of cuff fabric piece together; press seam open. Matching wrong sides and raw edges, fold cuff in half.
6. Matching raw edges and cuff seam to heel seam, place cuff over stocking. Beginning with pressed end of welting at cuff seam, pin welting along top of stocking. Trimming to fit, insert unfinished end of welting into folded end. Use zipper foot to sew around top of stocking as close to welting as possible. Press seam allowances to inside of stocking.
7. For hanging loop, fold ribbon in half. Tack loop inside stocking at heel seam. Fold top edge of lining ¹⁄₄" to wrong side; press. Place lining in stocking. Hand sew pressed edge of lining to seam allowance of welting. With ends of edging on back of stocking, tack top of crocheted edging to cuff just below welting.

STOCKING TOP

STOCKING BOTTOM

# CROCHETED ANGEL ORNAMENTS (Shown on page 68)

**For each ornament,** you will need bedspread weight (#10) white cotton thread, steel crochet hook size 6 (1.80), 1" plastic ring, nine 4mm silver beads, ³/₈"w silver ribbon, hand sewing needle, and white thread.

**Note:** Refer to **Crochet**, page 156, for abbreviations and general instructions.

## JOINING WITH SC
When instructed to join with sc, begin with a slip knot on hook. Insert hook in a stitch or space as indicated, YO and pull up a loop, YO and draw through both loops on hook.

## HEAD
**Rnd 1 (Right side):** Join thread to plastic ring with sc; work 40 **more** sc in ring; join with sl st to first sc: 41 sc.
Note: Mark last round as right side.
**Neck:** Ch 1, turn; sc in same st and in next 8 sc, leave remaining 32 sc unworked; do **not** finish off: 9 sc.

## RIGHT WING
**Row 1:** Ch 14, dc in sixth ch from hook, ch 1, skip next ch, ★ dc in next ch, ch 1, skip next ch; repeat from ★ 2 times **more**, sc in last ch; with **right** side facing, sl st in first sc on Neck.
**Row 2:** Ch 1, turn; sc in first sc, ch 1, (dc in next dc, ch 1) 4 times, skip next ch, dc in next ch: 5 ch-1 sps.
**Row 3:** Ch 4 (counts as first dc plus ch-1, now and throughout), turn; (dc in next dc, ch 1) 4 times, sc in last sc, sl st in **same** sc on Neck.
**Row 4:** Ch 1, turn; sc in first sc, (ch 1, dc in next dc) across.
**Row 5:** Ch 4, turn; (dc in next dc, ch 1) 4 times, sc in last sc, sl st in **next** sc on Neck.
**Row 6:** Repeat Row 4.
**Row 7:** Repeat Row 3.
**Row 8:** Repeat Row 4.
**Row 9:** Repeat Row 5; finish off.

## DRESS
**Row 1:** With **right** side facing, join thread with sl st in first dc on Row 9 of Right Wing; ch 23, dc in sixth ch from hook, ch 1, skip next ch, (dc in next ch, ch 1, skip next ch) 8 times; working in sts across Row 9, (dc in next dc, ch 1) 5 times, sc in last sc, sl st in same sc on Neck: 15 sps.
**Row 2:** Ch 1, turn; sc in first sc, ch 1, (dc in next dc, ch 1) 14 times, skip next ch, dc in next ch: 15 dc and 15 ch-1 sps.
**Row 3:** Ch 4, turn; (dc in next dc, ch 1) 14 times, sc in last sc, sl st in **next** sc on Neck.
**Row 4:** Ch 1, turn; sc in first sc, (ch 1, dc in next dc) across.
**Row 5:** Ch 4, turn; (dc in next dc, ch 1) 14 times, sc in last sc, sl st in **same** sc on Neck.
**Row 6:** Ch 1, turn; sc in first sc, (ch 1, dc in next dc) across.
**Rows 7 - 17:** Repeat Rows 3 - 6 twice, then repeat Rows 3 - 5 once **more**.
Finish off.

## LEFT WING
**Row 1:** With **right** side facing, skip first 10 dc on Row 17 of Dress and join with sl st in next dc; place marker around dc just worked into for Edging placement, ch 4, (dc in next dc, ch 1) 4 times, sc in last sc, sl st in **next** sc on Neck: 5 ch-1 sps.
**Row 2:** Ch 1, turn; sc in first sc, (ch 1, dc in next dc) across.
**Row 3:** Ch 4, turn; (dc in next dc, ch 1) 4 times, sc in last sc, sl st in **same** sc on Neck.
**Row 4:** Ch 1, turn; sc in first sc, (ch 1, dc in next dc) across.
**Row 5:** Ch 4, turn; (dc in next dc, ch 1) 4 times, sc in last sc, sl st in **next** sc on Neck.
**Row 6 - 9:** Repeat Rows 2 and 3 twice.
Finish off.

## EDGING
**To work Cluster:** Ch 3, YO, insert hook in third ch from hook, YO and pull up a loop, YO and draw through 2 loops on hook, YO, insert hook in same ch, YO and pull up a loop, YO and draw through 2 loops on hook, YO and draw through all 3 loops on hook.
With **right** side facing, join with sl st in marked dc on Dress; ch 2, dc in same st, (sl st, ch 2, dc) in top of dc at end of first 8 rows on Left Wing; working in sts across Row 9, (sl st, ch 2, hdc) in first 5 dc, sl st in last sc; working in unworked scs on Head, sl st in first 3 scs, work Cluster, (skip next 2 sc, dc in next sc, work Cluster) 8 times, skip next 2 sc, sl st in last 3 sc; working in free loops of beginning ch on Right Wing, (sl st, ch 2, hdc) in first ch (opposite sc), skip next ch, ★ (sl st, ch 2, hdc) in next ch, skip next ch; repeat from ★ 3 times more, (sl st, ch 2, dc) in next ch; (sl st, ch 2, dc) in top of dc at end of first 8 rows on Right Wing, sl st in top of dc at end of last row, ch 2; working in free loops of beginning ch on Row 1 of Dress, skip first ch, (sl st in next ch, ch 2, skip next ch) 9 times, (sl st, ch 2, dc) in next ch; (sl st, ch 2, dc) in top of dc at end of first 16 rows on Dress, sl st in top of dc at end of last row, ch 2; working in sts across Row 17, (sl st in next dc, ch 2) 9 times; join with sl st to joining sl st, finish off.

## ANGEL FINISHING
1. Weave ribbon through spaces on Row 1 of Dress and every other row. Weave ribbon through spaces next to Edging on Wings; use needle and thread to secure all ribbon ends.
2. Tie an 8" length of ribbon into a bow. Sew bow and beads to Angel.

# HOLLY-JOLLY FELT

*S*anta and his favorite reindeer team up to bring a sleighful of fun to your holiday decor
with our Holly-Jolly Felt collection. A sprinkling of hearts, stars, and polka-dot bows highlights
a tree covered with North Pole buddies, from topper to skirt and each branch in between. In a
fabulous flurry of felt, Santa and Rudy will dance and prance their way through your home on
charming pillows, irresistible stockings, a delightful mantel swag, and appealing gift bags.
Instructions for the projects shown here and on the following pages begin on page 80.

Settle into a cozy corner with lovable **Polar Pal Pillows** (*page 87*) boasting a Santa whose nose is as bright as his reindeer
buddy's! Dotted with a flurry of French-knot snowflakes and edged using pinking shears, the comfortable cushions are
embellished with blanket stitching and buttons.

Crowned with an appealing **Jolly Santa Tree Topper** *(page 82),* our **Holly-Jolly Felt Tree** *(page 80)* is covered with a merry assortment — **Floppy Star Ornaments** *(page 81),* a colorful wooden garland, wooden candy canes, polka-dot bows, multicolor lights, and glass ornaments. **Fun Felt Ornaments** *(page 80)* feature spiral wire hanging loops and include stars, hearts, Santas, and reindeer stuffed with fiberfill. *(Opposite, top)* For a lighthearted touch, accent your mantel with a **Starry Santa Garland** *(page 81). (Opposite, bottom)* Add a playful ending to your tree with our animated **Ring-Around-the-Tree Skirt** *(page 86).* Endearing Santas and reindeer encircle the skirt, which is finished with French-knot snowflakes.

Our star-studded **Jolly Santa Door Hanger** *(page 83)* serves as a merry reminder of the joyful season.

**Felt Gift Bags** *(page 81)*, embellished with our Santa and reindeer ornaments, hold special surprises for loved ones.

Each holding a heart or a star, the characters on our **Santa and Reindeer Stockings** *(page 84)* have a dimensional look that brings them to life!

# HOLLY-JOLLY FELT TREE
(Shown on page 75)

Colorful Santas and reindeer roam freely among bright stars and warm hearts on our Holly-Jolly Felt Tree.

We wrapped strands of multicolor lights around a seven-foot-tall artificial pine tree and draped brightly painted wooden garland along the branches.

A Jolly Santa Tree Topper (page 82) watches for good boys and girls, while Santas and reindeer play on the snow-studded background of our Ring-Around-the-Tree Skirt (page 86).

Our Fun Felt Ornaments with curly wire hangers are easy to make using simple embroidery stitches and fluffy stuffing. Floppy Star Ornaments tucked here and there add bursts of color to the felt array.

Simple bows tied from 28" lengths of 1 1/2"w white and red polka-dot ribbon, wooden candy canes, and red and green glass ornaments bring holiday cheer to our Holly-Jolly Felt Christmas.

# FUN FELT ORNAMENTS (Shown on page 76)

**For each ornament,** you will need tracing paper, desired colors of felt, black embroidery floss, polyester fiberfill, 12" of 18-gauge black craft wire, fabric glue, and a pencil.
**For heart or star,** you will **also** need a button.

**Note:** Cut one of each shape from desired color felt unless otherwise indicated. Refer to **Embroidery Stitches**, page 157, and use three strands of embroidery floss for all stitches unless otherwise indicated. Allow glue to dry after each application.

## REINDEER
**1.** Follow **Making Patterns**, page 158, to make small reindeer patterns, page 84. Use patterns to cut two background pieces and one of each remaining piece from felt.
**2.** Using Running Stitch, stitch head to one background and nose to muzzle. Work three small vertical Running Stitches below center of nose for mouth. Using Blanket Stitch, stitch antlers and muzzle in place. Using six strands of floss, work a French Knot for each eye.
**3.** Glue inner ears to head.
**4.** Matching edges and leaving bottom open for stuffing, work Blanket Stitch to join background pieces. Stuff with fiberfill and continue working Blanket Stitch to close opening.
**5.** For wire hanger, coil wire around pencil. Remove wire from pencil and stretch into curve shape. Bending wire ends as needed, hook one end of wire between background pieces at each side of ornament; glue to secure.

## SANTA
**1.** Follow **Making Patterns**, page 158, to make small Santa patterns. Use patterns to cut two background pieces and one of each remaining piece from felt.
**2.** Using Running Stitch, stitch head and hat to one background piece.
**3.** Glue face, cheeks, and hat trim to Santa head.
**4.** Using Blanket Stitch, stitch mustache in place. Work a Cross Stitch to secure center of hat star to background at top of hat. Using six strands of floss, work a French Knot for each eye.
**5.** Follow steps 4 and 5 of Reindeer to complete ornament.

## STAR
**1.** Trace small and large star patterns onto tracing paper. Use patterns to cut one small and two large stars from felt.
**2.** Sew button to center of small star. Using Running Stitch, stitch small star to center of one large star.
**3.** Follow steps 4 and 5 of Reindeer to complete ornament.

## HEART
**1.** Trace small star and heart patterns onto tracing paper. Use patterns to cut one star and two hearts from felt.
**2.** Sew button to center of star. Using Running Stitch, stitch star to one heart.
**3.** Follow steps 4 and 5 of Reindeer to complete ornament.

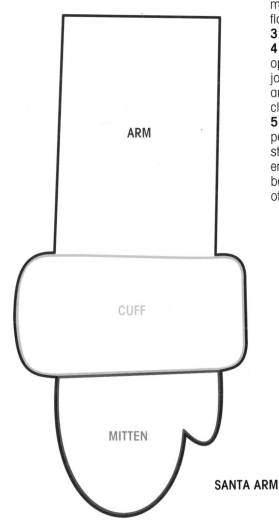

ARM

CUFF

MITTEN

SANTA ARM

HEART

## FLOPPY STAR ORNAMENTS

(Shown on page 76)

**For each ornament,** you will need tracing paper, four colors of felt, button, black embroidery floss, pinking shears, and fabric glue.

**Note:** Refer to **Embroidery Stitches,** page 157, and use three strands of floss for all embroidery stitches.

**1.** Trace small and large star patterns onto tracing paper.
**2.** Use patterns to cut one small star and two large stars from felt.
**3.** Work Running Stitch to sew small star to center of one large star. Sew button to center of small star. Match edges of large stars and work Blanket Stitch to sew edges together.
**4.** Center and glue large star on a 6¹/₂" square of felt. Using pinking shears and leaving a ¹/₂" border, cut out star.
**5.** Center and glue pinked star on an 8" square of remaining color felt. Using straight-edged scissors and leaving a ¹/₂" border, cut out star.

## STARRY SANTA GARLAND

(Shown on page 77)

**For each five-foot section of garland,** you will need 2¹/₈ yds. of 1"w red polka-dot ribbon, hot glue gun, one Santa and two Star Fun Felt Ornaments without wire hangers, and two 1" dia black buttons.

**1.** Cut one 16" length from ribbon; cut remaining ribbon in half. With 16" length at center, knot ribbon lengths together.
**2.** Center and glue Santa on right side of 16" ribbon length. Glue a star 2¹/₂" outside each knot on either side of Santa.
**3.** Glue a button to each knot.

## FELT GIFT BAGS

(Shown on page 78)

**For each gift bag,** you will need two 9" x 12" pieces of felt, black embroidery floss, pinking shears, 15" lengths of satin ribbon in assorted widths and colors, desired Fun Felt Ornament without hanger, and a safety pin.

**1.** Matching edges, place felt pieces together. Use three strands of floss and **Running Stitch,** page 157, to sew side and bottom edges together ¹/₄" inside edges. Use pinking shears to trim all edges of bag. Work running stitch along each top edge of bag.
**2.** Place gift in bag. Tie ribbon into a bow around bag. Pin ornament to bag.

LARGE STAR

SMALL STAR

HAT STAR

HAT

BACKGROUND

HAT TRIM

FACE

CHEEK

CHEEK

MUSTACHE

HEAD

**SMALL SANTA**

# JOLLY SANTA TREE TOPPER (Shown on page 76)

**You will need** tracing paper, desired colors of felt for Santa, two 9" x 12" pieces of felt for background, black embroidery floss, polyester fiberfill, $3/4$" dia. red shank button, two $1/4$" dia. black shank buttons, and fabric glue.

**Note:** Cut one of each shape from desired color of felt unless otherwise indicated. Refer to **Embroidery Stitches**, page 157, and use three strands of floss for all embroidery stitches unless otherwise indicated. Allow glue to dry after each application.

**1.** Follow **Making Patterns**, page 158, to make large Santa patterns. Use patterns to cut pieces from felt.
**2.** Glue face, cheeks, and hat trim to head. Using Blanket Stitch, stitch mustache in place. Sew buttons to face for eyes and nose.
**3.** Using Running Stitch, center and stitch head and hat to one background piece.

**4.** Matching wrong sides, pin background pieces together. Leaving a $1/4$" border, cut out Santa. Leaving bottom edges open for stuffing, use Blanket Stitch to join background pieces. Stuff with fiberfill and continue Blanket Stitch to close opening.

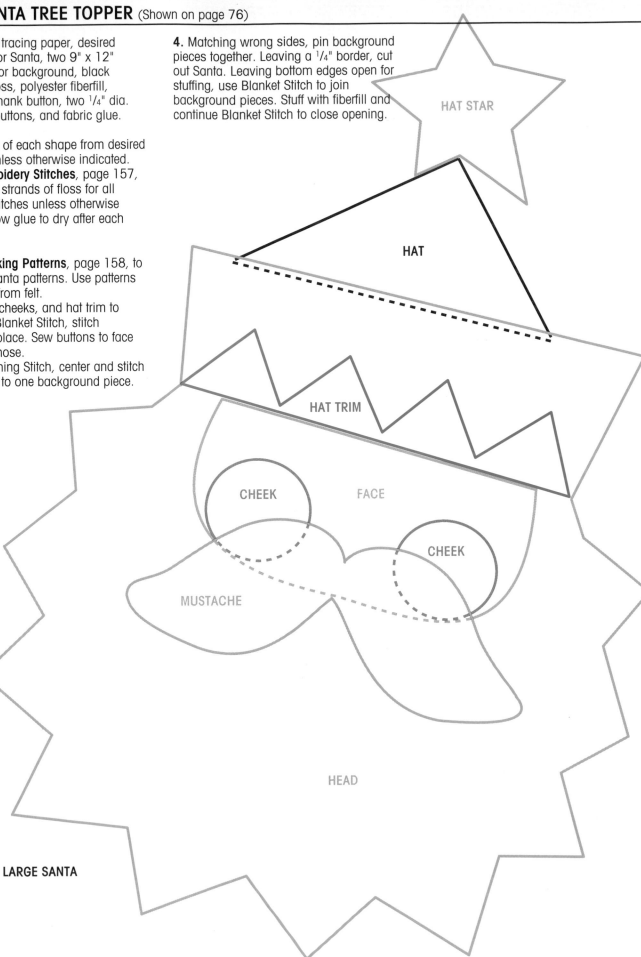

HAT STAR

HAT

HAT TRIM

CHEEK

FACE

CHEEK

MUSTACHE

HEAD

**LARGE SANTA**

# JOLLY SANTA DOOR HANGER (Shown on page 78)

**You will need** tracing paper, desired colors of felt, black embroidery floss, sewing thread to match felt, polyester fiberfill, buttons, and fabric glue.

**Note:** Refer to **Embroidery Stitches**, page 157, and use three strands of floss for all embroidery stitches unless otherwise indicated. Allow glue to dry after each application.

**1.** Follow Santa instructions, page 84, to make Santa without ornament.
**2.** Aligning arrows and dotted lines and following **Making Patterns**, page 158, make patterns for small star, page 81, and door hanger.
**3.** Use patterns to cut three small stars, page 81, and one each of hanger back, hanger front, belt, and belt buckle from felt.

**4.** Matching edges, work Blanket Stitch along outer edge of hanger front and knob opening to join hanger front to hanger back. Work Running Stitches along points of hanger and along edges of each star.
**5.** Using matching thread, stitch belt and belt buckle to hanger.
**6.** Arrange stars on hanger. Placing a button at center of each star, stitch through button and all layers to secure each star to hanger. Glue Santa to hanger.

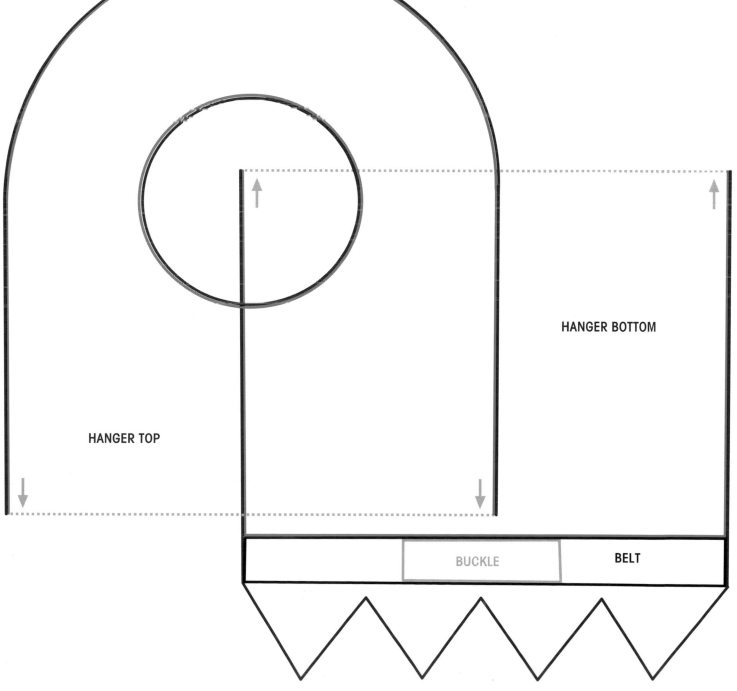

HANGER BOTTOM

HANGER TOP

BUCKLE     BELT

**You will need** tracing paper, desired colors of felt, black embroidery floss, sewing thread to match felt, polyester fiberfill, buttons, Fun Felt Star or Heart Ornament without hanger (page 80), and fabric glue.

**Note:** Refer to **Embroidery Stitches**, page 157, and use three strands of floss for all embroidery stitches unless otherwise indicated. Allow glue to dry after each application.

**STOCKING**

**1.** Aligning arrows and dotted lines, trace stocking top and stocking bottom patterns onto tracing paper. Use pattern to cut two stocking pieces from felt.
**2.** Trace small star, page 81, heel, toe, cuff, and hanger onto tracing paper. Use patterns to cut one each from felt.
**3.** Use pinking shears to trim inner edges of heel and toe pieces.
**4.** Use Running Stitch to sew star to toe and toe and heel to stocking front. Work Straight Stitches on cuff. Use matching thread to stitch cuff to top of stocking front.
**5.** Place stocking front and back wrong sides together. Use matching thread to sew along cuff edges. Use black floss to sew side and foot edges together.
**6.** Fold hanger in half. Place hanger ends on front of stocking. Place button over hanger ends. Stitch through button and all layers to secure.

**SANTA**

**1.** Follow **Making Patterns**, page 158, to make small Santa and Santa arm patterns, pages 80 and 81. Use patterns to cut two each head, hat, star, cuff, and mitten and one each hat trim, face, mustache, and cheeks from felt.
**2.** Glue face, cheeks, and hat trim to Santa head.
**3.** Using Blanket Stitch, stitch mustache in place. Using six strands of floss, work a French Knot for each eye.
**4.** Work Straight Stitches on each cuff. Matching edges, work Running Stitches along top edges of hat and a Cross Stitch at center of star to join pieces.
**5.** Matching edges and leaving an opening for stuffing, work Running Stitch to join head pieces. Stuff with fiberfill and continue Running Stitch to close opening.
**6.** Using matching thread, stitch hat to top of head and star to top of hat.

**7.** Using arm pattern, follow **Sewing Shapes**, page 158, to make two arms. Stuff with fiberfill and sew opening closed. Using matching thread, stitch one mitten and one cuff to each arm.
**8.** Arrange and glue arms to back of head. Sew ornament between hands. Glue Santa to front of stocking.

**REINDEER**

**1.** Follow **Making Patterns**, page 158, to make small reindeer and reindeer leg patterns. Use patterns to cut two each head and hoof and one each nose, muzzle, antlers, and inner ears from felt.
**2.** Using Running Stitch, stitch nose to muzzle and make three vertical stitches below center of nose for mouth. Using Blanket Stitch, stitch muzzle to head and stitch around each antler. Using six strands of floss, work a French Knot for each eye.
**3.** Matching edges and leaving an opening for stuffing, work Running Stitch to join head pieces. Stuff with fiberfill and continue Running Stitch to close opening.
**4.** Arrange and glue antlers and inner ear pieces on head.
**5.** Using leg pattern and hoof pieces, follow Steps 7 and 8 of Santa to complete reindeer stocking.

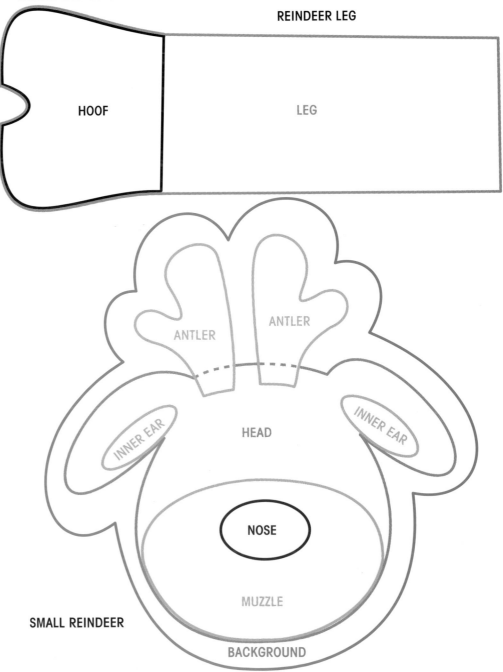

**REINDEER LEG**

HOOF

LEG

ANTLER

ANTLER

INNER EAR

INNER EAR

HEAD

NOSE

MUZZLE

**SMALL REINDEER**

BACKGROUND

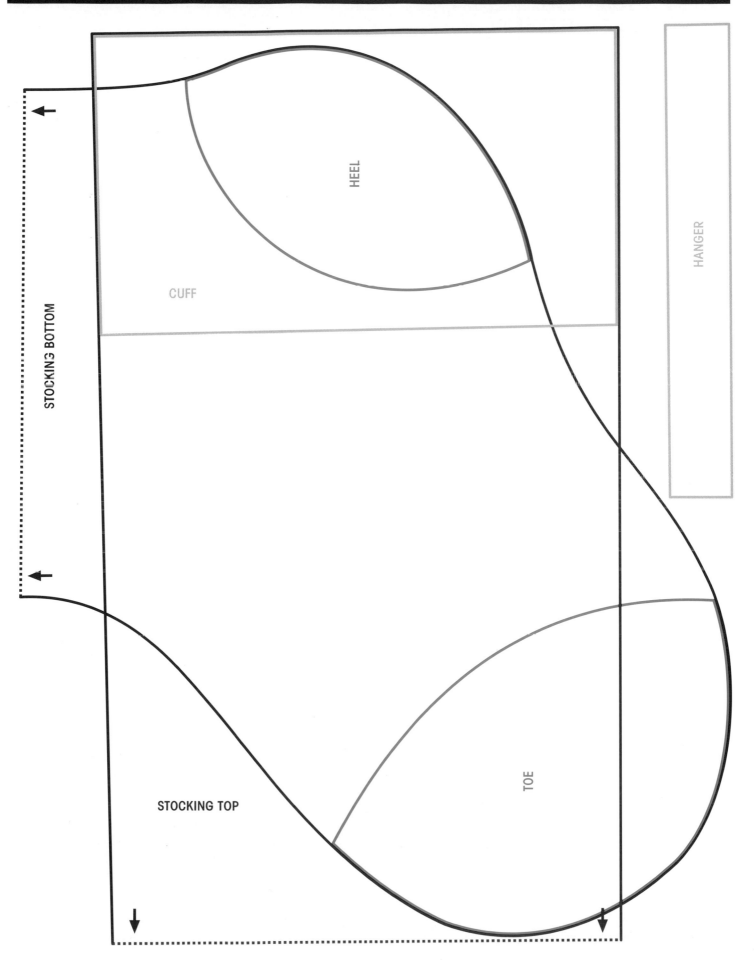

STOCKING BOTTOM

CUFF

HEEL

HANGER

STOCKING TOP

TOE

# RING-AROUND-THE-TREE SKIRT (Shown on page 77)

**You will need** one each 45" square of red, blue, and green felt; fabric marking pen; string; thumbtack; desired colors of felt for appliqués; white and black embroidery floss; tracing paper; fabric glue; and white worsted weight yarn.

**Note:** Refer to **Embroidery Stitches**, page 157, and use three strands of black floss for all embroidery stitches unless otherwise indicated.

**1.** Using a 2" measurement for inside cutting line and a 20$\frac{1}{2}$" measurement for outside cutting line, follow **Cutting a Fabric Circle**, page 157, to cut skirt front from blue felt square.
**2.** Using 2" for inside cutting line and 21$\frac{1}{2}$" for outside cutting line, follow Step 1 to cut skirt middle from red felt square.
**3.** Using 2" for inside cutting line and 22$\frac{1}{2}$" for outside cutting line, follow Step 1 to cut skirt backing from green felt square.
**4.** Matching center circles, layer skirt pieces; pin to secure. For opening, match

edges and fold skirt in half. Cut along one fold from center to outer edge through all layers. Work Running Stitches along opening edges and inside cutting line through all layers.
**5.** Trace edging pattern onto tracing paper. Working on back side of tree skirt, beginning at one side opening, and matching points of pattern to bottom edge of green layer, use pattern to mark points along outer edge of tree skirt. Cut points along drawn lines.
**6.** Stitching through all layers, work Blanket Stitches along edge of blue layer, Running Stitch along edge of red layer, and a Cross Stitch at center of each point on green layer.
**7.** Omitting backgrounds, follow **Making Patterns**, page 158, to make small reindeer and reindeer leg patterns, page 84; Santa arm and heart patterns, page 80; and large star and small Santa patterns, page 81.
**8.** Use patterns to cut pieces for four reindeer heads, eight reindeer legs, four Santa heads, eight Santa arms, four hearts, and three large stars from felt.

**9.** Work Blanket Stitches along thumb and hand of each Santa mitten and around edges of each heart, star, reindeer muzzle, antler, and Santa mustache.
**10.** Work Running Stitches along edges of each reindeer head, nose, leg, and hoof and Santa head, arm, and top edges of hat; Straight Stitches on cuff; and a Cross Stitch at center of each star for Santa hat. Using three strands of white floss, work Running Stitches along edges of each Santa cuff.
**11.** Arrange and glue muzzle, nose, antlers, and inner ears on each reindeer head; hooves on legs; face, hat trim, cheeks and mustache on each Santa head; and mittens and cuffs on arms. Allow to dry. Work three small, vertical Straight Stitches for mouth on each reindeer. Using six strands of black floss, work a French Knot for each eye on reindeer and Santa head.
**12.** Referring to Tree Skirt Diagram, arrange and glue reindeer and Santa heads; Santa hats, stars, and arms; reindeer legs and antlers; large stars; and hearts to skirt front. Allow to dry.
**13.** Using yarn, work French Knots as desired on tree skirt for snow.

**TREE SKIRT DIAGRAM**

86

# POLAR PAL PILLOWS (Shown on page 74)

**For each pillow,** you will need tracing paper, desired colors of felt for Santa (page 82) or Reindeer, one 10" square of felt for background, two 13" squares of felt for pillow front and back, black embroidery floss, white worsted weight yarn, polyester fiberfill, three $^3/_4$" dia buttons, pinking shears, and fabric glue.
**For Santa Pillow,** you will **also** need a $^3/_4$" dia. red shank button and two $^1/_4$" dia. black shank buttons.
**For Reindeer Pillow,** you will **also** need two $^3/_8$" dia. black shank buttons.

**Note:** Refer to **Embroidery Stitches**, page 157, and use three strands of embroidery floss for all stitches unless otherwise indicated. Allow glue to dry after each application.

## SANTA PILLOW

**1.** Follow Steps 1 - 4 of Holly Jolly Tree Topper, page 82, to stitch Santa $^1/_4$" from top at center of background piece.
**2.** Follow Pillow Finishing to complete pillow.

## REINDEER PILLOW

**1.** Follow **Making Patterns**, page 158, to make large reindeer patterns. Use patterns to cut pieces from felt.
**2.** Using Running Stitch, stitch head to background and nose to muzzle. Stitch three small vertical Running Stitches below center of nose for mouth. Glue inner ears to head. Using Blanket Stitch, stitch muzzle and antlers in place. Sew shank buttons to face for eyes.
**3.** Follow Pillow Finishing to complete pillow.

## PILLOW FINISHING

**1.** Trace large star, page 81, and heart pattern, page 80, onto tracing paper. Use patterns to cut two stars and one heart from felt. Sew a button to each shape. Arranging heart and stars at bottom of head, use Blanket Stitch to stitch in place.
**2.** Using white yarn, work scattered French Knots on background.
**3.** Use Blanket Stitch to stitch background to center of one 13" square. Matching wrong sides and edges, pin 13" squares together. Leaving an opening for stuffing, machine stitch squares together $^1/_4$" outside background. Use pinking shears to trim pillow edges. Stuff with fiberfill. Continue machine stitch to close opening.

ANTLER

ANTLER

INNER EAR

INNER EAR

HEAD

NOSE

LARGE
REINDEER

MUZZLE

# A FESTIVAL OF WREATHS

Adorned with a wealth of characters and colors, our festive wreaths graciously convey seasonal goodwill. Stylings from this eclectic collection, which range from elegant to whimsical, add beauty and warmth to home and hearth. Including designs with special appeal for lovers of nature, music, and cooking, our versatile wreaths offer handsome ways to deck your halls, doors, and walls. Whatever your fancy, you'll find an enchanting way to spread Christmas joy in our Festival of Wreaths! Instructions for the projects shown here and on the following pages begin on page 92.

Glowing with Yuletide grandeur, the **Elegant Angel and Roses Wreath** (*page 92*) is a gilded fantasy of gold-tipped roses and grape leaves, gold mesh bows, and a paper twist angel dressed in damask.

A delicious inspiration, the **Gingerbread Kitchen Wreath** *(page 93)* is a perfect place to display your favorite tools of the cooking trade. This treasure is all done up in vintage kitchen utensils, spice-trimmed gingerbread men, peppermint candies, and a sprightly gingham bow.

Capable of carrying your thoughts to a mountainside retreat, our **Lively Cardinal Wreath** *(page 93)* is all aflutter with jaunty redbirds, snow-frosted pinecones, red-berried holly, golden jingle bells, and a perky plaid bow.

Add a nostalgic touch to your Christmas trimmings with our **Fabric Poinsettia Wreath** *(page 92)*. A peppermint-striped bow highlights this wintry warmer, which is accented with fused fabric and felt poinsettias, flocked branches, and glittery garlands.

Enter the holiday season on a high note with our golden-tone **"Note-able" Nutcracker Wreath** *(page 93)* featuring a parade of nutcrackers in assorted colors and sizes. Delightful drums, antiqued sheet music, a red crinkle bow, and gilded musical notations complete the harmonious arrangement.

## ELEGANT ANGEL AND ROSES WREATH (Shown on page 88)

**You will need** a 20" dia. flocked artificial wreath, 10 gold artificial grape leaves, 2" dia. plastic foam egg, cream and peach paper twist, two 6" lengths of $^1/_8$" dia. wooden dowel, gold angel fleece for hair, 24" of $2^1/_4$"w gold and white damask wired ribbon, 2 yds. of $^5/_8$"w gold mesh wired ribbon, $3^1/_2$ yds. of 2"w gold mesh wired ribbon, 3 yds. of $1^1/_2$"w gold-edged sheer wired ribbon, 6" of gold wired cord, floral wire, wire cutters, three cream **Paper Twist Rose** centers (page 159) for buds, eight cream **Paper Twist Roses** (page 159), tracing paper, metallic gold acrylic paint, paintbrush, 2" wooden star, $2^2/_3$ yds. of gold bead garland, and a hot glue gun.

**1.** For angel head, cut foam egg in half lengthwise. Cut a 6" square from peach paper twist; untwist and flatten. Gluing edges of paper twist to flat side of one foam piece, cover head with paper twist. Glue flat side of head to one end of one dowel. Arrange and glue fleece to head for hair.
**2.** For angel dress, cut a 28" length of cream paper twist; untwist and flatten. Matching short edges, fold paper twist in half. Matching short edges, fold damask ribbon in half. Matching folded edges, place damask ribbon on top of paper twist. For waist, pinch ribbon and paper twist together $2^1/_2$" below folds; secure

with floral wire. Arrange and glue dress to dowel below head. Tie a 24" length of $^5/_8$"w ribbon into a bow around waist. Trim ribbon and paper twist ends as desired. Glue two gold leaves below bow.
**3.** For arms, cut a 12" length from 2"w gold mesh ribbon. Thread ribbon through paper twist twist at top of dress. Fold each end of arm $1^1/_2$" to back. For wrists, knot a length of $^5/_8$"w ribbon around each arm 1" from folded end; trim ends close to knots.
**4.** For halo, use gold cord to form a 2" dia. circle with a 2" stem; twist to secure. Glue stem to back of head.
**5.** For wings, cut a 15" length of cream paper twist twist; untwist and flatten. Matching short ends, fold in half. Trim ends diagonally and unfold. Pinch wings at center and secure with floral wire.
**6.** Use gold paint to paint star, remaining dowel, and highlights on wings, rosebuds, and roses; allow to dry.
**7.** Glue star to one end of dowel. Glue remaining end of dowel to one hand, wings to back of angel, and grape leaves to bases of roses.
**8.** For each bow, cut one 24" length each from sheer ribbon and 2"w gold mesh ribbon. Tie ribbon lengths together into a bow. Notch each ribbon end. Repeat to make a total of four bows.
**9.** Arrange bead garland, bows, angel, and roses on wreath; glue to secure.

## FABRIC POINSETTIA WREATH (Shown on page 90)

**You will need** a 24" dia. flocked artificial pine wreath, six 18" and six 8" squares of paper-backed fusible web, two 18" squares each of three different red print fabrics, two 8" squares each of three different green print fabrics, three 18" and three 8" squares of white felt, tracing paper, twenty-two 8" lengths of floral wire, 3 yds. of $2^1/_2$"w red and white striped wired ribbon with gold backing, 4 yds. of $2^3/_4$"w red taffeta ribbon, $2^1/_2$ yds. each of metallic red rope garland and clear iridescent bead garland, twelve 15mm gold beads, white flocked branches, garden clippers, and a hot glue gun.

**1.** Fuse web to wrong side of each fabric square. Fuse matching fabric squares to front and back of each felt square.
**2.** Trace leaf and poinsettia petal sections A, B, and C separately onto tracing paper; cut out. Use patterns to cut four each A, B, and C petal sections from red fabric-covered felt squares. Cut sixteen leaves from green fabric-covered felt squares.
**3.** For each poinsettia, layer petal sections from largest to smallest, rotating petals. Bend one length of floral wire in half. Insert wire ends through front center of poinsettia; twist to secure. For each leaf, insert one length of wire between fabric layers for stem. Arrange and glue four leaves to back of each poinsettia. Glue three beads to center of each poinsettia, covering wire.
**4.** Using striped ribbon, follow **Making a Bow**, page 159, to make a bow with eight 10" loops and two 5" streamers. Using taffeta ribbon, make a bow with six 14" loops and two 20" streamers. Glue striped bow to center of taffeta bow.
**5.** Cut flocked branches to desired lengths; insert and glue in wreath.
**6.** Arrange rope and bead garlands in wreath. Arranging as desired, wire bow and poinsettias to wreath.

LEAF

A

B

C

# GINGERBREAD KITCHEN WREATH
(Shown on page 89)

**You will need** an 18" dia. artificial pine wreath, tracing paper, yellow foam food trays, craft knife, floral wood tone spray, red and white paint pens, black permanent fine-point marker, whole allspice, whole cloves, floral wire, wire cutters, assorted kitchen utensils, 1 1/4 yds. of 2"w red and white checked wired ribbon, six artificial holly sprigs, peppermint disk candies, cinnamon sticks, and a hot glue gun.

**Note:** Allow wood tone spray and paint to dry after each application.

1. Trace gingerbread man pattern onto tracing paper; cut out. Draw around pattern three times on wrong side of foam trays. Use knife to cut out gingerbread men. Spray right side of each gingerbread man with wood tone spray.
2. For each gingerbread man, use red paint pen to paint feet, heart, and swirls for cheeks. Use white paint pen to paint a zigzag line across each arm. Use marker to draw "stitches" on each heart.
3. Glue allspice to each gingerbread man for eyes and buttons. For mouth, insert stems of cloves through foam; glue to secure.
4. Arrange utensils on wreath; wire in place. Tie ribbon into a bow. Arrange bow, gingerbread men, holly sprigs, cinnamon sticks, and candies on wreath; glue in place.

GINGERBREAD MAN

# "NOTE-ABLE" NUTCRACKER WREATH
(Shown on page 91)

**You will need** a 24" dia. artificial pine wreath with a foam base, red and green plaid and solid red wrapping paper, sheet music, wood tone spray, gold acrylic paint, paintbrush, floral pins, 4 1/2 yds. of 2 1/2"w red crinkle satin wired ribbon with gold trim, spool of floral wire, 4" long floral picks, wire cutters, six 2 1/4" dia. gold jingle bells, three 3" dia. drum ornaments, five 6"h and three 9"h nutcrackers, six gold musical symbol ornaments, and a hot glue gun.

1. Lightly spray wrapping paper and sheet music with wood tone spray; allow to dry. Tear twenty-five 4" squares each from wrapping paper and sheet music. Lightly brush gold paint along edges of solid red and sheet-music squares; allow to dry.
2. To make each paper cluster, layer one sheet music square on top of one or two wrapping paper squares. Insert a floral pin through center of layered papers. Loosely wrapping papers around thumb, push floral pin into foam base of wreath. Spacing evenly, repeat to add desired number of paper clusters to wreath.
3. For each bell, thread wire through loop of bell and center of one wrapping paper square; wire to floral pick.
4. Using wired ribbon, follow **Making a Bow**, page 159, to make a bow with ten 12" loops and two 10" streamers. Wire bow and drums to floral picks.
5. Using a length of wire to secure large nutcrackers to wreath and inserting floral picks into foam, arrange drums, bells, large nutcrackers, and bow on wreath.
6. Arrange and glue musical symbols and small nutcrackers around wreath.

# LIVELY CARDINAL WREATH
(Shown on page 89)

**You will need** a 24" dia. artificial pine wreath, tracing paper, red felt, black fabric scraps, gold fabric scraps, black embroidery floss, five 2 1/2" dia. gold jingle bells, 1 2/3 yds. of 3/4"w plaid ribbon, two 2 1/2 yd. lengths of 2 1/2"w plaid wired ribbon with gold backing, four 1" dia. gold glass ornaments, sixteen artificial holly sprigs, floral wire, wire cutters, seven flocked pinecones, gold glitter twigs, fabric glue, and a hot glue gun.

**Note:** Use hot glue for all gluing, unless otherwise indicated.

1. Trace cardinal patterns onto tracing paper; cut out. Use patterns to cut ten cardinal bodies and sixteen wings from red felt, five beaks from gold fabric, and five masks from black fabric.
2. For each body or wing, match edges of two felt pieces and use six strands of floss to work **Blanket Stitch**, page 157, to join edges.
3. For each bird, determine direction bird will face on wreath. Use fabric glue to glue mask, beak, and one wing to front of bird. For three birds, glue a second wing to back of bird.
4. Cut 3/4"w ribbon into five 12" lengths. Thread one length of ribbon through loop at top of each bell and tie into bow.
5. Using one length of 2 1/2"w ribbon, follow **Making a Bow**, page 159, to tie a bow with a 6" center loop, six 10" loops, and two 9" streamers. Arrange remaining ribbon length on wreath; glue in place.
6. Arrange and wire bow and bells to wreath. Arrange birds, ornaments, pinecones, holly sprigs, and gold twigs on wreath; glue to secure.

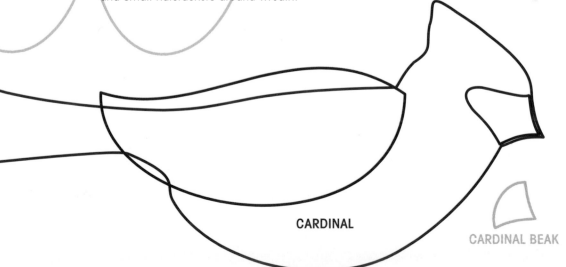

CARDINAL

CARDINAL BEAK

# THE SHARING
# OF CHRISTMAS

*The sharing of Christmas joy bestows abundant blessings on the giver as well as the receiver. Our charming fashions, lovely home decorations, and pretty, practical creations will please friends and loved ones alike. Convey seasonal goodwill to individuals of all ages with luxurious bath oils, an angelic crocheted afghan, and an appealing cross-stitched sampler. Remember the little ones with an adorable gown and blanket for baby and an appliquéd dress for a merry miss. Impress your friends with thoughtful gifts for the home, including hand-painted tableware, a festive frame or pillow, and cross-stitched towels and mugs. As you share your handiwork with the special people on your gift list, you can be assured of having a very blessed Christmas!*

*L*ayering simple appliqués makes our cheery handmade **Snowman Pillow** (page 104) *a quick and festive decoration.*

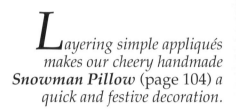

*I*n no time, you can cross stitch these cute **Winter Warmer Mugs and Towels** (page 113) *to share with special friends.*

*F*ashion a festive **Seasonal Sweatshirt Vest** (page 107) from an ordinary fleece top and fabric appliqués and present it to a deserving lady on your list.

*K*eep a buddy warm and toasty with our **Fleecy Winter Wear** (page 108), decorated with felt and fabric appliqués.

*A little miss will look especially charming in our **Appliquéd Knit Dress** (page 106). It's easy to make by fusing a few fabric cutouts onto a cotton knit dress and adding a plaid ruffle and trim.*

*W rap a bundle of joy in this **Sweet Baby Set** (page 107). The ensemble features a cotton knit gown and blanket that are decorated with fabric appliqués and rickrack trim.*

*O*ur attractive **Hand-Painted Holiday Tableware** (page 105) *is surprisingly easy to make. You just paint festive motifs on clear gold-rimmed glass dinnerware.*

*T*reat a friend to selections from our **Luxurious Bath Set** (page 109). *The collection includes rich bath oils, refreshing bath gel, and relaxing bath salts, all packaged in prettily adorned bottles.*

*E*asy-to-mix **Fragrant Bath Tea Bags** (page 109) possess the soothing and invigorating qualities of dried chamomile blossoms, mint leaves, and lavender.

*T*his cozy **Crocheted Angel Afghan** (page 110) is made of cloud-soft brushed acrylic yarn. Each block portrays an angel with popcorn-stitch wings.

*A **Fabric-Covered Photo Frame** (page 105), constructed from mat board, batting, holiday fabric, and shiny embellishments, is a merry way to display a favorite Christmas snapshot.*

*F*ill these hand-painted **Festive Flowerpots** (page 106) *with a sampling of sweets and nuts to surprise friends and neighbors.*

*H*ow sweet it is to greet guests with a **Gingerbread Doormat** (page 112)! *You create the cute design by spray painting over poster board cutouts.*

# SNOWMAN PILLOW (Shown on page 96)

**You will need** paper-backed fusible web; white, red, green, and black fabric scraps for appliqués; two 12½" squares of red checked flannel for pillow; stabilizer; clear thread; white and black embroidery floss; small silk holly leaf; one red and three black ⅜" dia. buttons; red colored pencil; 2 yds. of 5"w red checked fabric for ruffle (pieced as necessary); 1½" x 50" bias strip of green checked fabric for welting (pieced as necessary); 50" of ¼" dia. cord; polyester fiberfill; tracing paper; orange and black felt scraps; and fabric glue.

**Note:** Use a ¼" seam allowance for all sewing. Use three strands of floss and follow **Embroidery Stitches**, page 157, for all embroidery stitches unless otherwise indicated.

**1.** Trace nose and eye patterns onto tracing paper; cut out. Use patterns to cut pieces from felt.
**2.** Follow **Making Appliqués**, page 158, to make remaining snowman appliqués from fabric scraps.
**3.** For pillow front, arrange appliqués on right side of one flannel square, overlapping as necessary; fuse in place. Using clear thread, follow **Machine Appliqué**, page 158, to sew over raw edges of each appliqué. Glue eyes and nose to snowman; allow to dry.
**4.** Using white floss, stitch a ¾" and a ⅜" Cross Stitch for each snowflake on pillow front. Work a French Knot at each end of ¾" cross stitch. Using Stem Stitch and black floss, stitch snowman's mouth. Sew holly leaf and red button to hat and black buttons to snowman. Use red pencil to shade cheeks on snowman.
**5.** For welting, press one end of bias strip ½" to wrong side. Beginning ½" from folded end, center cord on wrong side of strip. Fold strip over cord. Beginning ½" from folded end, use a zipper foot to baste close to cord along length of strip. Trim seam allowance to ¼".
**6.** Matching raw edges and beginning with pressed end at center bottom of pillow front, pin welting to right side of pillow front. Trimming welting to fit, insert unfinished end of welting into folded end. Sewing as close to welting as possible, use a zipper foot to baste welting to pillow top.

**7.** Matching right sides, sew short edges of ruffle piece together; press seam open. Matching wrong sides and long edges, fold ruffle in half. Baste long raw edges of ruffle together. Pull basting thread, gathering ruffle to fit pillow top. Matching raw edges, pin ruffle to right side of pillow top.

**8.** Leaving an opening for stuffing and stitching as close to welting as possible, use zipper foot to sew right sides of pillow front and back together. Clip curves, turn right side out, and press. Stuff pillow with fiberfill; sew opening closed.

SNOWMAN

# FABRIC-COVERED PHOTO FRAME (Shown on page 102)

**You will need** a precut mat for frame front (we used an 8" x 10" mat with a 4½" x 6½" opening), a piece of mat board same size as precut mat for frame back, spray adhesive, mat board for easel, ½ yd. Christmas print fabric, batting, 38" of ¼" dia. red satin cord, 24" of 1½"w red satin wired ribbon, 18" of ⅜"w gold mesh ribbon, 1¼" dia. jingle bell, and hot glue gun.

**Note:** Use hot glue for all gluing unless otherwise indicated.

1. Use a pencil to draw around mat and mat opening on batting and wrong side of fabric. Cut out batting along drawn lines; glue to mat. Cut out fabric 1" outside drawn lines. Clip inner corners to within ¼" of drawn lines (**Fig. 1**).

**Fig. 1**

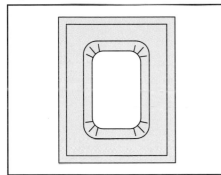

2. Center mat batting side down on wrong side of fabric. Fold fabric edges at opening of mat to back; glue in place. Fold corners of fabric diagonally over corners of mat; glue in place (**Fig. 2**). Fold remaining fabric edges to back of mat; glue in place.

**Fig. 2**

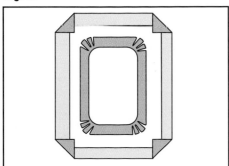

3. Beginning at center top edge, glue cord around outer edge of frame front.
4. Cut one piece of fabric 2" larger and a second piece of fabric ¼" smaller than frame back. Spray wrong sides of fabric pieces with adhesive. Center frame back on wrong side of large fabric piece. Fold outer corners diagonally over corners of frame back. Fold remaining fabric edges over edges of frame back. Center and smooth remaining fabric piece over raw edges of fabric on wrong side of frame back.
5. Matching wrong side of frame back to back of frame front, glue side and bottom edges of frame pieces together.
6. Measure height of frame; subtract 3". Cut a piece of mat board 2"w by the determined measurement. Cut one piece of fabric 1" larger and a second piece of fabric ¼" smaller than easel. Repeat Step 4 to cover easel with fabric pieces. Slightly bend top 1½" of easel toward right side. With bent end at top, matching bottom edges of easel and frame, and centering easel on back of frame, glue bent section of easel to back of frame.
7. Thread bell onto center of gold ribbon; tie ribbon into a bow. Thread bell onto center of satin ribbon; tie ribbon into a bow. Arrange and glue satin bow to top of frame over cord ends.

# HAND-PAINTED HOLIDAY TABLEWARE
(Shown on page 100)

**For each place setting,** you will need gold-rimmed clear glass dinner plate, salad plate, stemware, and rose bowl; red, green, and gold permanent enamel glass paint; tracing paper; removable tape; and small paintbrushes.

**Note:** Follow manufacturer's instructions to apply paints.

### ROSE BOWL AND STEMWARE
1. Trace holly pattern onto tracing paper.
2. Tape pattern on inside of glass. Working on outside of glass, paint leaves green and berries red. Remove pattern.
3. Use gold paint to paint veins on leaves and highlights on berries.

### PLATES
1. Trace holly or gift pattern onto tracing paper. With traced side down, tape pattern on front of plate.
2. Painting on wrong side of plate, paint gold highlights, red areas, then green areas.
3. Remove tape and pattern. Repeat for desired number of designs.

## APPLIQUÉD KNIT DRESS (Shown on page 99)

**You will need** a girl's cotton knit dress; black, green print, and plaid fabrics; $1/2$" dia. red shank button; clear thread; assorted buttons; paper-backed fusible web; stabilizer; and red thread for sewing buttons.

**Note:** Use a $1/4$" seam allowance for all sewing unless otherwise indicated.

1. Make a 3" vertical cut at center back of neck of dress. Measure around bottom edge of neckband, add 10". Cut a bias strip $1 1/2$"w by the determined measurement from plaid fabric. Press edges of strip $1/2$" to wrong side. Matching wrong sides and long edges, press strip in half.
2. For ruffle, measure around bottom edge of neckband. Cut a length of bias strip the determined measurement. Multiply measurement by $1 1/2$ and cut a piece of plaid fabric $3 1/4$"w by the determined measurement. Press short ends $1/4$" to wrong side; press $1/4$" to wrong side again. Repeat for one long edge. Baste along long raw edge. Pull basting threads to gather fabric to fit bias strip. Adjusting gathers as necessary, insert gathered edge of ruffle into fold of bias strip. Stitch edges of strip together,

catching ruffle in stitching. Pin ruffle along bottom edge of neckband; top stitch in place.
3. For back closure of dress, cut a 7" length from bias strip. Unfold strip and press ends $1/2$" to wrong side; refold strip. Pin strip over cut edge and sew in place. Cut a $2 1/2$" length from bias strip. Unfold strip and press ends $1/2$" to wrong side; refold strip. Sew along long edges. Matching short ends, fold strip in half. Sew short ends of loop to inside left edge of neckband at opening. Sew shank button to outside right edge of neckband.
4. For skirt border, measure around skirt 2" above bottom edge; add $1 1/2$". Cut a bias strip $1 1/4$"w by the determined measurement. Press long edges $1/4$" to wrong side. Press one end $1/2$" to wrong side. Beginning with raw end, pin strip around dress 2" above bottom edge, overlapping ends at back. Top stitch in place.
5. Follow **Making Appliqués**, page 158, to make three tree and three trunk appliqués. Arrange appliqués on front of dress, overlapping as necessary; fuse in place. Using clear thread, follow **Machine Appliqué**, page 158, to sew over edges of appliqués. Sew buttons to trees as desired.

## FESTIVE FLOWERPOTS
(Shown on page 103)

**For each flowerpot,** you will need a 5" dia. clay flowerpot with saucer; spray primer; white, red, and green acrylic paints; 1"w paintbrush; medium-point and fine-point gold paint pens; and clear acrylic spray sealer.

**Note:** Allow primer, paint, and sealer to dry after each application.

1. Spray flowerpot and saucer with primer.
2. Paint pot and saucer white. Paint bottom sections of pot and saucer with red or green paint.
3. Paint vertical stripes on rim of flowerpot.
4. Use medium paint pen to add a wavy line to edges of each stripe. Use fine paint pen to freehand paint star bursts to rims of pot and saucer.
5. Spray pot and saucer with sealer.

GINGERBREAD BOY

TREE

TRUNK

# SEASONAL SWEATSHIRT VEST (Shown on page 98)

**You will need** a women's sweatshirt (we used an extra large), seam ripper, tailor's chalk, plaid fabric for binding and elastic casing, assorted print fabrics for appliqués, paper-backed fusible web, stabilizer, clear thread, black permanent fine-point marker, red fabric paint, small paintbrush, 6" length of 1/16"w green satin ribbon, assorted buttons, 6" of 1/2"w elastic, and a safety pin.

**For background appliqués,** you will **also** need one 5" x 8" fabric rectangle for tree; 4 1/2" x 5 1/2" fabric rectangle, 1" x 5 1/2" fabric strip, and 1" x 6" fabric strip for gingerbread boy; two 3 1/2" x 4 1/2" fabric rectangles and one 1 3/4" x 4 1/2" fabric strip for hearts; and one 3 3/4" x 6 1/2" fabric rectangle and two 1" x 6 1/2" fabric strips for ornaments.

**Note:** Match wrong sides of fabric pieces and use a 1/4" seam allowance for all sewing unless otherwise indicated.

1. Use seam ripper to remove neckband, sleeves, and bottom ribbing from sweatshirt. If desired, shorten length of shirt. Cut shirt open vertically down center front.
2. Use chalk to mark 11" below neck on both sides of front opening. Draw a line from each mark to shoulder seam (**Fig. 1**); cut along drawn lines.

**Fig. 1**

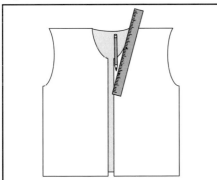

3. To enlarge armholes, mark shoulder seams 4 1/2" from neck edge. Following the curves of armhole openings, draw tapering lines from shoulder marks to bottoms of armholes (**Fig. 2**). Cut along drawn lines.

**Fig. 2**

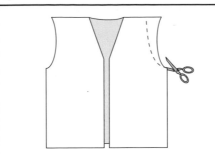

4. Stay-stitch along all edges of vest. Using 2 1/2"w bias strip, follow **Binding**, page 158, to bind raw edges of vest.
5. Follow **Making Appliqués**, page 158, to make five large star; three each small star, ornament, and cap; two heart; and one each tree, trunk, and gingerbread boy appliqués.
6. For gingerbread boy background, sew 5" strip to 5" edge of rectangle. Sew 6" strip to right side of rectangle. For heart background, sew one 4 1/2" edge of each rectangle to each 4 1/2" side of strip. For ornament background, sew one 6" strip to each 6" side of rectangle. Press edges of each background 1/4" to wrong side.
7. Arrange appliqués on backgrounds, overlapping as necessary; fuse in place. Using clear thread, follow **Machine Appliqué**, page 158, to sew over edges of appliqués. Use permanent marker to draw face on gingerbread boy. Thin red paint with water, paint cheeks on gingerbread boy. Tie ribbon into a bow; tack bow to gingerbread boy.
8. Arrange backgrounds on vest; top stitch in place. Arrange star appliqués on vest; fuse in place. Machine Appliqué over edges of stars. Sew buttons to vest as desired.
9. For elastic casing in back, cut a 1 1/2" x 9" strip from fabric. Press ends, then long edges 1/4" to wrong side. Mark 8 1/2" across center back 6" from bottom edge. Center strip over marked line. Sewing close to pressed edges, top stitch long edges in place. Use safety pin to thread elastic through casing. Catching one end of elastic in stitches, sew a button over one end of casing. Repeat to catch remaining end of elastic at opposite end of casing.

# SWEET BABY SET
(Shown on page 99)

**You will need** red rickrack, infant's cotton knit gown, cotton knit receiving blanket, assorted red and gold fabric scraps for appliqués, paper-backed fusible web, stabilizer, thread to match fabrics, and three 10" lengths of 1/4"w green satin ribbon.

1. Arrange and pin rickrack down front of gown. Cut rickrack 1" below hem. Fold rickrack 1/4" to wrong side and around bottom edge of hem; pin in place. Beginning at hem, sew rickrack to front of gown.
2. Beginning and ending at one corner, folding ends 1/2" to wrong side, and placing rickrack 1" from edges, pin rickrack along edges of blanket. Sew rickrack to blanket.
3. Follow **Making Appliqués**, page 158, to make eight small star and three gingerbread boy appliqués. Arrange two gingerbread boys and five small stars on gown and one gingerbread boy and three stars on one corner of blanket; fuse in place.
4. Follow **Machine Appliqué**, page 158, to stitch over edges of appliqués.
5. Tie ribbons into bows. Tack one bow to each gingerbread boy.

HEART

SMALL STAR

LARGE STAR

ORNAMENT

CAP

# FLEECY WINTER WEAR (Shown on page 98)

**You will need** 1 yd. of 60"w red fleece, tracing paper, green and gold felt, pinking shears, plaid fabric, gold embroidery floss, sixteen $5/8$" dia. buttons, and eight $3/8$" dia. jingle bells.

**For mittens**, you will **also** need 15" of $1/2$"w elastic and a safety pin.

**Note:** Using three strands of floss, follow **Embroidery Stitches**, page 157, for all embroidery stitches. Use a $1/4$" seam allowance for all sewing unless otherwise indicated.

## MUFFLER

**1.** Cut a 12" x 50" piece of fleece. Follow **Making Patterns**, page 158, to make star and border patterns. Use border pattern to cut two pieces from green felt. Use pinking shears to trim long straight edge of each border piece. Use star pattern to cut six stars from gold felt.

**2.** Cut two $2^1/2$" x 13" pieces of plaid fabric. Press long, then short edges of each fabric piece $1/2$" to wrong side.

**3.** For each end of muffler, place border across short edge of muffler with pointed edge of border $1^1/4$" from short end of muffler. Work Running Stitch along pointed edges of border through both layers. Use Straight Stitch to make a vertical stitch at each point.

**4.** Arrange three stars above border piece. Work Straight Stitch and French Knots as indicated on star pattern to stitch stars to muffler. For each star burst, stitch a 1" vertical Straight Stitch, a Cross Stitch across center of Straight Stitch, and a French Knot at each end of one stitch of cross stitch.

**5.** Place one fabric strip across border pieces $1/4$" below pinked edge. Work Running Stitch along each long edge of fabric strip through all layers.

**6.** For fringe, make 1" clips $1/4$" apart along short edge.

**7.** Sew buttons above Straight Stitches at points of border. Sew bells to points of border.

## MITTENS

**1.** Trace mitten and star patterns onto tracing paper; cut out. Leaving mittens open at wrist, follow **Sewing Shapes**, page 158, to make two mittens. Use star pattern to cut two stars from gold felt. Use pinking shears to cut two $2^3/4$" squares from green felt.

**2.** For each mitten, center star on square. Work Straight Stitch and French Knots as indicated on star pattern to stitch star to square.

**3.** Work one Cross Stitch and two French Knots to secure corners of square to mitten top.

**4.** Fold $1/4$" of straight edge of mitten to wrong side, fold $1/4$" to wrong side again; sew in place.

**5.** For elastic casing, cut a $1^1/4$" x 11" piece of plaid fabric. Press long, then short edges of fabric strip $1/4$" to wrong side. Beginning at thumb seam, pin strip around mitten $1^1/4$" from bottom edge. Work Running Stitch along long edges of fabric strip to sew strip to mitten.

**6.** Use safety pin to insert elastic in casing. Overlap elastic ends $1/4$"; sew ends together. Hand sew casing closed.

## HAT

**1.** Cut a 12" x 25" piece of fleece. Matching short edges, fold fleece in half. Sew short edges together.

**2.** Refer to **Fig. 1** to stitch curved seams across top corners of cap. Trim corners $1/2$" from curved seams. With seam at center back, fold hat flat. Refer to **Fig. 2** to sew $1/2$" x 3" darts at top of side folds.

**Fig. 1**

**Fig. 2**

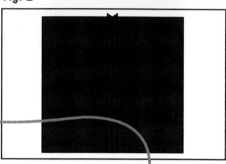

**3.** Matching darts and top edge, baste across top of hat from back seam to front curve. Pull basting thread to gather top edge of hat. Sew top edge of hat along gathers. Remove basting thread.

**4.** Using dotted line as bottom of pattern, follow **Making Patterns**, page 158, to make border pattern. Use pattern to cut border from a 28" strip of green felt. Use pinking shears to trim long straight edge of border.

**5.** Beginning with short edge at back seam and matching wrong sides and long edges, pin border around hat. Use Running Stitch to sew border to hat along points and pinked edge. Use Straight Stitch to make vertical stitches at points of border. Sew buttons above straight stitches at points of border. Turn hat right side out. Fold edge of hat up.

**6.** For pom-pom, cut a 3" x $3^1/2$" piece of fleece. Make $1^1/2$" cuts $1/4$" apart along short edges of piece. Matching long edges, fold fleece in half, fold in half again. Stitch center of pom-pom to top of hat.

STAR

MITTEN

BORDER

# LUXURIOUS BATH SET (Shown on page 100)

## WAX-SEALED BOTTLE
**You will need** a small glass bottle with cork stopper, wax crystals, gold crayon with paper removed, large can, saucepan, and a letter seal.

1. Follow recipe to prepare and fill bottle with Exotic Bath Salts, Sparkling Bath Gel, **or** Silky Bath Oil; cork bottle tightly.
2. Follow **Working with Wax**, page 159, to melt wax and crayon to a depth of 2". Dip cork and rim of bottle in melted wax until completely coated. Allowing wax to cool slightly, repeat until desired thickness is achieved. If desired, stamp letter seal in warm wax on top of cork; allow wax to harden.

## GOLD-SEALED BOTTLE
**You will need** a small glass bottle with cork stopper, 9" length of $1/2$"w gold mesh ribbon, gold sealing wax, and desired letter seal.

1. Follow recipe to prepare and fill bottle with Exotic Bath Salts, Sparkling Bath Gel, **or** Silky Bath Oil; cork bottle tightly.
2. Tie gold mesh ribbon into a knot around neck of bottle. Trim or notch ribbon ends.
3. (**Note:** Follow manufacturer's instructions to use gold sealing wax and letter seal.) Leaving $1/2$" of ribbon ends free, stamp seal on ribbon streamers and bottle.

## HEART-STAMPED BOTTLE
**You will need** a small glass bottle with cork stopper to fit a $1^1/2$" x $2^1/4$" design, gold leaf, gold spray paint, $1^1/2$" x $1^3/4$" rectangle of screen wire, 1" dia. heart-shaped rubber stamp, gold ink pad, $1^1/4$" square of decorative paper, $1^1/2$" x $2^1/4$" rectangle of gold wrapping paper, and a hot glue gun.

1. Follow manufacturer's instructions to apply gold leaf to entire bottle.
2. Spray paint screen gold; allow to dry. Stamp heart on decorative paper. Center and glue decorative paper to screen. Center and glue screen to gold wrapping paper; glue to front of bottle.
3. Follow recipe to prepare and fill bottle with Exotic Bath Salts, Sparkling Bath Gel, **or** Silky Bath Oil; cork bottle tightly.

## SCREEN-WRAPPED BOTTLE
**You will need** a small glass bottle with cork stopper, screen wire, gold spray paint, gold cord, hot glue gun, wax crystals, gold crayon with paper removed, large can, and saucepan.

1. Follow recipe to prepare and fill bottle with Exotic Bath Salts, Sparkling Bath Gel, **or** Silky Bath Oil; cork bottle tightly.
2. Measure around bottle; add 1". Measure height of bottle; subtract $1/2$". Cut a piece of screen the determined measurement. Spray paint screen gold; allow to dry.
3. Overlapping ends at back, wrap screen around bottle; glue to secure.
4. Follow Step 2 of Wax-Sealed Bottle to coat cork and rim with melted wax.
5. Tie cord into a bow around neck of bottle.

## GOLD CORD-WRAPPED BOTTLE
**You will need** a small glass bottle with cork stopper, gold cord, gold charm, and a hot glue gun.

1. Follow recipe to prepare and fill bottle with Exotic Bath Salts, Sparkling Bath Gel, **or** Silky Bath Oil; cork bottle tightly.
2. Beginning and ending at back of bottle, glue one end of cord at top of bottle neck. Wrap cord closely around bottle neck until desired amount of neck is covered. Trim end and glue to secure.
3. Cut a length of cord to drape around bottle. Spot glue center of cord length at center back of bottle. Bring ends to front of bottle. Glue charm to bottle over cord to secure ends together.

## STAR-SPANGLED BOTTLE
**You will need** a small glass bottle with cork stopper, gold glitter dimensional paint, wax crystals, gold crayon with paper removed, large can, saucepan, gold tassel, flat gold trim, and a hot glue gun.

1. Follow recipe to prepare and fill bottle with Exotic Bath Salts, Sparkling Bath Gel, **or** Silky Bath Oil; cork bottle tightly.
2. Use dimensional paint to paint stars on bottle; allow to dry.
3. Follow Step 2 of Wax-Sealed Bottle to coat cork and rim with melted wax.
4. Beginning and ending at back of bottle and working through hanging loop of tassel, glue one end of trim at top of bottle neck. Wrap trim around bottle neck three or four times. Trim end and glue to secure.

## EXOTIC BATH SALTS
**You will need** $1/2$ cup rock salt, skin-safe essential oil, and a funnel.

1. Combine rock salt with ten drops of essential oil.
2. Use funnel to pour salt mixture into bottle; cork bottle tightly.

## SPARKLING BATH GEL
**For bath gel,** you will need $1^1/3$ cups aloe vera gel, 1 teaspoon lanolin, fine gold glitter, and a funnel.

1. Mix gel and lanolin with a small amount of glitter.
2. Use funnel to pour mixture into bottle; cork bottle tightly.

## SILKY BATH OIL
**You will need** 16 oz. of almond oil, $1/2$ oz. of skin-safe essential oil, dried flowers and greenery (we used small dried rosebuds, dried Queen Anne's lace, and thin dried leaves), and a funnel.

1. Mix oils together.
2. Place desired dried items in bottle. (**Note:** If using a bottle with a narrow neck, soak dried items in oil mixture before placing them in bottle.)
3. Pour oil mixture into bottle; cork bottle tightly.

# FRAGRANT BATH TEA BAGS
(Shown on page 101)

**For tea bags,** you will need dried chamomile blossoms, $1/4$"w flat gold trim, 12" squares of gold tulle and sheer organza, and dried mint leaves for invigorating bath tea **or** dried lavender for soothing bath tea.

1. Using equal parts, mix chamomile blossoms with mint leaves or lavender.
2. For each tea bag, center one square of organza over one square of tulle. Place $1/4$ cup of desired tea mixture in center of squares. Gather edges of squares around tea. Wrap an 8" length of trim several times around gathers. Knot ends to secure.
3. To use: Place one bag in bathtub under warm running water.

# CROCHETED ANGEL AFGHAN (Shown on page 101)

**Finished Size:** 46" x 61"

**You will need,** 46 ounces (1,310 grams, 1,330 yards) of worsted weight brushed acrylic yarn, and size G (4.00 mm) crochet hook **or** size needed for gauge

**Note:** Refer to **Crochet**, page 156, for abbreviations and general instructions.

**GAUGE:** Each Square =15"
**Gauge Swatch:** 2³/₄" Square
Work same as Square through Rnd 2.

## STITCH GUIDE
### POPCORN
4 dc in st or sp indicated, drop loop from hook, insert hook in first dc of 4-dc group, hook dropped loop and draw through.

### REVERSE SINGLE CROCHET
Working from **left** to **right**, ★ insert hook in st or sp to right of hook (**Fig. 1**), YO and draw through, under and to left of loop on hook (2 loops on hook) (**Fig. 2**), YO and draw through both loops on hook (**Fig. 3**) (**Reverse Single Crochet made, Fig. 4**); repeat from ★ around.

**Fig. 1**          **Fig. 2**

**Fig. 3**          **Fig. 4**

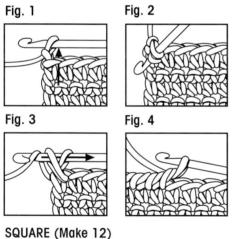

### SQUARE (Make 12)
Ch 6; join with sl st to form a ring.

**Rnd 1:** (Right side): Ch 3 **(counts as first dc, now and throughout)**, 2 dc in ring, (ch 3, 3 dc in ring) 3 times, ch 2, sc in first dc to form last ch-3 sp: 12 dc and 4 ch-3 sps.
**Note:** Loop a short piece of yarn around any stitch to mark Rnd 1 as **right** side.

**Rnd 2:** Ch 3, dc in same sp and in next 3 dc, (2 dc, ch 3, dc) in next ch-3 sp, ch 1, dc in next dc, work Popcorn in next dc, dc in next dc, ch 1, (dc, ch 3, dc) in next ch-3 sp, ch 1, dc in next dc, ch 1, skip next dc, dc in next dc, ch 1, (dc, ch 3, dc) in next ch-3 sp, ch 1, dc in next dc, work Popcorn in next dc, dc in next dc, ch 1, dc in same sp as first dc, ch 2, sc in first dc to form last ch-3 sp: 19 dc, 2 Popcorns, and 11 sps.
**Rnd 3:** Ch 3, dc in same sp and in next dc, ch 1, skip next 2 dc, (dc, ch 3, dc) in next dc, ch 1, skip next 2 dc, dc in next dc, (2 dc, ch 3, dc) in next ch-3 sp, † ch 1, dc in next dc, work Popcorn in next ch-1 sp, dc in next dc, ch 1, dc in next dc, work Popcorn in next ch-1 sp, dc in next dc, ch 1 †, (dc, ch 3, dc) in next ch-3 sp, ch 1, dc in next dc, skip next ch-1 sp, 5 dc in next ch-1 sp, skip next dc, dc in next dc, ch 1, (dc, ch 3, dc) in next ch-3 sp, repeat from † to † once, dc in same sp as first dc, ch 2, sc in first dc to form last ch-3 sp: 29 dc and 15 sps.
**Rnd 4:** Ch 3, dc in same sp and in next dc, ch 1, skip next 2 dc, dc in next dc, 9 dc in next ch-3 sp, dc in next dc, ch 1, skip next 2 dc, dc in next dc, (2 dc, ch 3, dc) in next ch-3 sp, ch 1, † dc in next dc, work Popcorn in next ch-1 sp, dc in next dc, ch 1 †, repeat from † to † 2 times **more**, (dc, ch 3, dc) in next ch-3 sp, (ch 1, dc in next dc) twice, skip next 2 dc, 5 dc in next dc, skip next 2 dc, (dc in next dc, ch 1) twice, (dc, ch 3, dc) in next ch-3 sp, ch 1, repeat from † to † 3 times, dc in same sp as first dc, ch 2, sc in first dc to form last ch-3 sp: 44 dc and 18 sps.
**Rnd 5:** Ch 4 **(counts as first dc plus ch 1, now and throughout)**, dc in next 3 dc, ch 1, hdc in next 5 dc, 2 hdc in next dc, hdc in next 5 dc, ch 1, dc in next 3 dc, ch 1, (dc, ch 3, dc) in next ch-3 sp, ch 1, † dc in next dc, work Popcorn in next ch-1 sp, dc in next dc, ch 1 †, repeat from † to † 3 times **more**, (dc, ch 3, dc) in next ch-3 sp, ch 1, (dc in next dc, ch 1) 3 times, skip next 2 dc, 5 dc in next dc, ch 1, skip next 2 dc, (dc in next dc, ch 1) 3 times, (dc, ch 3, dc) in next ch-3 sp, ch 1, repeat from † to † 4 times, dc in same sp as first dc, ch 2, sc in first dc to form last ch-3 sp: 41 dc and 26 sps.

**Rnd 6:** Ch 4, dc in next dc, ch 1, dc in next 3 dc, ch 2, skip next 2 hdc, hdc in next 3 hdc, 2 hdc in each of next 2 hdc, hdc in next 3 hdc, ch 2, skip next 2 hdc, dc in next 3 dc, ch 1, dc in next dc, ch 1, (dc, ch 3, dc) in next ch-3 sp, ch 1, † dc in next dc, work Popcorn in next ch-1 sp, dc in next dc, ch 1 †, repeat from † to † 4 times **more**, (dc, ch 3, dc) in next ch-3 sp, ch 1, dc in next dc, skip next ch-1 sp, 5 dc in next ch-1 sp, ch 1, skip next 4 dc, 5 dc in next dc, ch 1, skip next 2 ch-1 sps, 5 dc in next ch-1 sp, skip next dc, dc in next dc, ch 1, (dc, ch 3, dc) in next ch-3 sp, ch 1, repeat from † to † 5 times, dc in same sp as first dc, ch 2, sc in first dc to form last ch-3 sp: 53 dc and 26 sps.
**Rnd 7:** Ch 4, (dc in next dc, ch 1) 3 times, skip next dc, dc in next dc, 2 dc in next ch-2 sp, ch 2, skip next 2 hdc, sc in next 6 hdc, ch 2, 2 dc in next ch-2 sp, dc in next dc, ch 1, skip next dc, (dc in next dc, ch 1) 3 times, (dc, ch 3, dc) in next ch-3 sp, ch 1, † dc in next dc, work Popcorn in next ch-1 sp, dc in next dc, ch 1 †, repeat from † to † 5 times **more**, (dc, ch 3, dc) in next ch-3 sp, (ch 1, dc in next dc) twice, skip next 2 dc, 5 dc in next dc, ★ ch 1, skip next 4 dc, 5 dc in next dc; repeat from ★ once **more**, skip next 2 dc, (dc in next dc, ch 1) twice, (dc, ch 3, dc) in next ch-3 sp, ch 1, repeat from † to † 6 times, dc in same sp as first dc, ch 2, sc in first dc to form last ch-3 sp: 63 dc and 34 sps.
**Rnd 8:** Ch 4, (dc in next dc, ch 1) 5 times, skip next dc, dc in next dc, 2 dc in next ch-2 sp, ch 2, skip next 2 sc, sc in next 2 sc, ch 2, 2 dc in next ch-2 sp, dc in next dc, ch 1, skip next dc, (dc in next dc, ch 1) 5 times, (dc, ch 3, dc) in next ch-3 sp, ch 1, † dc in next dc, work Popcorn in next ch-1 sp, dc in next dc, ch 1 †, repeat from † to † 6 times **more**, (dc, ch 3, dc) in next ch-3 sp, ch 1, (dc in next dc, ch 1) 3 times, skip next 2 dc, 5 dc in next dc, ch 1, ★ skip next 4 dc, 5 dc in next dc, ch 1; repeat from ★ once **more**, skip next 2 dc, (dc in next dc, ch 1) 3 times, (dc, ch 3, dc) in next ch-3 sp, ch 1, repeat from † to † 7 times, dc in same sp as first dc, ch 2, sc in first dc to form last ch-3 sp: 73 dc and 44 sps.
**Rnd 9:** Ch 4, (dc in next dc, ch 1) 7 times, skip next dc, dc in next dc, 2 dc in

next ch-2 sp, ch 1, 2 dc in next ch-2 sp, dc in next dc, ch 1, skip next dc, (dc in next dc, ch 1) 7 times, (dc, ch 3, dc) in next ch-3 sp, ch 1, (dc in next dc, ch 1) 16 times, (dc, ch 3, dc) in next ch 3 sp, ch 1, dc in next dc, skip next ch-1 sp, 5 dc in next ch-1 sp, ch 1, ★ skip next 4 dc, 5 dc in next dc, ch 1; repeat from ★ 2 times **more**, skip next 2 ch-1 sps, 5 dc in next ch-1 sp, skip next dc, dc in next dc, ch 1, (dc, ch 3, dc) in next ch-3 sp, ch 1, (dc in next dc, ch 1) 16 times, dc in same sp as first dc, ch 2, sc in first dc to form last ch-3 sp: 87 dc and 61 sps.

**Rnd 10:** Ch 3, (dc in next dc, ch 1) 9 times, skip next dc, (dc in next dc, ch 1) twice, skip next dc, dc in next dc, (ch 1, dc in next dc) 8 times, (dc, ch 3, dc) in next ch-3 sp, ch 1, (dc in next dc, ch 1) 18 times, (dc, ch 3, dc) in next ch-3 sp, ch 1, (dc in next dc, ch 1) twice, skip next 2 dc, 5 dc in next dc, ch 1, ★ skip next 4 dc, 5 dc in next dc, ch 1; repeat from ★ 3 times **more**, skip next 2 dc, (dc in next dc, ch 1) twice, (dc, ch 3, dc) in next ch-3 sp, ch 1, (dc in next dc, ch 1) 18 times, dc in same sp as first dc, ch 2, sc in first dc to form last ch-3 sp: 93 dc and 71 sps.

**Rnd 11:** Ch 4, skip next dc, dc in next dc, (dc in next ch-1 sp and in next dc) 19 times, ch 1, skip next dc, (dc, ch 3, dc) in next ch-3 sp, ch 1, dc in next dc, (dc in next ch-1 sp and in next dc) 19 times, ch 1, (dc, ch 3, dc) in next ch-3 sp, ch 1, (dc in next dc, ch 1) 3 times, skip next 2 dc, 5 dc in next dc, ch 1, ★ skip next 4 dc, 5 dc in next dc, ch 1; repeat

from ★ 3 times **more**, skip next 2 dc, (dc in next dc, ch 1) 3 times, (dc, ch 3, dc) in next ch-3 sp, ch 1, dc in next dc, (dc in next ch-1 sp and in next dc) 19 times, ch 1, dc in same sp as first dc, ch 2, sc in first dc to form last ch-3 sp: 156 dc and 22 sps.

**Rnd 12:** Ch 4, dc in next dc and in each ch-1 sp and each dc across to next ch-3 sp, ch 1, (dc, ch 3, dc) in ch-3 sp, ch 1, dc in each dc and in each ch-1 sp across to next ch-3 sp, ch 1, (dc, ch 3, dc) in ch-3 sp, ch 1, (dc in next dc, ch 1) 4 times, skip next 2 dc, 5 dc in next dc, ch 1, ★ skip next 4 dc, 5 dc in next dc, ch 1; repeat from ★ 3 times **more**, skip next 2 dc, (dc in next dc, ch 1) 4 times, (dc, ch 3, dc) in next ch-3 sp, ch 1, dc in each dc and in each ch-1 sp across, ch 1, dc in same sp as first dc, ch 2, sc in first dc to form last ch-3 sp: 170 dc and 24 sps.

**Rnd 13:** Ch 4, dc in next dc and in each ch-1 sp and each dc across to next ch-3 sp, ch 1, (dc, ch 3, dc) in ch-3 sp, ch 1, dc in next dc and in each ch-1 sp and each dc across to next ch 3 sp, ch 1, (dc, ch 3, dc) in next ch-3 sp, (ch 1, dc in next dc) 5 times, ch 2, skip next 2 dc, sl st in next dc, ch 2, ★ sc in next ch-1 sp, ch 2, skip next 2 dc, sl st in next dc, ch 2; repeat from ★ 3 times **more**, skip next 2 dc, (dc in next dc, ch 1) 5 times, (dc, ch 3, dc) in next ch-3 sp, ch 1, dc in each dc and in each ch-1 sp across, ch 1, dc in same sp as first dc, ch 2, sc in first dc to form last ch-3 sp: 159 dc and 30 sps.

**Rnd 14:** Ch 4, † (dc in next dc, ch 1) twice, (skip next st, dc in next dc, ch 1) across to next ch-3 sp, (dc, ch 3, dc) in ch-3 sp, ch 1 †, repeat from † to † once **more**, (dc in next dc, ch 1) 6 times, place marker around last dc made to mark bottom edge, skip next ch, dc in next ch, ch 1, skip next sl st, dc in next ch, ch 1, skip next ch, ★ dc in next sc, ch 1, skip next ch, dc in next ch, ch 1, skip next sl st, dc in next ch, ch 1, skip next ch; repeat from ★ 3 times **more**, (dc in next dc, ch 1) 6 times, (dc, ch 3, dc) in next ch-3 sp, ch 1, (dc in next dc, ch 1) twice, (skip next st, dc in next dc, ch 1) across, dc in same sp as first dc, ch 3; join with sl st to first dc, finish off: 112 dc and 112 sps.

## ASSEMBLY

Assemble Afghan by forming three vertical strips of four Squares each. Join Squares as follows:
With right sides together, match sps on bottom edge of one Square to top edge of next Square. Working through both thicknesses, join yarn with sl st in first corner ch-3 sp; (ch 1, sl st in next sp) across; finish off.
Join strips together in same manner.

## EDGING

With right side facing, join yarn with sl st in any st; working from **left** to **right**, work Reverse Single Crochet in each dc and in each ch-1 sp around, working 3 Reverse Single Crochet in each corner ch-3 sp; join with sl st to first st, finish off.

## GINGERBREAD DOORMAT (Shown on page 103)

**You will need** tracing paper, poster board, 1"w masking tape, a 30"w x 18"h coir (coconut husk fiber) doormat, spray adhesive, red spray paint, white and green acrylic paint, small paintbrush, and pencil with unused eraser.

**1.** Trace gingerbread man pattern onto tracing paper; cut out. Use pattern to cut three gingerbread men from poster board.
**2.** Apply a strip of tape 1 1/2" inside each edge of doormat. Lightly apply spray adhesive to one side of each gingerbread man. Arrange gingerbread men on doormat adhesive side down to hold in place.

**3.** Spray paint doormat red; allow to dry. Remove gingerbread men and masking tape. Use white acrylic paint to paint zigzags on border and gingerbread men. Use eraser end of pencil and acrylic paints to add white dots to gingerbread men for eyes and buttons and green dots to border. Allow to dry.

GINGERBREAD MAN

## WINTER WARMER WALL HANGING
(Shown on page 97)

**You will need** an 8" x 14" piece of white Aida (14 ct); embroidery floss (refer to color key); #24 tapestry needle; two each 2 1/4" x 11 3/4" and 2 1/4" x 14 1/4" strips, 7" x 10" piece of fabric for hanging sleeve, and one 11 3/4" x 17 1/2" backing piece of red checked flannel; two each 1 1/2" x 8 1/2" and 1 1/2" x 12" strips of green check fabric; 11 3/4" x 17 1/2" piece of batting; four 1" dia. white buttons; and an 11" length of 1/4" dia. wooden dowel.

**Note:** Use 1/4" seam allowance for all sewing unless otherwise indicated.

**1.** Following **Cross Stitch**, page 156, and using three strands of floss for Cross Stitch and one strand of floss for Backstitch and French Knot, work Winter Warmer Wall Hanging design on Aida cloth. Trim finished stitched piece to 6" x 12".
**2.** For wall hanging front, match right sides and raw edges and sew long green strips to sides of cross-stitched piece. Repeat to sew short green strips to top and bottom of cross-stitched piece.
**3.** Repeat Step 2 to sew red strips to sides, then top and bottom of wall hanging front. Center batting piece on wrong side of backing. Center wrong side of wall hanging front on batting. Pin front, batting, and backing together. Use three strands of black floss to sew buttons to corners of sampler.
**4.** Press short edges of hanging sleeve fabric piece 1/4" to wrong side. Press 1/4" to wrong side again; stitch in place. Matching wrong sides and long edges, fold piece in half. Match raw edges to center top back of wall hanging; pin in place. Taking care not to stitch through to design, tack folded edge in place.
**8.** Using a 2"w bias strip, follow **Binding**, page 158, to bind wall hanging.
**9.** Insert dowel into hanging sleeve.

# WINTER WARMER MUGS

(Shown on page 96)

**For each mug,** you will need one red Crafter's Pride® Stitch-a-Mug™ with 14 ct white Vinyl Weave™ insert, DMC embroidery floss (refer to color key), and a #24 tapestry needle.

**1.** Centering design 2¹/₂" from short edge of insert, use three strands of floss and follow **Cross Stitch,** page 156, to stitch snowman or snow woman from Winter Warmer Wall Hanging chart. Beginning at one short edge of insert and leaving three unworked threads between border and long edges, stitch red heart border along long edges of insert.
**2.** Place stitched piece in mug. Remove stitched piece before washing mug.

# WINTER WARMER TOWELS

(Shown on page 96)

**You will need** a white fingertip towel with 14 ct Aida insert, DMC embroidery floss (refer to color key), and #24 tapestry needle.

**1.** Using three strands of floss, follow **Cross Stitch,** page 156, to stitch tree border or verse of Winter Warmer Wall Hanging chart in center of Aida inserts.
**2.** Center and stitch red and black border above and below stitched design, repeating as needed to work border to approximately ¹/₂" from towel edges.

**Winter Warmer Wall Hanging**

| X | DMC | B'ST | ANC. | COLOR |
|---|-----|------|------|-------|
| ▦ | 310 | ╱ | 403 | black |
| ◒ | 415 | | 398 | grey |
| ■ | 433 | | 358 | brown |
| ■ | 666 | | 46 | red |
| ✳ | 701 | | 227 | green |
| ★ | 826 | | 161 | blue |
| ▣ | 827 | | 160 | lt blue |
| ◈ | 3716 | | 25 | pink |
| ● | 310 | | | French Knot |

**STITCH COUNT (51w x 137h)**

| | | | |
|---|---|---|---|
| 14 count | 3³/₄" | x | 9⁷/₈" |
| 16 count | 3¹/₄" | x | 8⁵/₈" |
| 18 count | 2⁷/₈" | x | 7⁵/₈" |
| 22 count | 2³/₈" | x | 6¹/₄" |

# THE TASTES OF CHRISTMAS

The delightful tastes of Christmas transform this season into a flavorful festival of palate-pleasing foods! Our holiday recipes will help you create a mouth-watering brunch, a well-seasoned supper, delicious desserts, and treats that are perfect for sharing as Yuletide presents. There are fabulous make-ahead foods that give you time to thoroughly enjoy your guests, and family favorites from the kitchens of our own employees. These dishes are so yummy you'll want to serve them again and again before the next holiday season rolls around. So turn the pages and join us for a taste-tempting trip through a merry wonderland of delectable dishes!

# NEW ENGLAND HOLIDAY BRUNCH

*Softly swirling snow, newly arrived guests, and heavily laden sideboards paint a nostalgic picture of a festive New England meal. This bold-spirited region and its rich culinary heritage set the tone for a grand assortment of succulent foods. Begin the feast with a beverage flavored with fruit from the area's marshy cranberry bogs and top it off with a traditional Massachusetts holiday dessert, Marlborough Pie. For a heartwarming, palate-pleasing Yuletide brunch that promises to be long remembered, choose from dishes inspired by the land of our Pilgrim forefathers.*

Tinged with saffron and accented with a kaleidoscope of rice and vegetables, Paella is a mouth-watering dish served in the two-handled pan from which it derives its name. This version of the popular Spanish creation blends sausage, artichoke hearts, and marinated shrimp and chicken with seasonings.

# PAELLA

*Marinate chicken and shrimp in advance.*

- 1/2 cup plus 2 tablespoons olive oil, divided
- 3 tablespoons freshly squeezed lemon juice
- 4 cloves garlic, divided and minced
- 1 tablespoon chopped fresh thyme leaves
- 1 teaspoon ground black pepper
- 1/4 teaspoon salt
- 2 pounds boneless chicken breasts, cut into large bite-size pieces
- 1/2 pound medium shrimp, peeled and deveined with tails left on
- 1/2 pound chorizo sausage, sliced
- 1 cup chopped onion
- 3 plum tomatoes, peeled and quartered
- 1 jar (4 ounces) whole pimiento, drained and cut into strips
- 2 cups uncooked arborio rice
- 1 can (14 ounces) quartered artichoke hearts, drained
- 1/4 cup chopped fresh parsley
- 1 tablespoon paprika
- 1 tablespoon drained capers
- 1/2 teaspoon saffron
- 1/2 cup white wine
- 3 cups hot chicken broth
- 1 package (10 ounces) frozen small green peas, thawed
- Chopped fresh parsley to garnish

In a large container, combine 1/4 cup plus 2 tablespoons olive oil, lemon juice, 2 cloves minced garlic, thyme, black pepper, and salt. Add chicken and shrimp to marinade; cover and chill 3 to 5 hours, stirring occasionally.

Remove shrimp from marinade; drain. In a 13-inch-diameter paella pan or heavy skillet, heat remaining 1/4 cup olive oil. Stirring constantly, cook shrimp in oil over medium-high heat about 2 minutes or just until shrimp turns pink. Transfer to a bowl. Remove chicken pieces from marinade; drain. Turning frequently, cook in pan about 15 minutes or until browned. Transfer to another bowl. Stirring frequently, cook sausage in pan about 4 minutes or until browned. Transfer sausage to bowl containing shrimp. Reduce heat to medium. Cook onion and remaining 2 cloves minced garlic in pan 4 minutes or until onion is translucent. Add tomatoes and pimiento; continue to cook 5 minutes. Add rice, artichoke hearts, 1/4 cup chopped parsley, paprika, and capers; stir until blended. Add saffron to wine. Stir wine mixture, hot chicken broth, and chicken pieces into rice mixture. Increase heat to medium-

An elegant beverage with a festive twist, Cranberry Champagne Cocktail imparts a golden glow to the holiday table. From flaky crust to creamy topping, Savory Tomato and Olive Pastries are rich, full-bodied delicacies.

high. Bring liquid to a boil. Reduce heat to medium. Cover and simmer about 15 minutes or until liquid is absorbed and rice is tender. Stir in shrimp, sausage, and peas. Remove from heat. Cover pan and let stand 15 minutes before serving. Garnish with parsley.
**Yield:** 10 to 12 servings

## SAVORY TOMATO AND OLIVE PASTRIES

- 6 ounces cream cheese, softened
- 1/3 cup finely chopped green onions
- 1/3 cup finely chopped fresh mushrooms
- 1/2 teaspoon ground black pepper
- 1 sheet frozen puff pastry, thawed
- 6 ounces thinly sliced Provolone cheese
- 3/4 cup dried tomatoes marinated in olive oil, drained and cut into strips
- 1 can (2 1/4 ounces) sliced black olives, drained

Preheat oven to 400 degrees. In a medium bowl, beat cream cheese until fluffy. Stir in green onions, mushrooms, and pepper. On a lightly floured surface,

use a lightly floured rolling pin to roll out pastry into a 10 1/2-inch square. Cut pastry in half. Transfer pastry pieces to an ungreased baking sheet. Dampen edges of pastries with water. Fold edges of pastries 1/2 inch and press to seal. Spread cream cheese mixture over pastries. Place cheese slices over cream cheese mixture. Sprinkle with tomatoes and olives. Bake 15 to 17 minutes or until cheese melts and pastries are golden brown. Let stand 5 minutes. Cut each pastry in half lengthwise, then cut into 1-inch slices. Serve warm.
**Yield:** about 3 dozen appetizers

## CRANBERRY CHAMPAGNE COCKTAIL

- 1/4 cup cranberry-flavored liqueur
- 2 tablespoons Grand Marnier liqueur
- 1 tablespoon sweet vermouth
- 1 bottle (750 ml) champagne, chilled

In a 2-quart container, combine cranberry liqueur, Grand Marnier, and vermouth. Add champagne to mixture. Serve immediately.
**Yield:** about 3 1/2 cups cocktail

## CHEESY TRIANGLE PUFFS

- 1 container (16 ounces) small-curd cottage cheese
- 2 cups all-purpose flour
- 1/2 teaspoon baking powder
- 3/4 cup butter or margarine, softened
- 1 tablespoon lemon pepper

In a large bowl, beat cottage cheese, flour, baking powder, butter, and lemon pepper with an electric mixer until well blended. Divide dough into fourths. Wrap in plastic wrap and chill 2 hours or until firm.

Preheat oven to 350 degrees. On a heavily floured surface, use a floured rolling pin to roll out one fourth of dough into a 10-inch square. Cut dough into 2-inch squares. Cut each square in half diagonally, forming 2 triangles. Transfer to a lightly greased baking sheet. Bake 12 to 14 minutes or until lightly browned. Repeat with remaining dough. Serve warm.

**Yield:** about 16 1/2 dozen puffs

## ROSEMARY-SWEET POTATO SOUP

- 2 cans (14 1/2 ounces each) chicken broth
- 1 pound fresh sweet potatoes, peeled and sliced (about 2 medium sweet potatoes)
- 1 3/4 cups carrots, sliced (about 2 large carrots)
- 2 teaspoons finely chopped fresh rosemary leaves
- 2 tablespoons butter or margarine
- 1 1/4 cups chopped onion
- 1 large clove garlic, minced
- 1/2 cup orange juice
- 1/2 teaspoon salt
- 1/4 teaspoon ground white pepper
  Pinch ground red pepper
  Chopped fresh rosemary leaves to garnish

In a Dutch oven over medium-high heat, combine chicken broth, sweet potatoes, carrots, and 2 teaspoons rosemary. Bring to a boil. Reduce heat to low, cover and simmer 20 minutes or until vegetables are tender.

In a medium skillet, combine butter, onion, and garlic over medium heat. Stirring constantly, cook 8 minutes or until onion is translucent; transfer to a large food processor. Reserving liquid, transfer vegetables from sweet potato mixture to food processor; process until smooth. Stir puréed mixture back into

Light and delicate Cheesy Triangle Puffs offer a hint of lemon. Rosemary-Sweet Potato Soup is a flavorful mixture of puréed vegetables.

liquid. Stir in orange juice, salt, and peppers. Return to low heat; cook 10 minutes or until heated through. Garnish each serving with rosemary.

**Yield:** about 6 cups soup

## TURKEY QUICHE LORRAINE

- 1 unbaked 9-inch pie crust
- 8 slices bacon
- 1/4 cup finely chopped onion
- 1 1/2 cups (about 6 ounces) shredded Gruyère cheese
- 1 cup diced cooked turkey
- 1 1/2 cups half and half
- 4 eggs
- 1/2 teaspoon dry mustard
- 1/4 teaspoon salt

Preheat oven to 350 degrees. Bake crust 8 minutes or until lightly browned. Cook bacon in a medium skillet until crisp; remove bacon, reserving 1 tablespoon drippings in skillet. Drain and crumble bacon; set aside. Sauté onion in reserved drippings over medium-low heat until tender. Sprinkle cheese, turkey, bacon, and onion into bottom of pie crust. In a medium bowl, beat half and half, eggs, dry mustard, and salt until well blended. Pour egg mixture into pie crust. Bake 40 to 50 minutes or until a knife inserted in center of quiche comes out clean. Let stand 5 minutes before serving. Serve warm.

**Yield:** about 8 servings

*(Clockwise from bottom left)* Turkey Quiche Lorraine updates a versatile favorite. A faint touch of citrus and flecks of dill add zip to Lemon-Dill Biscuits. Tangy Minted Cranberry-Pear Relish blends sweetened fresh cranberries and pears, lemon juice, and chopped mint.

## LEMON-DILL BISCUITS

- 2 cups all-purpose flour
- 1 tablespoon baking powder
- 1/4 teaspoon salt
- 1/4 teaspoon ground black pepper
- 1/3 cup chilled butter or margarine, cut into pieces
- 3/4 cup milk
- 1 tablespoon chopped fresh dill weed
- 1 teaspoon grated lemon zest

Preheat oven to 425 degrees. In a medium bowl, combine flour, baking powder, salt, and pepper. Using a pastry blender or 2 knives, cut butter into dry ingredients until mixture resembles coarse meal. In a small bowl, combine milk, dill weed, and lemon zest. Add to dry ingredients; stir just until moistened. On a lightly floured surface, use a floured rolling pin to roll out dough to 1/2-inch thickness. Use a 2-inch-diameter biscuit cutter to cut out biscuits. Transfer to an ungreased baking sheet. Bake 11 to 13 minutes or until golden brown. Serve warm.

**Yield:** about 1 1/2 dozen biscuits

## MINTED CRANBERRY-PEAR RELISH

- 1 package (12 ounces) fresh cranberries
- 2 fresh unpeeled pears, cored and coarsely chopped
- 2 cups sugar
- 1/4 cup freshly squeezed lemon juice
- 1/4 cup chopped fresh mint leaves
  Whole fresh mint leaves to garnish

Process all ingredients in a food processor until finely chopped. Transfer to an airtight container; cover and chill. To serve, garnish with whole mint leaves.

**Yield:** about 4 cups relish

With a sprinkling of nuts and dates, Stuffed Baked Apples taste as yummy as they look! Served chilled, festive Zucchini Medley layers sliced fresh mozzarella cheese with vegetables that have been marinated and baked.

## STUFFED BAKED APPLES

    5   unpeeled red baking apples
    1/2 cup apple juice
    1/2 cup applejack
    2   tablespoons lemon juice
    1   cup firmly packed brown sugar
    1/4 cup butter or margarine
    1   teaspoon ground cinnamon
    2/3 cup chopped walnuts, toasted
    2/3 cup chopped dates
    1   teaspoon vanilla extract
    1   to 2 tablespoons cornstarch

Preheat oven to 350 degrees. Cut apples in half through stem end. Trim 1/2 inch peel from apples. Core and place in an ungreased 9 x 13-inch baking pan. In a medium saucepan, combine next 6 ingredients. Stirring constantly, cook over medium heat until sugar dissolves. Remove from heat. Stir in walnuts, dates, and vanilla. Spoon mixture over apples. Cover and bake 45 to 50 minutes or until apples are tender, spooning syrup over apples every 10 minutes. Transfer apples to a serving dish. Measure remaining syrup and transfer to a small saucepan. Using 1 tablespoon cornstarch for each cup apple syrup, combine cornstarch with an equal amount of water in a small bowl. Bring syrup to a boil over medium heat. Stir in cornstarch mixture. Stirring constantly, cook until syrup thickens. Spoon over baked apples. Serve warm.
**Yield:** 10 servings

## ZUCCHINI MEDLEY

    1   cup olive oil
    2   tablespoons chopped fresh thyme
        leaves
    2   tablespoons chopped fresh
        tarragon leaves
    2   tablespoons chopped fresh basil
        leaves
    2   cloves garlic, minced
    1   teaspoon salt
    1/2 teaspoon crushed red pepper flakes
    1/8 teaspoon ground black pepper
    4   unpeeled zucchini, sliced
        lengthwise
    2   sweet red peppers, cut into rings
    5   plum tomatoes, peeled and sliced
    4   ounces fresh mozzarella cheese
        (packed in water), sliced

In a medium bowl, combine first 8 ingredients. Place zucchini, pepper rings, and marinade in a large resealable plastic bag. Let stand at room temperature 2 hours, turning frequently to coat vegetables.

Preheat oven to 350 degrees. Reserving marinade, place zucchini and peppers on an ungreased broiler pan. Chill marinade. Bake vegetables 30 minutes, turning after 15 minutes. Cool on pan 10 minutes. Store in an airtight container in refrigerator until ready to serve.

To serve, alternate zucchini, tomatoes, cheese, and peppers on serving platter. Brush vegetables with reserved marinade.
**Yield:** 6 to 8 servings

## HAZELNUT COFFEE CAKE

### CAKE

    1   cup butter or margarine, softened
    1 1/3 cups granulated sugar
    3   eggs
    1 1/2 teaspoons vanilla extract
    2 1/2 cups sifted cake flour
    1   teaspoon baking powder
    1   teaspoon baking soda
    1/8 teaspoon salt
    1 1/3 cups sour cream
    1 1/4 cups chopped hazelnuts, toasted
    1/2 cup firmly packed brown sugar
    1   teaspoon ground cinnamon

### ICING

    2   ounces bittersweet baking
        chocolate
    4   teaspoons hazelnut-flavored liqueur
    1   tablespoon light corn syrup

Preheat oven to 325 degrees. For cake, cream butter and granulated sugar in a large bowl until fluffy. Add eggs and vanilla; beat until smooth. In a medium bowl, combine cake flour, baking powder, baking soda, and salt. Alternately beat dry ingredients and sour cream into creamed mixture, beating just until blended. Spoon one-third of batter into bottom of a greased and floured 9-inch springform pan with a tube insert. In a small bowl, combine hazelnuts, brown sugar, and cinnamon. Sprinkle one-third of hazelnut mixture over batter. Continue layering batter and hazelnut mixture, ending with hazelnut mixture. Bake 55 to 65 minutes or until a toothpick inserted in center of cake comes out clean. Cool cake in pan on a wire rack 10 minutes. Run a knife around edge of pan; remove sides of pan. Cool completely. Carefully remove bottom of pan; transfer cake to a serving plate.

For icing, place chocolate, liqueur, and corn syrup in top of a double boiler over hot water. Stirring frequently, cook until chocolate melts and mixture is smooth. Drizzle chocolate mixture over cake. Store in an airtight container.
**Yield:** about 16 servings

*(From left)* Sliced almonds embedded in white icing give lemony Pinecone Cookies their prickly appearance. Drizzled with a stunning chocolate glaze, light-textured Hazelnut Coffee Cake has a crunchy topping that's echoed in the tasty filling. Delicious either warm or cold, handsome Marlborough Pie adds tasty apples, whipping cream, sherry, and cinnamon to a rich custard.

# PINECONE COOKIES

## COOKIES
- ³/₄ cup butter or margarine, softened
- ¹/₂ cup sugar
- 1 egg
- 1 tablespoon freshly squeezed lemon juice
- ¹/₂ teaspoon grated lemon zest
- ¹/₂ teaspoon vanilla extract
- 1³/₄ cups all-purpose flour
- ¹/₄ teaspoon salt

## ICING
- 4 cups sifted confectioners sugar
- 2 tablespoons plus 2 teaspoons water
- 2 tablespoons freshly squeezed lemon juice
- ¹/₂ teaspoon grated lemon zest
- ¹/₂ teaspoon vanilla extract
- 1¹/₂ cups sliced almonds, toasted

For cookies, cream butter and sugar in a large bowl until fluffy. Add egg, lemon juice, lemon zest, and vanilla; beat until smooth. In a small bowl, combine flour and salt. Add dry ingredients to creamed mixture; stir until a soft dough forms. Divide dough in half. Wrap in plastic wrap and chill 2 hours or until dough is firm enough to handle.

Preheat oven to 375 degrees. On a lightly floured surface, use a floured rolling pin to roll out dough to ¹/₄-inch thickness. Use a 2¹/₂-inch-wide by 3¹/₂-inch-long oval crinkled-edge cookie cutter to cut out cookies. Transfer to a greased baking sheet. Bake 8 to 10 minutes or until bottoms are lightly browned. Transfer cookies to a wire rack to cool.

For icing, combine confectioners sugar, water, lemon juice, lemon zest, and vanilla in a medium bowl; beat until smooth. Working with 3 cookies at a time, spread icing on cookies. Before icing hardens, place almonds on cookies to resemble pinecones. Let icing harden. Store in a single layer in an airtight container.

**Yield:** about 2 dozen cookies

# MARLBOROUGH PIE

- 4 eggs
- 1 cup sugar
- 1 cup whipping cream
- ¹/₄ cup cream sherry
- 1 tablespoon butter, melted
- ¹/₂ teaspoon ground cinnamon
- ¹/₈ teaspoon salt
- 2 cups unpeeled, cored, and finely chopped Granny Smith apples
- 1 unbaked 9-inch pie crust

Preheat oven to 400 degrees. In a medium bowl, beat eggs and sugar until smooth. Add whipping cream, sherry, melted butter, cinnamon, and salt; beat until well blended. Stir in apples. Pour into crust. Bake 10 minutes. Reduce temperature to 350 degrees. Bake 40 to 50 minutes or until center is firm. Let stand 1¹/₂ hours before serving. Store in an airtight container in refrigerator.

**Yield:** about 8 servings

# Ski Lodge Supper

*Whether you live in Maine or Miami, you can create a setting with the cozy atmosphere
of a ski lodge for your holiday meal. Our collection of hearty and flavorful dishes is rich in
well-seasoned items influenced by foods from south of the border and fresh from the country's
heartland. To satisfy appetites stimulated by an exhilarating day on the slopes or a
cliff-hanger football game, our mountain-high menu is a surefire crowd pleaser!*

Turkey Enchiladas with Sweet Red Pepper Sauce add a festive touch to a Mexican standard. A good use for leftover turkey, the cilantro-garnished dish is flavored with Monterey Jack and Cheddar cheeses as well as sour cream. Golden Citrus Cider Punch is a sweet, slightly tangy blend of lemon-lime and apple. For a stronger beverage, serve bottled draft cider.

## TURKEY ENCHILADAS WITH SWEET RED PEPPER SAUCE

- 3 sweet red peppers
- 1/2 cup plus 3 tablespoons finely chopped onion, divided
- 2 cloves garlic, minced
- 2 tablespoons vegetable oil
- 1 can (28 ounces) crushed tomatoes
- 1 can (14 1/2 ounces) chicken broth
- 1/2 teaspoon salt
- 1/2 teaspoon ground cumin
- 1/4 teaspoon dried oregano leaves, crushed
- 4 cups finely chopped cooked turkey
- 1 container (8 ounces) sour cream
- 20 corn tortillas (6 inches in diameter)
- 4 cups combined shredded Monterey Jack and Cheddar cheeses, divided
  Chopped fresh cilantro to garnish

To roast red peppers, cut in half lengthwise; remove seeds and membranes. Place, skin side up, on an ungreased baking sheet; flatten with hand. Broil about 3 inches from heat 12 to 15 minutes or until skin is evenly blackened. Immediately seal peppers in a plastic bag and allow to steam 10 to 15 minutes. Remove charred skin. Cut peppers into 1/2-inch x 1-inch strips.

In a heavy large saucepan, sauté 1/2 cup onion and garlic in oil over medium-high heat until vegetables are tender. Stir in pepper strips, tomatoes, chicken broth, salt, cumin, and oregano. Bring mixture to a boil. Stirring frequently, reduce heat to medium-low and simmer about 20 minutes or until sauce thickens.

Preheat oven to 375 degrees. Spread 2/3 cup sauce in each of 2 greased 7 x 11-inch baking dishes. In a medium bowl, combine turkey, remaining 3 tablespoons chopped onion, and sour cream. Soften tortillas in a microwave according to package directions. Place 2 rounded tablespoons turkey mixture and 2 tablespoons cheese on each tortilla. Tightly roll up tortillas and place, seam side down, in baking dishes. Spoon remaining sauce down each side of baking dishes, covering ends of tortillas. Sprinkle remaining cheese over middle of enchiladas. Bake 12 to 15 minutes or until heated through and cheese melts. Garnish with cilantro. Serve warm.

**Yield:** 20 enchiladas

What a culinary surprise — Christmas Pasta Snacks are crisp and crunchy instead of al dente! To make this tasty treat, lightly sauté colorful tree-shaped pasta, then sprinkle with spiced-up Parmesan cheese. Terrific as an appetizer, Seafood-Stuffed Jalapeños (*recipe on page 124*) have a not-too-spicy shrimp and crab filling. The crunchy buttermilk coating goes well with our zesty horseradish sauce.

## CITRUS CIDER PUNCH

*We made apple cider ice cubes to serve in our punch.*

- 1 gallon apple cider, chilled
- 1 can (12 ounces) frozen limeade concentrate
- 1 can (12 ounces) frozen lemonade concentrate
- 1 bottle (2 liters) lemon-lime soft drink, chilled
  Lemon and lime slices and maraschino cherries with stems to garnish

In a 2-gallon container, combine cider and concentrates. Stir until concentrates thaw. Stir in soft drink. Garnish servings with lemon and lime slices and maraschino cherries. Serve immediately.

**Yield:** about 27 cups punch

## CHRISTMAS PASTA SNACKS

- 2 tablespoons grated Parmesan cheese
- 1 teaspoon ground cumin
- 3/4 teaspoon ground oregano
- 3/4 teaspoon salt
- 1/2 teaspoon garlic powder
  Vegetable oil
- 8 ounces tree-shaped pasta, cooked, drained, and patted dry

In a small bowl, combine cheese, cumin, oregano, salt, and garlic powder. In a heavy medium saucepan, heat oil to 375 degrees. Stirring occasionally, deep fry 1 cup pasta 4 to 5 minutes or until pasta is golden brown and oil stops bubbling. Drain on paper towels. Transfer warm pasta to lightly greased aluminum foil. Sprinkle about 2 teaspoons cheese mixture over warm pasta. Repeat with remaining pasta and cheese mixture. Cool completely and store in an airtight container.

**Yield:** about 4 1/2 cups snack mix

# SEAFOOD-STUFFED JALAPEÑOS (Shown on page 123)

### HORSERADISH SAUCE
1 1/2  cups sour cream
3/4  cup mayonnaise
4  to 5 tablespoons prepared horseradish

### PEPPERS
30  medium jalapeño peppers
1  package (8 ounces) cream cheese, softened
1  can (6 ounces) small shrimp, drained
1  can (6 ounces) crabmeat, drained
2  tablespoons finely chopped onion
1  tablespoon Worcestershire sauce
1  tablespoon freshly squeezed lemon juice
1/4  teaspoon garlic powder
1  cup buttermilk
1  egg, beaten
1 1/2  cups corn flake crumbs
3/4  cup self-rising cornmeal mix
Vegetable oil

For horseradish sauce, combine sour cream, mayonnaise, and horseradish in a small bowl. Cover and chill 4 hours to let flavors blend.

For peppers, cut peppers in half lengthwise and seed (protect hands with gloves). To blanch peppers, cover with water in a large saucepan. Cover and bring to a boil over medium-high heat; boil 5 minutes. Being careful to avoid steam, drain peppers and rinse with cold water. Drain on paper towels.

In a medium bowl, combine cream cheese, shrimp, crabmeat, onion, Worcestershire sauce, lemon juice, and garlic powder; beat until well blended. Transfer cream cheese mixture to a quart-size resealable plastic bag. Cut off 1 corner of bag and pipe mixture into each pepper half. Place on a baking sheet lined with waxed paper; freeze about 1 hour or until filling is frozen.

Combine buttermilk and egg in a small bowl. In a medium bowl, combine corn flake crumbs and cornmeal mix. Dip each pepper into buttermilk mixture and roll in crumb mixture. Return to baking sheet. Cover and freeze 1 hour.

To serve, heat oil to 350 degrees in a heavy medium saucepan. Removing about 6 peppers at a time from freezer, deep fry peppers about 2 minutes or until golden brown. Drain on paper towels. Serve warm with sauce.

**Yield:** about 2 1/2 cups sauce and 5 dozen appetizers

Elegant Pear and Spinach Salad is a choice blend of textures and flavors. For an unforgettable start to your meal, top this unique salad with Mango Buttermilk Dressing, a creamy accent with a hint of curry.

# PEAR AND SPINACH SALAD

12  cups washed and torn fresh spinach
3  avocados
3  cans (15 1/4 ounces each) pear slices in heavy syrup, drained
2  cups fresh grapefruit segments (about 3 grapefruit)
1  cup (4 ounces) shredded Cheddar cheese
1/3  cup sliced almonds, toasted and coarsely chopped

Place 1 cup spinach on each serving plate. Peel each avocado and cut into 12 slices. Arrange about 3 slices each of pear, grapefruit, and avocado on each plate. Garnish each serving with about 1 tablespoon cheese and 1 teaspoon almonds. Serve with Mango Buttermilk Dressing.
**Yield:** 12 servings

# MANGO BUTTERMILK DRESSING

*Chilled jars of mango slices can be found in the produce department.*

1  cup mayonnaise
1/4  cup buttermilk
1/2  teaspoon curry powder
1  cup finely chopped mango
1  tablespoon chopped fresh parsley
2  teaspoons finely chopped onion

In a small bowl, combine mayonnaise, buttermilk, and curry powder; whisk until well blended. Stir in mango, parsley, and onion. Serve with Pear and Spinach Salad.
**Yield:** about 2 cups dressing

# HEARTY CORN CHOWDER

¼ cup butter or margarine
1¼ cups chopped sweet red pepper
½ cup finely chopped celery
½ cup chopped onion
3 cups peeled and diced potatoes
1 can (14½ ounces) chicken broth
2¼ cups half and half, divided
3 tablespoons all-purpose flour
2 packages (10 ounces each) frozen
   whole kernel corn, thawed
1 teaspoon salt
½ teaspoon ground white pepper

In a large Dutch oven, melt butter over medium-high heat. Add red pepper, celery, and onion; sauté until tender. Add potatoes and chicken broth; bring to a boil. Reduce heat to medium-low. Cover and cook 15 minutes or until potatoes are tender.

In a medium bowl, combine ¼ cup half and half and flour; whisk until smooth. Whisk in remaining 2 cups half and half. Stir corn, half and half mixture, salt, and white pepper into soup. Increase heat to medium. Stirring frequently, cook 15 minutes longer or until heated through and thickened. Serve warm.

**Yield:** about 8½ cups soup

# BLACK BEAN SALSA

1 can (15 ounces) black beans,
   rinsed and drained
1 cup seeded and chopped fresh
   plum tomatoes
1 cup chopped sweet yellow pepper
½ cup chopped fresh cilantro
½ cup sliced green onions
1 jalapeño pepper, seeded and
   chopped
3 tablespoons freshly squeezed lime
   juice
1 tablespoon olive oil
1 tablespoon red wine vinegar
1 clove garlic, minced
1 teaspoon salt
½ teaspoon ground cumin
   Tortilla chips to serve

In a medium bowl, combine beans, tomatoes, yellow pepper, cilantro, green onions, and jalapeño pepper. In a small bowl, combine lime juice, olive oil, vinegar, garlic, salt, and cumin; stir until blended. Pour lime juice mixture over bean mixture and gently toss. Cover and chill 2 hours to let flavors blend. Serve with tortilla chips.

**Yield:** about 3½ cups salsa

Hearty Corn Chowder is a rich, filling dish that's good to the last yummy drop. Chilled to combine its distinct tastes, colorful Black Bean Salsa is a sauce with "wow!" An excellent make-ahead dish, cheesy Green Chili Rice Timbales have just the right amount of zip to complement our enchiladas.

# GREEN CHILI RICE TIMBALES

*Timbales may be made ahead and chilled.*

1 can (4 ounces) whole green chiles,
   drained
2 cans (4½ ounces each) chopped
   green chiles, drained
½ cup salsa
½ teaspoon salt
½ teaspoon ground cumin
6 cups hot cooked rice
1 cup (4 ounces) shredded Monterey
   Jack cheese
1 cup (4 ounces) shredded mild
   Cheddar cheese

Preheat oven to 325 degrees. Slice whole green chiles into twenty-two ½-inch-wide strips. Cross 2 strips in bottom of each of 11 greased 6-ounce baking cups. In a large bowl, combine chopped green chiles, salsa, salt, and cumin; stir until blended. Stir in rice and cheeses. Spoon rice mixture into prepared baking cups. Cover and chill until ready to serve.

To serve, bake covered 25 to 30 minutes or until heated through. Let stand 5 minutes. Invert onto serving plates; serve warm.

**Yield:** 11 servings

A sumptuous butter and honey mixture is brushed between three layers of sour cream-moistened Honey Spice Cake. Toasted pecan pieces are pressed into the sides for a rustic finish.

## HONEY SPICE CAKE

**CAKE**
- ¹/₂ cup butter or margarine, softened
- ¹/₂ cup granulated sugar
- ¹/₂ cup firmly packed brown sugar
- 1 container (8 ounces) sour cream
- 3 eggs
- ¹/₄ cup honey
- 1³/₄ cups plus 2 tablespoons all-purpose flour
- 2 teaspoons ground cinnamon
- 1 teaspoon baking soda
- ¹/₂ teaspoon ground allspice
- ¹/₂ teaspoon salt
- ³/₄ cup chopped pecans, toasted

**SYRUP**
- ¹/₄ cup honey
- 2 tablespoons butter or margarine

**ICING**
- 1 cup firmly packed brown sugar
- ³/₄ cup butter or margarine
- 1 tablespoon light corn syrup
- ¹/₃ cup milk
- 1 teaspoon vanilla extract
- 2¹/₄ cups sifted confectioners sugar
- 1 cup finely chopped pecans, toasted

Preheat oven to 325 degrees. For cake, grease three 8-inch round cake pans and line bottoms with waxed paper; set aside. In a large bowl, cream butter and sugars until well blended. Add sour cream, eggs, and honey; beat until smooth. In a medium bowl, combine flour, cinnamon, baking soda, allspice, and salt. Add dry ingredients to creamed mixture; beat until well blended. Stir in pecans. Pour batter into prepared pans. Bake 20 to 25 minutes or until a toothpick inserted in center of cake comes out clean. Cool in pans 10 minutes. Remove from pans and cool completely on a wire rack.

For syrup, combine honey and butter in a small saucepan over medium heat. Stir constantly until butter melts. Brush syrup between cake layers.

For icing, combine brown sugar, butter, and corn syrup in a heavy medium saucepan. Whisking constantly, cook over medium heat until mixture comes to a full boil (about 8 minutes); boil 5 minutes. Turn off heat, leaving pan on burner. Slowly whisk in milk and vanilla until smooth. Transfer to a heatproof bowl and let cool 20 minutes. Place bowl of icing in a larger bowl filled with ice. Beat in confectioners sugar, beating until mixture is smooth and begins to hold its shape (about 3 minutes). Spread icing on top and sides of cake. Press pecans into sides of cake. Let icing harden. Store in an airtight container.

**Yield:** 12 to 14 servings

126

## ORANGE-WALNUT PIE

**CRUST**

1¼ cups all-purpose flour
½ teaspoon salt
½ teaspoon grated orange zest
⅓ cup vegetable shortening
3 to 4 tablespoons cold orange juice

**FILLING**

3 eggs
1 cup light corn syrup
½ cup sugar
¼ teaspoon salt
¼ cup butter or margarine, melted
½ teaspoon orange extract
1 cup chopped walnuts

For crust, combine flour, salt, and orange zest in a medium bowl. Using a pastry blender or 2 knives, cut in shortening until mixture resembles coarse meal. Sprinkle with orange juice; mix until a soft dough forms. On a lightly floured surface, use a floured rolling pin to roll out dough. Transfer to a 9-inch pie plate and use a sharp knife to trim edge of dough. Flute edge of dough.

Preheat oven to 400 degrees. For filling, beat eggs, corn syrup, sugar, and salt in a medium bowl until blended. Add melted butter and orange extract; beat until well blended. Stir in walnuts. Pour mixture into prepared crust. Bake 10 minutes. Reduce temperature to 350 degrees. Bake 35 to 40 minutes longer or until center is almost set. Cool completely. Store in an airtight container in refrigerator.
**Yield:** about 8 servings

## FROSTED CINNAMON BARS

½ cup butter or margarine, softened
3 cups sugar, divided
1 egg
1 egg yolk
1 teaspoon vanilla extract
1½ cups all-purpose flour
1 tablespoon ground cinnamon
½ teaspoon baking powder
¼ teaspoon salt
2 egg whites
2 cups finely chopped pecans

Preheat oven to 325 degrees. Line a 10½ x 15½-inch jellyroll pan with aluminum foil, extending foil over ends of pan. In a large bowl, cream butter and 1 cup sugar until fluffy. Add egg, egg yolk, and vanilla; beat until well blended. In a small bowl, combine flour, cinnamon, baking powder, and salt. Stir dry ingredients into creamed mixture. Use

A walnut version of the ever-popular pecan pie, Orange-Walnut Pie has a delightful citrus taste from flaky crust to exquisite filling. Frosted Cinnamon Bars have a meringue-like covering with a pecan-flavored crunch.

lightly greased hands to press mixture into bottom of prepared pan. In a medium bowl, beat egg whites until foamy. Gradually add remaining 2 cups sugar; beat about 3 minutes or until well blended (sugar will not dissolve). Fold in pecans. Spread topping evenly over crust.

Bake 26 to 30 minutes or until top is lightly browned and firm to touch. Cool in pan on a wire rack. Lift from pan using ends of foil. Use a serrated knife and a sawing motion to cut into 2-inch squares. Store in an airtight container.
**Yield:** about 3 dozen bars

# HOLIDAY TRADITIONS

*What a fabulous festival of foods we enjoy at Christmas — a mouth-watering parade of yummy cookies and candies topped off by a savory feast of turkey, dressing, and pies! As generation after generation of celebrants passes along "secret" recipes for their wonderful holiday dishes, culinary traditions from one household to another take on a distinctive flair. In this section, you will find cherished dishes from very special families — those of Leisure Arts employees. This sentimental sampling is sure to include selections to add to your own family's medley of festive favorites.*

Test kitchen coordinator Nora Faye Taylor *(second from left)* and her daughter, publications director Carla Bentley *(right)*, enjoy making Fresh Apple and Orange Cake with four generations of their family. Nora Faye's mother, Etta Mae Spencer *(third from left)*, "invented" this moist cake in the 1940's. Seven-year-old Samantha Bentley *(left)* stirs dry ingredients, while her grandfather, Don Taylor *(in window)*, waits in the den for the tasty treat.

Fresh Apple and Orange Cake has a tasty "frosting" of chopped fruits.

## FRESH APPLE AND ORANGE CAKE

### CAKE

- $^1/_2$ cup butter or margarine, softened
- $1^3/_4$ cups sugar
- 2 eggs
- $1^1/_2$ teaspoons vanilla extract
- $2^3/_4$ cups all-purpose flour
- $2^1/_2$ teaspoons baking powder
- $^1/_2$ teaspoon salt
- $1^1/_4$ cups milk

### FILLING

- 3 unpeeled navel oranges
- 3 unpeeled apples, cored and quartered
- $1^1/_4$ cups sugar
- 2 tablespoons orange-flavored liqueur (optional)

Preheat oven to 350 degrees. For cake, grease three 8-inch round cake pans and line bottoms with waxed paper. In a large bowl, cream butter and sugar until fluffy. Add eggs and vanilla; beat until smooth. In a medium bowl, combine flour, baking powder, and salt. Alternately add dry ingredients and milk to creamed mixture; beat until well blended. Pour batter into prepared pans. Bake 23 to 28 minutes or until a toothpick inserted in center of cake comes out clean. Cool in pans 10 minutes. Remove from pans and cool completely on a wire rack.

For filling, peel and quarter 2 oranges. Quarter remaining unpeeled orange. Process oranges in a large food processor until coarsely chopped. Add apples; process until fruit is finely chopped. Transfer fruit to a large bowl. Stir in sugar and liqueur. Spread about 1 cup filling between each layer. Press remaining filling over top and sides of cake. Cover and chill 3 hours before serving.
**Yield:** 12 to 14 servings

## SNOWFLAKE MOUSSE WITH CRIMSON RASPBERRY SAUCE

*Serving this snowy mousse with its crimson
sauce in parfait glasses gives the light,
elegant dessert a very Christmasy look,
according to designer Becky Werle.*

### MOUSSE

- 1 envelope unflavored gelatin
- $1^1/_4$ cups milk
- 1 cup sugar
- $^1/_2$ teaspoon salt
- 1 teaspoon vanilla extract
- 1 package (6 ounces) fresh frozen sweetened coconut
- 2 cups whipping cream, whipped

### RASPBERRY SAUCE

- 1 package (12 ounces) frozen red raspberries, thawed and crushed
- $^1/_2$ cup red currant jelly
- $1^1/_2$ teaspoons cornstarch

For mousse, sprinkle gelatin over milk in a medium saucepan; let stand 1 minute. Stirring constantly over medium heat, add sugar and salt; stir until sugar dissolves. Bring to a boil. Transfer mixture to a large heatproof bowl. Chill about 30 minutes or until partially set (mixture will appear thin). Stir in vanilla and coconut. Fold in whipped cream. Spoon into an oiled 7-cup mold. Cover and chill 4 hours or until firm.

For raspberry sauce, combine raspberries, jelly, and cornstarch in a medium saucepan. Stirring constantly, cook over medium heat about 15 minutes or until mixture thickens. Strain and cool. Serve over mousse.
**Yield:** about 12 servings

*Flavorful Chicken-Rice Soup brings back memories of a happy childhood tradition for photo stylist Aurora Huston. "My mother always served this soup for our family of nine children when we came back from Midnight Mass on Christmas Eve. Then, after we ate the soup, we opened our presents. We were too excited to wait until morning!" The recipe for this traditional Filipino soup varies, but Aurora's family prefers this thicker version.*

Soy sauce and ginger lend an exotic flavor to Chicken-Rice Soup.

## CHICKEN-RICE SOUP

1 tablespoon vegetable oil
3 cloves garlic, minced
1 medium onion, finely chopped
1 teaspoon finely chopped fresh ginger
1 1/2 pounds boneless chicken, cut into 1-inch pieces
2 tablespoons soy sauce
6 cups water
1 cup uncooked rice
1 1/2 teaspoons salt
1/2 teaspoon ground black pepper
Finely sliced green onions to garnish

Place oil in a large Dutch oven over medium heat. Stirring frequently, sauté garlic until lightly browned. Add onion and ginger; cook 1 minute. Add chicken and soy sauce; cook 3 minutes. Stir in water, rice, salt, and pepper. Cover and reduce heat to medium-low. Stirring occasionally, simmer about 40 minutes. Reduce heat to low; continue to cook 20 minutes longer or until soup is very thick. Garnish servings with sliced green onions.
**Yield:** about 8 cups soup

## STRAWBERRY PRETZEL SALAD

*This versatile dish can be served as either a salad or a dessert, says senior editor Laura Holyfield.*

### CRUST
2 cups finely crushed pretzels (about 3 cups pretzel sticks)
3/4 cup melted butter or margarine
1 tablespoon sugar

### FILLING
1 package (8 ounces) cream cheese, softened

1 cup sifted confectioners sugar
1 container (12 ounces) frozen non-dairy whipped topping, thawed

### TOPPING
1 package (6 ounces) strawberry gelatin
2 cups boiling water
2 packages (10 ounces each) frozen sweetened sliced strawberries, thawed

Preheat oven to 400 degrees. For crust, combine pretzels, melted butter, and sugar in a small bowl. Press into bottom of a 9 x 13-inch baking dish. Bake 8 minutes. Cool on a wire rack.

For filling, combine cream cheese and confectioners sugar in a medium bowl; beat until well blended. Fold in whipped topping. Spread mixture on cooled crust. Cover and chill 1 hour or until firm.

For topping, combine strawberry gelatin, boiling water, and strawberries in a medium bowl; stir until gelatin dissolves. Cool about 45 minutes. Pour over cream cheese mixture. Cover and chill 2 hours or until firm. Cut into 2-inch squares.
**Yield:** about 2 dozen servings

## CRANBERRY SALAD

*Add a personal touch to this attractive salad, a favorite of associate editor Jenny Daniels and her family, by shaping it in an heirloom gelatin mold.*

1 envelope unflavored gelatin
1/4 cup cold water
1 package (3 ounces) raspberry gelatin
3/4 cup boiling water
1 can (16 ounces) jellied cranberry sauce
1 container (16 ounces) sour cream

In a small bowl, sprinkle gelatin over water; let stand 1 minute. In a medium bowl, combine raspberry gelatin and boiling water; stir until gelatin dissolves. Stir in softened gelatin mixture; set aside. Process cranberry sauce in a food processor until smooth. Add sour cream; process just until blended. Whisk cranberry mixture into gelatin. Pour into a lightly oiled 5-cup mold. Cover and chill 4 hours or until firm.
**Yield:** about 10 servings

For four generations, the family of designer Anne Stocks has brightened their holiday tables with colorful Candied Apples. "My great-grandmother had a huge apple tree in her backyard," Anne recalls. "So in late August or September, we made candied apples and canned them in pretty jars for the winter, then prepared applesauce and froze it for the spring and summer. I remember how beautiful the candied apples looked in Grandma's crystal bowl at Christmas." Anne and her family appreciate the lovely accent these crimson apples add to the table at both brunch and dinner.

## CANDIED APPLES

  8  cooking apples (we used Rome
     apples)
1³/₄ cups sugar
³/₄  cup water
  1  package (9 ounces) small red
     cinnamon candies

Peel, core, and cut apples into eighths. In a Dutch oven, combine sugar, water, and candies. Stirring constantly, cook over medium heat about 10 minutes or until candies dissolve. Add apples and bring to a boil. Cook about 7 minutes or until apples are tender; cool. Cover and store in refrigerator. Serve chilled.
**Yield:** about 6¹/₂ cups apples

## CHEESY SPINACH CASSEROLE

*A fan of spinach dip, managing editor Linda Trimble experimented until she found just the right combination of ingredients for this versatile casserole.*

  3  packages (10 ounces each) frozen
     chopped spinach, cooked and
     squeezed dry
  1  tube (6 ounces) jalapeño pepper
     pasteurized process cheese,
     softened
  1  container (16 ounces) sour cream
  1  can (14 ounces) artichoke hearts
     packed in water, drained and
     finely chopped
  1  can (8 ounces) sliced water
     chestnuts, drained and finely
     chopped
  1  envelope onion soup mix
  2  cups purchased herb-seasoned
     stuffing

Crimson Candied Apples are a festive complement to Yuletide meals.

Preheat oven to 350 degrees. In a large bowl, combine spinach and cheese until well blended. Stir in sour cream, artichoke hearts, water chestnuts, and soup mix. Spread mixture in a greased 9 x 13-inch baking dish. Sprinkle with stuffing. Bake 30 minutes or until heated through. Serve warm.
**Yield:** about 14 servings

## MOTHER'S CHICKEN AND DRESSING

*In this kid-friendly dressing, production assistant Nelwyn Gray's mother omits the sage and "hides" the vegetables by mashing them.*

### CORN BREAD
  2  cups white cornmeal
  1  cup all-purpose flour
  1  teaspoon baking soda
  1  teaspoon salt
1¹/₂ cups buttermilk
  3  eggs, beaten

### DRESSING
  1  recipe corn bread, crumbled
  3  to 4 slices white bread with crusts
     **or** 3 to 4 biscuits, crumbled

  1  chicken (about 4 pounds), cooked
     and boned, reserving broth
¹/₄  cup butter or margarine
  3  ribs celery, chopped
  1  large white onion, chopped
  3  eggs, beaten
  2  or 3 green onions, chopped
¹/₂  teaspoon salt
¹/₂  teaspoon ground black pepper

Preheat oven to 400 degrees. For corn bread, combine all ingredients in a large bowl. Pour into a greased 10-inch ovenproof skillet. Bake 30 minutes or until golden brown. Remove from skillet and cool on a wire rack.

Preheat oven to 325 degrees. For dressing, combine corn bread and white bread in a large bowl. Pour 2 to 3 cups chicken broth over bread mixture to moisten; set aside. In a medium skillet, melt butter over medium heat. Sauté celery and white onion until celery is tender and onion is translucent. Stir into bread mixture. Stir in eggs, green onions, salt, and pepper. Place chicken in a greased 9 x 13-inch baking pan. Spoon dressing over chicken. Bake 50 to 60 minutes or until top is golden brown.
**Yield:** about 10 servings

## AUNT RUTH'S CHEESE GRITS

- 1 cup quick-cooking grits
- 1 tube (6 ounces) pasteurized process cheese food with garlic
- 1/2 cup butter or margarine
- 1 container (8 ounces) sour cream
- 3/4 cup milk
- 2 eggs
- 1/8 teaspoon ground red pepper
- 1 cup (4 ounces) shredded sharp Cheddar cheese

Preheat oven to 375 degrees. Cook grits in a large saucepan according to package directions; remove from heat. Add garlic cheese and butter; stir until smooth. In a medium bowl, combine sour cream, milk, eggs, and red pepper; beat until well blended. Gradually stir sour cream mixture into grits mixture. Pour into a greased 2-quart baking dish. Covering with aluminum foil after 30 minutes, bake 50 to 60 minutes or until center is almost set. Uncover grits; sprinkle top with Cheddar cheese and bake 4 minutes longer or until cheese melts. Let stand 15 minutes before serving. Serve warm.
**Yield:** 10 to 12 servings

## CORNISH GAME HENS

*To keep the hens' drumsticks moist, senior production artist Roberta Aulwes arranges foil around them. Roberta pays special attention to the drumsticks because her daughter likes them best.*

- 4 Cornish game hens
- 1 teaspoon salt
- 1/4 teaspoon ground black pepper
- 1/4 cup dried rosemary leaves
- 1/4 cup dried sage leaves

Preheat oven to 350 degrees. Rinse hens and pat dry with paper towels. With

Aunt Ruth's Cheese Grits have a hint of garlic and red pepper.

a sharp knife, carefully prick skin in several places. Sprinkle hens with salt and pepper. In a small bowl, crush rosemary and sage. Rub herbs inside and over hens. Place hens, breast side up, in a greased shallow baking pan. Loosely cover with aluminum foil and roast hens about 45 minutes. Uncover hens; baste with drippings and bake 15 minutes longer or until juices run clear when thickest part of thigh is pierced with a fork. Serve warm.
**Yield:** 8 servings

## REFRIGERATOR YEAST ROLLS

*Making these rolls ahead of time eases Christmas cooking chores for production artist Leslie Loring Krebs.*

- 2 packages dry yeast
- 2 cups warm water
- 6 1/2 cups all-purpose flour, divided
- 1/2 cup sugar
- 2 teaspoons salt
- 1 egg
- 1/4 cup vegetable shortening
  Vegetable cooking spray
  Melted butter

In a small bowl, dissolve yeast in warm water. In a large bowl, combine 2 cups flour, sugar, and salt. Add yeast mixture to flour mixture; beat 2 minutes or until well blended. Beat in egg and shortening. Adding 1 cup at a time, beat in 2 cups flour. Stir in remaining 2 1/2 cups flour by hand. Turn onto a lightly floured surface and knead about 5 minutes or until dough becomes smooth and elastic. Place in a large bowl sprayed with cooking spray, turning once to coat top of dough. Cover and let rise until doubled in a warm place (80 to 85 degrees) about 2 hours or dough can rise in refrigerator overnight. (Dough may be stored in refrigerator up to 1 week.)

Turn dough onto a lightly floured surface and punch down. For cloverleaf rolls, shape dough into 1 1/4-inch balls. Place 3 balls of dough in each cup of a greased muffin pan. Spray tops of dough with cooking spray, cover, and let rise in a warm place 1 to 1 1/2 hours or until doubled in size.

Preheat oven to 350 degrees. Bake 18 to 22 minutes or until golden brown. Brush with melted butter and serve warm.
**Yield:** about 2 dozen rolls

## GLASS CANDY

*We used the following food colorings and flavors for our candies: orange (combine yellow and red food coloring) with orange extract, yellow with lemon extract, red with cinnamon oil, and green with spearmint or wintergreen oil.*

- 2 cups sugar
- 1 cup water
- 1/4 teaspoon cream of tartar
- 1 tablespoon extract **or**
       1 teaspoon flavored oil
  Liquid food coloring
  Confectioners sugar

Butter sides of a large saucepan. Combine sugar, water, and cream of tartar in pan. Stirring constantly, cook over medium-low heat until sugar dissolves. Using a pastry brush dipped in hot water, wash down any sugar crystals on sides of pan. Attach a candy thermometer to pan, making sure thermometer does not touch bottom of pan. Increase heat to medium and bring to a boil. Cook, without stirring, until mixture reaches hard-crack stage (approximately 300 to 310 degrees). Test about 1/2 teaspoon mixture in ice water. Mixture will form brittle threads in ice water and will remain brittle when removed from the water. Remove from heat and stir in extract or oil and a few drops food coloring. Pour mixture onto a lightly greased baking sheet. Cool completely.

Break candy into pieces. Roll pieces in confectioners sugar, shaking off excess sugar. Store in an airtight container.
**Yield:** about 1 pound candy

Flavorful Glass Candy is tinted to resemble stained glass.

## MICROWAVE PECAN PRALINES

*These quick and delicious pralines are a specialty of associate editor Jenny Daniels' mother.*

- 2 cups sugar
- 1 1/2 cups chopped pecans
- 3/4 cup buttermilk
- 2 tablespoons butter or margarine
- 1/4 teaspoon salt
- 1/2 teaspoon baking soda
- 1 teaspoon vanilla extract

(**Note:** We tested this recipe in a 700-watt microwave.) In a 4-quart microwave-safe bowl, combine sugar, pecans, buttermilk, butter, and salt. Cook, uncovered, on high power (100%) 12 minutes, stirring every 4 minutes with a wooden spoon. Stir in baking soda (mixture will foam). Cook on high power (100%) 1 minute longer or until mixture is a caramel color (watch closely to prevent mixture from boiling over bowl). Add vanilla; beat with a wooden spoon about 3 minutes or until mixture begins to thicken. Quickly drop by teaspoonfuls onto greased foil to form about 2-inch-diameter pralines. Cool completely. Store in an airtight container.
**Yield:** about 3 1/2 dozen pralines

## PUMPKIN-EGGNOG PIE

1 can (15 ounces) pumpkin
2 eggs
$3/4$ cup plus 1 tablespoon sugar
1 teaspoon ground cinnamon
$1/2$ teaspoon ground ginger
$1/4$ teaspoon ground nutmeg
$1/4$ teaspoon ground cloves
$1/2$ teaspoon salt
$1 1/2$ cups eggnog
1 unbaked 9-inch pie crust

Preheat oven to 425 degrees. In a medium bowl, beat pumpkin, eggs, sugar, spices, and salt until smooth. Slowly stir in eggnog. Pour into crust; bake 15 minutes. Reduce heat to 350 degrees. Bake 35 to 40 minutes longer or until a knife inserted in center comes out clean. Cool; cover and store in refrigerator.
**Yield:** about 8 servings

## PEANUT BUTTER PIE

*Because of the light, chiffon-like texture of this pie, production assistant Lylln Craig favors it over pumpkin or apple.*

1 envelope unflavored gelatin
1 cup milk
$1/4$ teaspoon salt
$1/4$ cup plus 2 tablespoons sugar, divided
2 eggs, separated
$1/2$ cup smooth peanut butter
$1/4$ cup water
$1/8$ teaspoon cream of tartar
1 container (12 ounces) frozen non-dairy whipped topping, thawed
1 baked 9-inch pie crust

For a traditional treat with a gingery twist, try Pumpkin-Eggnog Pie.

In a heavy medium saucepan, sprinkle gelatin over milk; let stand 1 minute. Add salt and 2 tablespoons sugar; stir until sugar dissolves. Stir in egg yolks. Whisking constantly, cook over medium heat until mixture boils. Remove from heat; stir in peanut butter. Pour into a medium heatproof bowl. Place plastic wrap directly on surface of custard. Chill 45 minutes.

Place egg whites, remaining $1/4$ cup sugar, water, and cream of tartar in top of a double boiler over simmering water. Whisking constantly, cook mixture until a thermometer registers 160 degrees (about 10 minutes). Transfer to a large bowl; cool. Beat until soft peaks form. Fold in whipped topping and custard. Spoon into crust; cover and chill 3 hours or until firm.
**Yield:** about 8 servings

## ITALIAN CREAM CAKE

*This cake is a coconut lover's delight! Production assistant Nelwyn Gray uses coconut in both the cake and its icing, but her mother likes to leave it out of the cake.*

### CAKE
$1/2$ cup butter or margarine, softened
$1/2$ cup vegetable shortening
2 cups sugar
5 egg yolks
1 teaspoon vanilla extract
2 cups all-purpose flour

1 teaspoon baking soda
1 cup buttermilk
1 can ($3 1/2$ ounces) flaked coconut
5 egg whites, beaten until stiff

### ICING
1 package (8 ounces) cream cheese, softened
$1/2$ cup butter or margarine, softened
1 tablespoon vanilla extract
6 cups sifted confectioners sugar
2 to 3 tablespoons milk
$1 1/2$ cups chopped pecans
1 can ($3 1/2$ ounces) flaked coconut

Preheat oven to 350 degrees. For cake, grease and flour three 8-inch round cake pans. In a large bowl, beat butter and shortening until smooth. Add sugar; beat until fluffy. Add egg yolks and vanilla; beat until smooth. In a small bowl, combine flour and baking soda. Alternately beat dry ingredients and buttermilk into creamed mixture. Stir in coconut. Fold in beaten egg whites. Spread batter into prepared pans. Bake 25 to 30 minutes or until a toothpick inserted in center of cake comes out clean. Cool in pans 10 minutes. Remove from pans and cool on a wire rack.

For icing, beat cream cheese, butter, and vanilla in a large bowl until fluffy. Beat in confectioners sugar and milk. Stir in pecans and coconut. Spread between layers and on top and sides of cake. Cover and store in refrigerator.
**Yield:** 12 to 14 servings

Making beautiful, delicious Norwegian cookies is a skill handed down from mother to daughter and granddaughter in senior editor Andrea Ahlen's family. Every Christmas, Andrea and her daughter make several types of candies and cookies for gifts and at-home treats, including two from her grandmother. Lemon Krumkake are made with a special iron (Andrea's is about 25 years old!) that can be found in catalogs or some department stores. Although considered a Christmas treat, this whipped cream-filled rolled cookie is typically served year-round. Baked in a wreath shape with a sprinkling of coarse sugar, the Berlinerkranser have a lovely holiday look to them. Andrea remembers how wonderful these cookies tasted when her grandmother made them, and she insists that "No one made Berlinerkranser as good as my grandmother!"

Lemon Krumkake and Berlinerkranser make handsome presents.

## LEMON KRUMKAKE

*Experience has taught Andrea Ahlen that the easiest way to fill these cookies is with whipped cream from an aerosol can.*

    3   eggs
    ¹/₂ cup sugar
    ¹/₂ cup butter or margarine, melted
    ¹/₂ cup all-purpose flour
    1   teaspoon lemon extract
        Sweetened whipped cream

In a medium bowl, combine eggs and sugar; beat well. Stir in melted butter. Add flour and extract; stir until smooth. Place about 2 teaspoons batter on a preheated, greased krumkake iron; bake until lightly browned on both sides. Quickly roll around a krumkake roller (wooden cone) to shape cookie. Cool cookies on a wire rack. Store in an airtight container. Fill with whipped cream and serve.
**Yield:** about 3 dozen cookies

## BERLINERKRANSER

    4    hard-cooked egg yolks
    4    uncooked egg yolks
    1    cup granulated sugar
    3    cups butter, softened
    6¹/₂ cups all-purpose flour
    1    egg white, slightly beaten
         White coarse decorating sugar

Preheat oven to 350 degrees. In a large bowl, finely crumble hard-cooked egg yolks. Add uncooked egg yolks; beat until smooth. Gradually beat in granulated sugar. Alternately beat or knead in butter and flour. Shape dough into 1¹/₂-inch balls and place on a baking sheet. Chill 15 minutes.

Roll balls into 6-inch-long ropes; transfer to a greased baking sheet. Cross ends of each rope to form a wreath. Brush each cookie with egg white and sprinkle with coarse sugar. Bake 17 to 22 minutes or until bottoms are lightly browned. Store in an airtight container.
**Yield:** about 6 dozen cookies

## PUMPKIN CRÈME BRÛLÉE

*This "awesome" pumpkin dessert, which is chilled after baking, is a great make-ahead treat, according to managing editor Beth M. Knife.*

    1¹/₄ cups whipping cream
     ¹/₂ vanilla bean, split lengthwise
       5 egg yolks
     ¹/₂ cup canned pumpkin

    6   tablespoons granulated sugar
    2   tablespoons orange-flavored
        liquour
    1   teaspoon ground nutmeg
    ¹/₄ cup firmly packed brown sugar
    ¹/₂ teaspoon ground cinnamon

Preheat oven to 350 degrees. In a heavy small saucepan, bring whipping cream to a boil over medium-high heat. Remove from heat. Scrape seeds from vanilla bean into whipping cream; add bean. Let stand 20 minutes; discard bean.

In a medium bowl, whisk egg yolks, pumpkin, granulated sugar, liqueur, and nutmeg until smooth. Gradually whisk in whipping cream. Pour into five 4-ounce ramekins. Place in a 9 x 13-inch baking pan; fill pan halfway with hot water. Bake 25 to 30 minutes or until center is almost set. Cool 1 hour; cover and chill. (Can be made 1 day ahead.)

To serve, combine brown sugar and cinnamon in a small bowl. Sprinkle about 1 tablespoon over each brûlée; broil until sugar melts. Serve warm.
**Yield:** 5 servings

# HOLIDAY FOODS ON THE GO

*From office parties to potlucks to impromptu gatherings, holiday entertaining can be heavenly when you have a wealth of yummy make-ahead dishes on hand. These zippy appetizers, luscious desserts, and delightful entrée let you display your culinary talents — and still have time to enjoy the merriest of all seasons!*

A jazzed-up version of a Sunday dinner favorite, Mexican Rolled Meat Loaf wraps a zesty ground beef-sausage mixture around a colorful collection of vegetables and cheese. For maximum visual appeal, top the meat loaf slices with salsa and cheese and garnish with cilantro.

# MEXICAN ROLLED MEAT LOAF

*Serving is easy when meat loaf is made a day ahead.*

- ¹/₂ cup chopped onion
- ¹/₂ cup chopped celery
- ¹/₄ cup chopped sweet red pepper
- ¹/₄ cup chopped green pepper
- 2 tablespoons chopped sweet yellow pepper
- 4 cloves garlic, minced
- 2 tablespoons vegetable oil
- ¹/₂ cup drained whole kernel yellow corn
- ¹/₂ cup chopped fresh cilantro
- 1 pound lean ground beef
- 1 pound lean breakfast sausage
- 1¹/₄ cups salsa, divided
- ³/₄ cup plain bread crumbs
- 2 eggs
- 1¹/₂ teaspoons ground cumin
- 1 teaspoon chili powder
- ¹/₂ teaspoon salt
- ¹/₂ teaspoon ground black pepper
- 2 cups (8 ounces) shredded Monterey Jack cheese, divided
  Fresh cilantro to garnish

In a medium skillet, combine onion, celery, red pepper, green pepper, yellow pepper, and garlic in oil over medium-high heat. Stirring constantly, cook about 10 minutes or until vegetables are tender. Stir in corn and chopped cilantro; set aside.

Preheat oven to 350 degrees. In a large bowl, combine beef, sausage, ¹/₂ cup salsa, bread crumbs, eggs, cumin, chili powder, salt, and black pepper. Press meat mixture into a 10 x 14-inch rectangle on plastic wrap. Spread vegetable mixture over meat mixture to within 1 inch of edges. Sprinkle with 1 cup cheese. Beginning at 1 long edge and using plastic wrap to hold shape, roll up meat mixture jellyroll style; press to seal edge and ends. Transfer roll, seam side down, to a 10¹/₂ x 15¹/₂-inch jellyroll pan. Bake 50 to 55 minutes or until juices run clear. Cool 30 minutes. Cover and chill 4 hours or overnight.

Preheat oven to 300 degrees. To serve, cut meat loaf into 1-inch slices. Arrange slices on a heatproof serving dish. Spoon remaining ³/₄ cup salsa over slices. Cover with aluminum foil and bake 30 minutes. Uncover and sprinkle with remaining 1 cup cheese; bake 5 minutes longer or until cheese melts. Garnish with cilantro; serve warm.

**Yield:** about 12 servings

Crisp and nutty, Spicy Cheese Crackers receive a bit of "bite" from red pepper. An invigorating complement to Yuletide dishes, slushy Freezer Margaritas are mixed ahead of time and frozen overnight.

# SPICY CHEESE CRACKERS

- 2 jars (5 ounces each) pasteurized process sharp cheese spread
- ²/₃ cup butter or margarine, softened
- 1 teaspoon ground red pepper
- 1 teaspoon salt
- 2 cups all-purpose flour
- ³/₄ cup finely chopped pecans

In a large bowl, beat cheese spread, butter, red pepper, and salt until well blended. Add flour, ¹/₂ cup at a time, using hands to knead until all flour is incorporated. Knead in pecans. Divide dough into thirds. Shape each piece into an 8-inch-long log. Wrap in plastic wrap and chill overnight.

Preheat oven to 350 degrees. Cut logs into ¹/₈-inch slices. Transfer to a lightly greased baking sheet. Bake 8 to 10 minutes or until lightly browned. Serve warm or at room temperature. Store in a cookie tin.

**Yield:** about 13¹/₂ dozen crackers

# FREEZER MARGARITAS

- 2 cups water
- 1 cup sugar
- 1¹/₂ cups freshly squeezed lime juice (about 8 limes)
- 1¹/₂ cups tequila
- ³/₄ cup Triple Sec liqueur
  Lime zest to garnish

In a small saucepan, combine water and sugar over high heat. Stirring frequently, bring mixture to a boil. Remove syrup from heat and cool 1 hour.

In a 2-quart freezer container, combine syrup, lime juice, tequila, and liqueur. Cover and freeze overnight. To serve, spoon into glasses and garnish with lime zest.

**Yield:** about 6¹/₂ cups margaritas

*(From left)* Creamy Onion Puffs, seasoned with blue cheese and a touch of hot sauce, are savory hors d'oeuvres. Garnished with red and green peppers, festive Confetti Eggs are enriched with cream cheese and sour cream. Smoked Tuna Spread is a quick make-ahead appetizer.

## CONFETTI EGGS

8 hard-cooked eggs, shelled
1 package (3 ounces) cream cheese
¼ cup sour cream
2 tablespoons finely chopped celery
2 tablespoons finely chopped
    green pepper
2 tablespoons finely chopped sweet
    red pepper
1 tablespoon white wine vinegar
2 teaspoons minced onion
¼ to ½ teaspoon salt
¼ teaspoon ground black pepper
  Chopped sweet red and green
    peppers to garnish

Cut eggs in half lengthwise; transfer yolks to a medium bowl. Add cream cheese and sour cream to yolks; beat until smooth. Stir in celery, peppers, vinegar, onion, salt, and black pepper. Spoon about 1 tablespoon yolk mixture into each egg white. Garnish with red and green peppers. Store in an airtight container in refrigerator.
**Yield:** 16 servings

## ONION PUFFS

*This a good make-ahead appetizer.*

1 cup mayonnaise
1 package (8 ounces) cream cheese,
    softened
1 package (4 ounces) blue cheese,
    crumbled
2 tablespoons chopped fresh parsley
2 tablespoons minced onion
½ teaspoon finely minced garlic
¼ teaspoon hot pepper sauce
⅛ teaspoon ground white pepper
2 loaves (12 ounces each) sliced rye
    cocktail bread

In a medium bowl, combine mayonnaise, cream cheese, blue cheese, parsley, onion, garlic, pepper sauce, and white pepper. Cover and chill 2 hours to let flavors blend.

Use a 2-inch round cookie cutter to cut out bread. Spread 1 teaspoon cheese mixture onto each bread round. Place on an ungreased baking sheet. Cover and chill until ready to serve.

Preheat oven to 400 degrees. To serve, uncover appetizers and bake 10 to 15 minutes or until tops are puffy and lightly browned. Serve warm.
**Yield:** about 5 dozen puffs

## SMOKED TUNA SPREAD

1 package (8 ounces) cream cheese,
    softened
3 tablespoons drained capers
1 tablespoon minced onion
⅛ teaspoon ground red pepper
1 can (6 ounces) smoked tuna,
    drained
  Crackers to serve

In a medium bowl, beat cream cheese until fluffy. Stir in capers, onion, and red pepper. Gently stir in tuna. Cover and chill 2 hours to let flavors blend. Serve with crackers.
**Yield:** about 1½ cups spread

## SPECIAL PUMPKIN PIE

*Bake frozen pie a day ahead and chill.*

- 1 frozen 9-inch (2 pounds, 5 ounces) pumpkin pie
- 2 packages (3 ounces each) cream cheese, softened
- 1/4 cup sifted confectioners sugar
- 1/4 cup sour cream
- 1 tablespoon rum **or** 2 teaspoons rum extract
- 1/2 teaspoon vanilla extract
  Toasted walnut halves to garnish

Bake pumpkin pie according to package directions; cool. Cover and chill overnight.

In a small bowl, beat cream cheese and confectioners sugar until fluffy. Add sour cream, rum, and vanilla; beat until smooth. Spread topping over chilled pie. Garnish with walnut halves. Store in an airtight container in refrigerator.
**Yield:** about 8 servings

## DOUBLE CHOCOLATE DREAMS

- 16 ounces semisweet baking chocolate, chopped
- 1 cup butter or margarine, cut into pieces
- 1/3 cup strongly brewed coffee
- 1 1/2 cups sugar
- 4 eggs
- 1 teaspoon vanilla extract
- 1/2 cup all-purpose flour
- 1 cup chopped walnuts
- 1 package (6 ounces) white baking chocolate, coarsely chopped

Preheat oven to 375 degrees. Line a 9 x 13-inch baking pan with aluminum foil, extending foil over ends of pan; grease foil. In top of a double boiler, combine semisweet chocolate, butter, and coffee. Stirring frequently, cook over hot, not simmering, water until chocolate melts. Remove from heat; cool 15 minutes.

Place sugar in a large bowl. Add eggs, 1 at a time, beating well after each addition. Beat in vanilla. Gradually stir in cooled chocolate mixture and flour just until blended. Stir in walnuts and white chocolate. Pour into prepared pan. Bake 25 to 30 minutes or until center is set. Cool in pan on a wire rack. Cover and chill overnight.

Use ends of foil to lift brownies from pan. Cut into 1-inch squares. Store in an airtight container in refrigerator.
**Yield:** about 7 dozen brownies

*(Clockwise from top)* Special Pumpkin Pie, a quick-and-easy holiday delight, has a lusciously creamy rum-tinged topping. Rich and fudgy Double Chocolate Dreams feature chunks of white chocolate and melt-in-your-mouth middles. Finely textured Almond Pound Cakes add a distinctive flavor to an ever-popular dessert.

## ALMOND POUND CAKES

*These cakes freeze well.*

- 1 cup butter or margarine, softened
- 1 1/2 cups sugar
- 4 eggs
- 2 teaspoons almond extract
- 2 cups all-purpose flour
- 1 teaspoon baking powder
- 1/2 teaspoon salt
- 1/2 cup milk

Preheat oven to 350 degrees. Grease and flour four 3 1/4 x 5 3/4-inch loaf pans. In a large bowl, cream butter and sugar until fluffy. Add eggs, 1 at a time, beating well after each addition. Beat in almond extract. In a small bowl, combine flour, baking powder, and salt. Alternately beat dry ingredients and milk into creamed mixture, beating until well blended. Spread batter into prepared pans. Bake 33 to 37 minutes or until a toothpick inserted in center of cake comes out clean. Cool in pans 10 minutes. Remove from pans and cool completely on a wire rack. Store in an airtight container.
**Yield:** 4 cakes

139

# Angel Food

*Create your own seventh heaven when you treat a gathering of friends and family to the most celestial desserts ever! Our fabulous collection of goodies will satisfy anyone's sweet tooth — and we've even included a few low-fat items. With so many extravagant delicacies, it's not easy to choose a favorite. You'll want to share each and every one of them with the "angels" who grace your holiday table.*

Billowy swirls of white icing finish this decadent Lady Baltimore Cake, which features a fruity filling. Light in texture and rich in flavor, the traditional cake is just right for entertaining family and special friends.

# LADY BALTIMORE CAKE

### FRUIT FILLING
- 1 cup chopped dried figs
- $1/2$ cup chopped golden raisins
- $1/2$ cup orange juice

### CAKE
- 1 cup butter or margarine, softened
- 2 cups sugar
- 1 teaspoon grated orange zest
- 3 cups sifted cake flour
- 1 tablespoon baking powder
- $1/4$ teaspoon salt
- $1/2$ cup orange juice
- $1/2$ cup water
- 2 teaspoons vanilla extract
- 8 egg whites

### ICING
- $1 1/2$ cups sugar
- 5 tablespoons water
- 2 egg whites
- 2 tablespoons light corn syrup
- $1/4$ teaspoon cream of tartar
- 1 teaspoon vanilla extract
- 1 cup chopped pecans

For fruit filling, combine figs, raisins, and orange juice in a small bowl; set aside.

Preheat oven to 350 degrees. For cake, grease three 9-inch round cake pans. Line bottom of pans with waxed paper; grease waxed paper. In a large bowl, cream butter, sugar, and orange zest. In a medium bowl, combine cake flour, baking powder, and salt. In a small bowl, combine orange juice, water, and vanilla. Alternately add dry ingredients and orange juice mixture to creamed mixture, beating until well blended. In a medium bowl, beat egg whites until stiff peaks form. Fold egg whites into batter; pour into prepared pans. Bake 20 to 25 minutes or until a toothpick inserted in center of cake comes out clean. Cool in pans 10 minutes. Remove from pans and cool completely on a wire rack.

For icing, drain fruit mixture; set aside. In top of a double boiler, combine sugar, water, egg whites, corn syrup, and cream of tartar. Beat with an electric mixer until sugar is well blended. Place over simmering water; beat about 7 minutes or until soft peaks form. Remove from heat and add vanilla. Continue beating 2 minutes longer or until icing is desired consistency. In a medium bowl, fold fruit mixture and pecans into 1 cup icing. Spread filling between layers. Ice top and sides of cake with remaining icing. Store in an airtight container in refrigerator.
**Yield:** about 12 servings

Delicate and unmistakably sweet, Heavenly Angel Cookies live up to their name. These buttery, melt-in-your-mouth cookies are embellished with ethereal icing so they look as good as they taste.

## HEAVENLY ANGEL COOKIES

### COOKIES
- $3/4$ cup butter or margarine, softened
- 1 package (3 ounces) cream cheese, softened
- $1 3/4$ cups sifted confectioners sugar
- 1 egg
- $1/2$ teaspoon vanilla extract
- $1/2$ teaspoon almond extract
- 2 cups all-purpose flour
- $3/4$ teaspoon baking powder

### ICING
- 3 cups sifted confectioners sugar
- $2 1/2$ to 3 tablespoons water
- 2 teaspoons light corn syrup
- $1/2$ teaspoon vanilla extract
  Pink paste food coloring

For cookies, cream butter, cream cheese, and confectioners sugar in a large bowl. Beat in egg and extracts. In a small bowl, combine flour and baking powder. Add dry ingredients to creamed mixture; stir until a soft dough forms.

Divide dough into fourths. Wrap in plastic wrap and chill 2 hours or until firm enough to handle.

Preheat oven to 350 degrees. On a lightly floured surface, use a floured rolling pin to roll out one fourth of dough to $1/8$-inch thickness. Use a 4-inch-wide by $4 1/4$-inch-high angel-shaped cookie cutter to cut out cookies. Transfer to an ungreased baking sheet. Bake 7 to 9 minutes or until bottoms are lightly browned. Transfer cookies to a wire rack to cool.

For icing, combine confectioners sugar, water, corn syrup, and vanilla in a medium bowl; tint pink. Spoon icing into a pastry bag fitted with a small round tip. Pipe hair, face, and wing design onto each cookie. Use a medium tip to outline and fill in dresses with icing. Allow icing to harden. Store in a single layer in an airtight container.
**Yield:** about $1 1/2$ dozen cookies

## CRANBERRY ANGEL DESSERT

- 1 cup fresh cranberries
- 1/2 unpeeled orange, seeded
- 1 package (3 ounces) cranberry gelatin
- 1/3 cup boiling water
- 1/3 cup cold water
- 1 package (16 ounces) angel food cake mix
- 2 containers (8 ounces each) fat-free frozen whipped topping, thawed
- 1/2 teaspoon orange extract
  Fresh cranberries and orange zest to garnish

Process 1 cup cranberries and orange half in a food processor until coarsely ground. Transfer to a small bowl; cover and chill.

In a medium bowl, combine gelatin and boiling water; stir until gelatin dissolves. Stir in cold water; cover and chill 30 minutes, stirring after 15 minutes. Stir in chilled cranberry mixture. Cover and chill up to 2 hours.

Preheat oven to 350 degrees. Line bottom of a 9 x 13-inch baking pan with waxed paper. Prepare cake mix according to package directions. Pour batter into prepared pan. Bake 30 to 35 minutes or until top is golden brown and cake pulls away from sides of pan. Cool cake in pan.

Remove cake from pan and cut in half horizontally. Place bottom layer on a serving plate. Spread gelatin mixture over bottom layer. Replace top layer. Place whipped topping in a medium bowl. Sprinkle orange extract over topping; fold into topping. Ice cake with whipped topping. Garnish cake with cranberries and orange zest.

**Yield:** about 20 servings

**1 serving (1 slice):** 143 calories, 0.1 gram fat, 2.4 grams protein, 31.7 grams carbohydrate

## COCONUT CREAMS WITH PINEAPPLE RUM SAUCE

### COCONUT CREAMS

- 1 envelope unflavored gelatin
- 1/4 cup cold water
- 1/2 cup shredded unsweetened frozen coconut
- 3 eggs
- 1/2 cup sugar
- 1/8 teaspoon salt
- 1 1/4 cups milk
- 1 1/2 teaspoons vanilla extract
- 1 cup whipping cream

Light, fluffy cake is layered with fruity gelatin to make flavorful low-fat Cranberry Angel Dessert *(top)*. Pineapple Rum Sauce bathes our luscious Coconut Creams with sweetness.

### SAUCE

- 1 can (15 1/4 ounces) pineapple tidbits in juice
- 1 1/2 tablespoons cornstarch
- 1/2 cup sugar
- 1/4 cup coconut-flavored rum

For coconut creams, sprinkle gelatin over water in a small bowl; let stand. Process coconut in a food processor until finely chopped. In a small bowl, beat eggs, sugar, and salt until well blended. Combine egg mixture, coconut, and milk in top of a double boiler over simmering water. Stirring constantly, cook about 15 minutes or until mixture coats the back of a spoon. Stir in gelatin mixture and vanilla; continue stirring 1 minute or until gelatin dissolves. Remove from heat.

Transfer custard to a medium heatproof bowl; chill 35 minutes or until thickened, stirring every 5 minutes.

In a medium bowl, beat whipping cream until stiff peaks form. Fold whipped cream into chilled custard mixture. Spoon into lightly oiled 1/2-cup shortcake molds. Cover and chill 1 hour.

For sauce, combine 2 tablespoons pineapple juice and cornstarch in a small bowl. In a heavy small saucepan, combine pineapple, remaining juice, and sugar. Stirring constantly, bring to a boil over medium-high heat. Add cornstarch mixture; cook 3 minutes or until sauce thickens. Remove from heat. Stir in rum; cool. Unmold custards onto serving plates; top with sauce.

**Yield:** about 9 servings

# FRUIT CUPS WITH LEMON YOGURT SAUCE

1   can (15¼ ounces) pineapple
     tidbits in juice, drained
1   can (15 ounces) mandarin
     oranges in light syrup, drained
1   jar (10 ounces) maraschino
     cherries, drained and chopped
1   package (8 ounces) Neufchâtel
     cheese, softened
1   container (8 ounces) nonfat lemon
     yogurt
¾   cup plus 1½ teaspoons sifted
     confectioners sugar, divided
12  sheets frozen phyllo pastry, thawed
     and divided
     Butter-flavored vegetable cooking
     spray

In a medium bowl, combine pineapple, oranges, and cherries. Cover and chill.

In a medium bowl, beat cheese until fluffy. Add yogurt and ¾ cup confectioners sugar; beat until smooth. Cover and chill.

Preheat oven to 350 degrees. Stack 6 pastry sheets. Cover remaining pastry with a damp cloth. Spray top layer with cooking spray. Cut pastry into 5-inch squares. Working with 1 stack of pastry squares at a time, arrange layers with corners staggered. Place in every other cup of a greased 12-cup muffin pan. Bake 5 to 7 minutes or until lightly browned. Transfer pastries to a wire rack to cool. Repeat with remaining 6 pastry sheets.

To serve, sift remaining 1½ teaspoons confectioners sugar over pastries. Spoon 1 rounded tablespoon yogurt sauce into each pastry. Spoon ¼ cup fruit into each pastry cup. Top fruit with 1 rounded tablespoon yogurt sauce. Serve immediately.

**Yield:** about 12 servings

**1 serving (1 pastry):** 172 calories, 3.8 grams fat, 4.3 grams protein, 31.1 grams carbohydrate

# LEMON-RASPBERRY POUND CAKE

## SAUCE
1¼  cups seedless raspberry jam
1½  cups whipping cream
3   tablespoons raspberry liqueur

## CAKE
½   cup seedless raspberry jam
2   cups butter or margarine, softened
2½  cups sugar
8   eggs

Fruit Cups with Lemon Yogurt Sauce *(left)* offer a less sinful way to enjoy holiday pastries! Lemon-Raspberry Pound Cake is served atop a tantalizing raspberry sauce made with jam and liqueur.

3¼  cups all-purpose flour
½   teaspoon baking powder
¼   teaspoon salt
1   tablespoon freshly squeezed lemon
     juice
1½  teaspoons lemon extract

For sauce, melt jam in a small saucepan over medium-low heat. Remove from heat and slowly whisk in whipping cream. Whisk in liqueur. Transfer to an airtight container and chill.

Preheat oven to 325 degrees. For cake, beat jam in a small bowl with an electric mixer just until smooth; set aside. In a large bowl, cream butter and sugar. Add eggs, 1 at a time, beating well after each addition. Sift flour, baking powder, and salt into a medium bowl. Add dry ingredients to creamed mixture; beat until

well blended. Beat in lemon juice and lemon extract. Pour half of batter into a greased and floured 10-inch tube pan with a removable bottom. Spoon half of jam over batter. Repeat with remaining batter and jam. Gently swirl batter with a knife, pulling up from bottom through batter and folding over. Bake 1 hour 25 minutes to 1 hour 40 minutes or until a toothpick inserted in center of cake comes out clean. Cool cake in pan 15 minutes. Run a knife around edge of pan; remove sides of pan. Allow cake to cool completely. Run knife around bottom of cake; transfer to a cake plate.

To serve, spoon about 2 tablespoons sauce onto each serving plate. Place a slice of cake on sauce.

**Yield:** about 16 servings cake and 2½ cups sauce

# BANANA-ORANGE SPONGE CAKE

### CAKE
1¼ cups sugar, divided
2 egg yolks
1 tablespoon orange juice
1 teaspoon grated orange zest
1 teaspoon vanilla extract
¾ cup mashed bananas
1¾ cups sifted cake flour
½ teaspoon salt
7 egg whites
½ teaspoon cream of tartar

### GLAZE
1½ cups sifted confectioners sugar
2 tablespoons light corn syrup
2 tablespoons orange juice
½ teaspoon grated orange zest

Preheat oven to 325 degrees. For cake, beat 1 cup sugar, egg yolks, orange juice, orange zest, and vanilla in a large bowl until mixture is fluffy and lightens in color. Add bananas; beat until well blended. In a small bowl, combine flour and salt. Gradually fold dry ingredients into banana mixture. In a medium bowl, beat egg whites until soft peaks form. Gradually add remaining ¼ cup sugar and cream of tartar; beat until stiff peaks form. Stir 1 cup egg white mixture into banana mixture to lighten batter. Fold remaining egg white mixture into batter. Spoon batter into an ungreased 10-inch tube pan with a removable bottom. Bake 50 to 60 minutes or until the top of cake springs back when lightly touched. Invert pan onto a bottle to cool. Remove cake from pan and place on a serving plate.

For glaze, combine confectioners sugar, corn syrup, orange juice, and orange zest in a small bowl; stir until smooth. Drizzle glaze over cake.
**Yield:** 16 servings

**1 serving (1 slice):** 170 calories, 0.8 gram fat, 2.9 grams protein, 38.9 grams carbohydrate

# PEANUT BUTTER CREAM PIE

### FILLING
⅔ cup firmly packed brown sugar
2 tablespoons all-purpose flour
4 eggs
½ cup smooth peanut butter
2 cups half and half
1½ teaspoons vanilla extract

### COCOA CRUST
1 cup all-purpose flour
3 tablespoons cocoa

Drizzled with orange glaze, this Banana-Orange Sponge Cake *(top)* makes a delightfully light finale to a holiday feast. Peanut Butter Cream Pie is a rich dessert bursting with creamy chocolate and nutty flavors.

2 tablespoons firmly packed brown sugar
2 tablespoons granulated sugar
¼ teaspoon salt
⅓ cup chilled butter or margarine
1 egg

### TOPPING
1 cup whipping cream
¼ cup sugar
2 tablespoons shaved semisweet baking chocolate
Shaved chocolate to garnish

For filling, combine brown sugar and flour in top of a double boiler. Add eggs and peanut butter; beat until well blended. Add half and half; beat until smooth. Stirring constantly, cook over simmering water about 30 minutes or until mixture thickens and has the consistency of pudding. Stir in vanilla. Transfer filling to a bowl. Place plastic wrap directly on surface of filling. Chill 2 hours. Chill a medium bowl and beaters from an electric mixer in freezer.

Preheat oven to 400 degrees. For cocoa crust, combine flour, cocoa, sugars, and salt in a medium bowl. Using a pastry blender or 2 knives, cut in butter until mixture resembles coarse meal. Add egg; stir until well blended. Between sheets of plastic wrap, roll out dough to ⅛-inch thickness. Transfer to a 9-inch pie plate and use a sharp knife to trim edge of dough. Flute edge of dough. Chill crust 15 minutes.

Prick bottom of pie crust with a fork. Bake 12 to 15 minutes or until firm. Cool completely on a wire rack.

To serve, spoon filling into crust. For topping, beat whipping cream in chilled bowl until soft peaks form. Gradually add sugar and beat until stiff peaks form. Fold in 2 tablespoons shaved chocolate. Spread topping onto pie. Garnish with chocolate.
**Yield:** about 8 servings

# CARAMEL BROWNIE SUNDAES

*Caramel sauce is best if made early in the day and chilled.*

## CARAMEL SAUCE
- 2 cups sugar
- 1/2 cup water
- 1 1/2 cups whipping cream
- 1 quart vanilla ice cream, softened

## BROWNIES
- 1/3 cup butter or margarine, softened
- 1 1/2 cups firmly packed brown sugar
- 2 eggs
- 1 1/4 teaspoons vanilla extract
- 1 1/3 cups all-purpose flour
- 1 teaspoon baking powder
- 1/8 teaspoon salt
- 1 cup chopped pecans, toasted
  Toasted pecan halves to garnish

For caramel sauce, combine sugar and water in a heavy large saucepan over medium heat. Stir constantly until sugar dissolves. Using a pastry brush dipped in hot water, wash down any sugar crystals on sides of pan. Increase heat to medium-high. Swirling pan occasionally, cook without stirring until syrup is dark golden brown (about 10 minutes). Remove from heat. Using a long-handle whisk, slowly whisk in whipping cream. Return to medium heat. Whisking constantly, cook about 3 minutes or until color darkens. (Sauce will thicken as it cools.) Pour sauce into a heatproof container. Cool to room temperature. Cover and store in refrigerator. Spread ice cream into a 9-inch square baking pan. Cover and freeze 4 hours or until firm.

Preheat oven to 350 degrees. For brownies, cream butter and brown sugar in a large bowl until fluffy. Add eggs and vanilla; beat until smooth. In a small bowl, combine flour, baking powder, and salt. Add dry ingredients to creamed mixture; stir until well blended. Stir in chopped pecans. Spread batter into a greased 9-inch square baking pan. Bake 33 to 38 minutes or until crust starts to pull away from sides of pan. Cool in pan. Cut into 2-inch squares.

For each sundae, place 1 brownie on a serving plate. Cut ice cream into 2-inch squares. Place 1 ice cream square on brownie. Spoon 2 tablespoons caramel sauce over sundae. Garnish with a pecan half.

**Yield:** about 16 servings

For an elegant presentation, serve divine Caramel Brownie Sundaes topped with a rich homemade sauce and pecan halves. Refreshingly robust cups of Cappuccino Mousse will please coffee lovers.

## CAPPUCCINO MOUSSE

- 1 teaspoon unflavored gelatin
- 1/4 cup cold water
- 1 tablespoon instant espresso powder
- 1 can (14 ounces) sweetened condensed milk
- 1 teaspoon vanilla extract
- 1 cup whipping cream
  Whipped cream and ground cinnamon to garnish

Chill a medium bowl and beaters from an electric mixer in freezer. Sprinkle gelatin over water in a small saucepan; let stand 1 minute. Stirring constantly, cook over low heat until gelatin dissolves. Add espresso powder, stirring constantly until powder dissolves. Remove from heat. In a large bowl, combine sweetened condensed milk, vanilla, and espresso mixture; stir until well blended. In chilled bowl, beat whipping cream until stiff peaks form. Fold into espresso mixture. Spoon into cups; cover and chill.

To serve, garnish with whipped cream and sprinkle with cinnamon.

**Yield:** about 6 servings

# Sweets in Toyland

*Visions of sugarplums and a wonderland of playthings create a magical formula for Christmas excitement. For sweets to please kids of all ages, start with childhood favorites, from crispy rice cereal and peanut butter to chocolate and cherries. The result is a delightful collection of melt-in-your-mouth treats. Shaped into prancing reindeer, cuddly teddy bears, and clever cowboy gear, these goodies are guaranteed to make dreams come true.*

For a sure holiday hit, serve crunchy Maple Clusters *(left)* enriched with walnuts, whipping cream, and maple syrup. Decorated with candied cherries and crushed peppermints, Christmas Fudge makes a pretty package.

# CHRISTMAS FUDGE

- 2 cups sugar
- 3/4 cup evaporated milk
- 3 tablespoons butter or margarine
- 1/2 teaspoon salt
- 3 cups miniature marshmallows
- 1 package (11 1/2 ounces) milk chocolate chips
- 1 1/2 teaspoons vanilla extract
  Candied cherry halves and peppermint pieces to decorate

Line a 9 x 13-inch baking pan with aluminum foil, extending foil over sides of pan; grease foil. Butter sides of a heavy large saucepan. Combine sugar, evaporated milk, butter, and salt in pan. Stirring constantly, cook over medium-low heat until sugar dissolves. Using a pastry brush dipped in hot water, wash down any sugar crystals on sides of pan. Attach a candy thermometer to pan, making sure thermometer does not touch bottom of pan. Increase heat to medium and bring to a boil. Cook, without stirring, until mixture reaches soft-ball stage (approximately 234 to 240 degrees). Test about 1/2 teaspoon mixture in ice water. Mixture will easily form a ball in ice water but will flatten when held in your hand. Remove from heat. Add marshmallows, chocolate chips, and vanilla; stir until smooth. Pour into prepared pan. Chill 2 hours.

Use ends of foil to lift fudge from pan. Cut into 1-inch squares. Decorate fudge with cherries and peppermint. Store in an airtight container in refrigerator.

**Yield:** about 7 1/2 dozen pieces fudge

# MAPLE CLUSTERS

- 1 cup firmly packed brown sugar
- 1 cup granulated sugar
- 1/2 cup maple syrup
- 1/2 cup whipping cream
- 1 tablespoon light corn syrup
- 1/8 teaspoon salt
- 1 tablespoon butter or margarine
- 1 teaspoon vanilla extract
- 2 cups chopped walnuts

Butter sides of a heavy large saucepan. Combine sugars, maple syrup, whipping cream, corn syrup, and salt in pan. Stirring constantly, cook over medium-low heat until sugars dissolve. Using a pastry brush dipped in hot water, wash down any sugar crystals on sides of pan. Attach a candy thermometer to pan, making sure thermometer does not touch bottom of pan. Increase heat to medium and bring to a boil. Cook, without stirring,

Dancer and Prancer will never be as handsome as our Fun Reindeer Cookies! Prepared with almond and vanilla, these buttery cookies are carefully iced and embellished with festive spots and Rudolph-red noses and collars.

until mixture reaches 234 degrees. Test about 1/2 teaspoon mixture in ice water. Mixture will easily form a ball in ice water but will flatten when held in your hand. Remove from heat and stir in butter, vanilla, and walnuts. Using medium speed of an electric mixer, beat until candy thickens and begins to lose it gloss (about 3 minutes). Drop by teaspoonfuls onto waxed paper; cool completely. Store in an airtight container.

**Yield:** about 5 dozen candies

# FUN REINDEER COOKIES

### COOKIES

- 3/4 cup butter or margarine, softened
- 1/2 cup sugar
- 1 egg
- 1 teaspoon almond extract
- 1/2 teaspoon vanilla extract
- 1 3/4 cups all-purpose flour
- 3 tablespoons cornstarch
- 1/2 teaspoon baking powder
- 1/8 teaspoon salt

### ICING

- 2 3/4 cups sifted confectioners sugar
- 1/4 cup warm water
- 2 tablespoons meringue powder
- 1 teaspoon almond extract
  Red, green, brown, and copper paste food coloring

Preheat oven to 350 degrees. For cookies, cream butter and sugar in a large bowl until fluffy. Add egg and extracts; beat until smooth. In a small bowl, combine remaining ingredients. Add dry ingredients to creamed mixture; stir until a soft dough forms. On a lightly floured surface, use a floured rolling pin to roll out dough to 1/4-inch thickness. Use a 4 1/2 x 2 3/4-inch reindeer-shaped cookie cutter to cut out cookies. Transfer to a greased baking sheet. Bake 10 to 12 minutes or until bottoms are lightly browned. Transfer cookies to a wire rack to cool.

For icing, beat all ingredients at high speed of an electric mixer in a medium bowl 10 to 12 minutes or until stiff. Place 1/4 cup icing in each of 2 small bowls; tint red and green. Tint remaining icing using brown and a small amount of copper food coloring. Adding 1/4 teaspoon water at a time, add enough water to each icing until icing begins to flow from a spoon (about 3/4 teaspoon water in red and green and about 3 3/4 teaspoons water in brown). Spoon each icing into a pastry bag fitted with a small round tip. Outline and fill in each reindeer with brown icing. Let icing set up 30 minutes. Pipe green icing onto each reindeer for spots and eye. Pipe red icing for collar and nose. Let icing harden. Store in an airtight container.

**Yield:** about 1 1/2 dozen cookies

For a cowboy-style Christmas, fill up the chuck wagon with spicy Western Cookies! These boots, stars, and hats are edged in red icing and flavored with molasses. A kid-pleasing, pop-in-your-mouth treat, Porcupine Candies are a jumble of cocoa-flavored rice cereal, chocolate-covered raisins, and slivered almonds.

## WESTERN COOKIES

    1   cup butter or margarine, softened
   3/4  cup plus 2 tablespoons sugar
    1   egg
    3   tablespoons molasses
    1   teaspoon vanilla extract
   2 1/2 cups all-purpose flour
    1   tablespoon ground cinnamon
   1 1/2 teaspoons baking powder
   1/2  teaspoon salt
   1/2  teaspoon ground cloves
    2   tubes (4 1/4 ounces each) red
        decorating icing

For cookies, cream butter and sugar in a large bowl until fluffy. Add egg, molasses, and vanilla; beat until smooth. In a medium bowl, combine flour, cinnamon, baking powder, salt, and cloves. Add dry ingredients to creamed mixture; stir until a soft dough forms.

Divide dough into thirds and wrap in plastic wrap; chill 1 hour.

Preheat oven to 375 degrees. On a lightly floured surface, use a floured rolling pin to roll out dough to slightly thicker than 1/8 inch. Use about 1 3/4-inch-wide Western-shaped cookie cutters to cut out cookies (we used a hat, boot, and star). Place 1 inch apart on an ungreased baking sheet. Bake 4 to 6 minutes or until bottoms are lightly browned. Transfer cookies to a wire rack to cool.

Transfer icing into a pastry bag fitted with a small round tip. Pipe icing onto cookies. Let icing harden. Store in an airtight container.
**Yield:** about 13 dozen cookies

## PORCUPINE CANDIES

    5   cups cocoa-flavored crispy rice
        cereal
    1   cup chocolate-covered raisins
   1/2  cup slivered almonds
    3   cups miniature marshmallows
   1/4  cup butter or margarine
   1/2  teaspoon vanilla extract

In a large bowl, combine cereal, raisins, and almonds. Combine marshmallows and butter in a large saucepan. Stirring constantly, cook over low heat until smooth. Remove from heat. Stir in vanilla. Pour marshmallow mixture over cereal mixture; stir until well coated. Use greased hands to shape cereal mixture into 1 1/2-inch balls. Place on greased waxed paper; cool completely. Store in an airtight container in a cool place.
**Yield:** about 3 dozen candies

## CREAMY CHERRY BROWNIES

- 1 jar (16 ounces) maraschino cherries, divided
- 1 package (22 1/2 ounces) fudge brownie mix and ingredients to prepare brownies
- 1 package (3 ounces) cream cheese, softened
- 6 tablespoons butter or margarine, softened
- 2 1/4 cups sifted confectioners sugar

Preheat oven to 350 degrees. Drain cherries, reserving syrup. Line a 9 x 13-inch baking pan with aluminum foil, extending foil over ends of pan; grease foil. To prepare brownie mix, use reserved syrup plus enough water to equal water measurement in recipe. In a large bowl, combine brownie mix and required ingredients; stir until blended. Stir in 1 cup cherries. Spread mixture into prepared pan. Bake 27 to 30 minutes or until brownies begin to pull away from sides of pan and are firm. Cool in pan.

Finely chop remaining cherries; drain on paper towels and pat dry. In a medium bowl, beat cream cheese and butter until fluffy. Stir in confectioners sugar and chopped cherries. Spread icing over brownies. Cover and chill 2 hours or until icing is firm.

Lift brownies from pan using ends of foil. Cut into 2-inch squares. Store in an airtight container in refrigerator.
**Yield:** about 2 dozen brownies

## PEANUT BUTTER BALLS

- 1 1/4 cups smooth peanut butter
- 2/3 cup butter or margarine, softened
- 1 teaspoon vanilla extract
- 1 package (16 ounces) confectioners sugar
- 8 ounces chocolate candy coating
- 1 package (6 ounces) semisweet chocolate chips
  Chocolate sprinkles

In a large bowl, beat peanut butter, butter, and vanilla until well blended. Gradually beat in confectioners sugar. Shape mixture into 1-inch balls and place on a baking sheet lined with waxed paper. Chill 45 minutes or until firm.

In top of a double boiler, melt candy coating and chocolate chips over hot water. Dip peanut butter balls into melted chocolate. Return to baking sheet; sprinkle with chocolate sprinkles. Chill until chocolate hardens. Store in an airtight container in refrigerator.
**Yield:** about 6 1/2 dozen candies

Ideal for a tea party, our Creamy Cherry Brownies feature fluffy cream cheese icing atop fudgy morsels. Picture-perfect Peanut Butter Balls, with yummy peanutty centers, are first dipped in chocolate, then topped with chocolate sprinkles.

# BROWN SUGAR COOKIES

### COOKIES

- 1/2 cup butter or margarine, softened
- 1 cup firmly packed brown sugar
- 1 egg
- 1 teaspoon vanilla extract
- 1 1/2 cups all-purpose flour
- 1/2 teaspoon baking powder
- 1/2 teaspoon ground cinnamon
- 1/4 teaspoon salt

### ICING

- 1 1/2 cups sifted confectioners sugar
- 1 1/2 tablespoons cocoa
- 2 tablespoons milk
- 1/2 teaspoon vanilla extract

In a large bowl, cream butter and brown sugar until fluffy. Add egg and vanilla; beat until smooth. In a small bowl, combine flour, baking powder, cinnamon, and salt. Add dry ingredients to creamed mixture; stir until a soft dough forms. Divide dough in half. Wrap in plastic wrap and chill 2 hours.

Preheat oven to 375 degrees. On a lightly floured surface, use a floured rolling pin to roll out dough to 1/8-inch thickness. Use a 3 1/4 x 4-inch bear-shaped cookie cutter to cut out cookies. Transfer to an ungreased baking sheet. Bake 4 to 6 minutes or until edges are lightly browned. Transfer cookies to a wire rack to cool.

For icing, combine confectioners sugar, cocoa, milk, and vanilla in a small bowl; stir until smooth. Spoon icing into a pastry bag fitted with a medium petal tip. Pipe icing onto neck of each bear for scarf. Use a small round tip to pipe icing onto bear for eyes, nose, ear, and scarf fringe. Let icing harden. Store in an airtight container.

**Yield:** about 1 1/2 dozen cookies

# BAKED BOSTON PEANUTS

- 2 cups raw Spanish peanuts
- 1 cup sugar
- 1/2 cup water
- 1 teaspoon salt

Preheat oven to 350 degrees. In a heavy medium skillet, cook peanuts, sugar, and water over medium heat until all liquid is absorbed and peanuts are coated with sugar (about 20 minutes). Sprinkle with salt. Transfer to a greased 10 1/2 x 15 1/2-inch jellyroll pan. Bake 10 minutes, stirring after 5 minutes. Spread on aluminum foil to cool. Store in an airtight container.

**Yield:** about 4 cups peanuts

As cute as their furry, full-sized friends, these "beary" sweet Brown Sugar Cookies have cocoa-flavored scarves. Irresistibly crunchy, Baked Boston Peanuts are made by baking sugar-coated peanuts.

# CRISPY CHRISTMAS TREES

*Let the kids press mixture into cookie cutters and decorate trees.*

4¹/₂ cups miniature marshmallows
3 tablespoons butter or margarine
¹/₈ teaspoon green liquid food coloring
6 cups crispy rice cereal
  Small red cinnamon candies

Lightly grease twenty-two 3¹/₂ by 3¹/₄-inch tree-shaped cookie cutters and place on a greased baking sheet. Combine marshmallows and butter in a heavy Dutch oven over medium heat; stir until smooth. Tint mixture green. Stir in cereal. When cool enough to handle, use lightly greased hands to press about ¹/₄ cup of mixture into each cookie cutter. Press candies onto trees. Store in an airtight container in a cool place.
**Yield:** 22 trees

# PEANUT PLANK CANDY

3¹/₂ cups sugar
1 cup dark corn syrup
³/₄ cup whipping cream
5 cups chopped salted peanuts
1 tablespoon vanilla extract
¹/₂ teaspoon baking soda

Line a 10¹/₂ x 15¹/₂-inch jellyroll pan with aluminum foil, extending foil over ends of pan; grease foil. Butter sides of a heavy Dutch oven. Combine sugar, corn syrup, and whipping cream in pan. Stirring constantly, cook over medium-low heat until sugar dissolves. Using a pastry brush dipped in hot water, wash down any sugar crystals on sides of pan. Attach a candy thermometer to pan, making sure thermometer does not touch bottom of pan. Continuing to stir constantly, increase heat to medium and bring to a boil. Stir in peanuts. Cook, without stirring, until mixture reaches soft-ball stage (approximately 234 to 240 degrees). Test about ¹/₂ teaspoon mixture in ice water. Mixture will easily form a ball in ice water but will flatten when held in your hand. Remove from heat and stir in vanilla and baking soda (mixture will foam). Beat about 3 minutes or until candy begins to thicken. Pour into prepared pan; cool. Use foil to lift candy from pan. Cut into 1 x 2-inch pieces. Store in an airtight container.
**Yield:** about 6 dozen pieces candy

Packed into tree-shaped cookie cutters and trimmed with red cinnamon candies, Crispy Christmas Trees *(top)* make great party favors. Peanut Plank Candy, made with whipping cream and corn syrup, features crunchy chunks of peanut. Rolled in sugar and cinnamon before baking, Chocodoodles add a chocolate twist to the traditional snickerdoodle cookie recipe.

# CHOCODOODLES

1 cup butter or margarine, softened
1¹/₂ cups plus 3 tablespoons sugar, divided
2 eggs
1 teaspoon vanilla extract
2¹/₄ cups all-purpose flour
¹/₂ cup cocoa
2³/₄ teaspoons ground cinnamon, divided
1 teaspoon cream of tartar
1 teaspoon baking soda
¹/₄ teaspoon salt

Preheat oven to 375 degrees. In a large bowl, cream butter and 1¹/₂ cups sugar until fluffy. Add eggs and vanilla; beat until smooth. In a medium bowl, combine flour, cocoa, 1 teaspoon cinnamon, cream of tartar, baking soda, and salt. Add dry ingredients to creamed mixture; stir until a soft dough forms. In a small bowl, combine remaining 3 tablespoons sugar and 1³/₄ teaspoons cinnamon. Shape dough into 1-inch balls and roll in sugar mixture. Place balls 2 inches apart on a lightly greased baking sheet. Bake 6 to 8 minutes or until bottoms are lightly browned. Transfer cookies to a wire rack to cool. Store in an airtight container.
**Yield:** about 7 dozen cookies

Dazzle friends and relatives with delectable offerings from your kitchen. You can present a fun-loving stocking cake, some palate-pleasing truffles, or pretty cakes baked in fancy loaf pans. Whether trimmed in holiday greenery, wrapped in elegant fabric, or covered with luscious icing, our sweet remembrances are certain to be a hit!

What a jolly gift! Santa's Stocking Cake is overflowing with a festive array of candies, cookies, and decorative flourishes. A moist, chocolaty cake is hidden beneath the bright, fluffy icing.

## SANTA'S STOCKING CAKE

### CAKE

- 3/4 cup butter or margarine, softened
- 2 cups sugar
- 3 eggs
- 2 teaspoons vanilla extract
- 2 cups sifted cake flour
- 3/4 cup cocoa
- 1 1/2 teaspoons baking soda
- 1 teaspoon salt
- 1/2 teaspoon baking powder
- 1 1/2 cups buttermilk

### ICING

- 6 cups sifted confectioners sugar
- 1/2 cup vegetable shortening
- 1/2 cup butter or margarine, softened
- 5 to 6 tablespoons milk
- 2 teaspoons vanilla extract
- 1/4 teaspoon salt
  Red powdered food coloring

Refer to page 25 for stocking pattern. Preheat oven to 350 degrees. For cake, line bottom of a 9 x 13-inch baking pan with waxed paper; grease waxed paper and sides of pan. In a large bowl, cream butter and sugar until fluffy. Add eggs and vanilla; beat until smooth. In a medium bowl, combine cake flour, cocoa, baking soda, salt, and baking powder. Alternately beat dry ingredients and buttermilk into creamed mixture, beating until well blended. Pour batter into prepared pan. Bake 35 to 40 minutes or until a toothpick inserted in center of cake comes out clean. Cool in pan on a wire rack.

Remove cake from pan. Use pattern to cut out stocking. For cuff, cut a 3 x 8-inch piece from remaining cake. Place stocking and cuff on a foil-covered board.

For icing, combine all ingredients in a large bowl; beat until smooth and fluffy. Place 1 3/4 cups icing in a small bowl. Tint remaining icing red. Spread red icing on stocking and white icing on cuff.
**Yield:** about 18 servings

## CAKE TOPPERS

**You will need** assorted candies (wrapped and unwrapped), stick candies, purchased cookies, silk greenery pick, 1 yd of 1 1/4"w plaid ribbon, 6" of 1/16"w green ribbon, 12" of 1/8"w red ribbon, 6" lengths of floral wire, toothpicks, 1 3/4" x 3" piece of heavy white paper, black fine-point marker, hole punch, and craft glue.

For a tempting present, whip up a batch of Orange Coconut Truffles and fill a charming tissue-lined basket. The balls of rich, smooth chocolate cream are rolled in toasted coconut for a lovely finish.

**1.** For candy picks, use floral wire to wire groups of 3 to 5 candies to toothpicks.
**2.** For stocking hanger pick, cut an 8" length from plaid ribbon. Wire ribbon ends to a toothpick.
**3.** For bow pick, refer to **Making a Bow**, page 159, to tie remaining plaid ribbon into a bow. Wire bow to a toothpick.
**4.** For tag, cut one short end of paper to a point. Punch hole near pointed end of tag. Glue pieces of green and red ribbon to tag. Write message on tag. Use remaining red ribbon to tie tag to bow pick.
**5.** Insert picks, cookies, and stick candies into cake at top end of stocking.

## ORANGE-COCONUT TRUFFLES

- 2 egg yolks
- 1/4 cup whipping cream
- 1 package (12 ounces) semisweet chocolate chips
- 1/2 cup butter or margarine, softened
- 3 tablespoons cream cheese, softened
- 1/3 cup Grand Marnier liqueur
- 2 cups flaked coconut, toasted

Whisking constantly, cook egg yolks and whipping cream in top of a double boiler over simmering water until mixture reaches 160 degrees on a thermometer (about 8 minutes). Transfer egg mixture to a small bowl. Melt chocolate chips in top of double boiler. Remove from heat and add butter; stir until smooth. Beat egg yolk mixture into chocolate mixture (mixture will begin to thicken). Beat cream cheese and liqueur into chocolate mixture until smooth. Transfer to an airtight container; chill 3 hours or until firm.

Shape mixture into 1-inch balls. Roll in coconut. Store in an airtight container in refrigerator.
**Yield:** about 4 dozen truffles

Brushed with a sweet glaze, delicious Banana-Walnut Cakes are especially appealing when baked in fancy loaf pans. For an elegant presentation, fashion a gift bag from a beautiful fabric napkin, tie with gold cord, and accent with a pretty tag.

## BANANA-WALNUT CAKES

### CAKES
1 cup butter or margarine, softened
1 cup sugar
2 cups mashed bananas (about 4 medium bananas)
2 eggs
1 teaspoon vanilla extract
2 cups all-purpose flour
1 1/2 teaspoons baking soda
1/2 teaspoon ground cinnamon
1/4 teaspoon ground cardamom
1 cup coarsely chopped walnuts
1 cup flaked coconut

### GLAZE
1/2 cup sugar
1/4 cup butter or margarine
2 tablespoons water
2 tablespoons banana-flavored liqueur

Preheat oven to 325 degrees. For cakes, cream butter and sugar in a large bowl until fluffy. Add bananas, eggs, and vanilla; beat until well blended. In a small bowl, combine flour, baking soda, cinnamon, and cardamom. Add dry ingredients to creamed mixture; stir until well blended. Stir in walnuts and coconut. Spoon batter into a greased decorative 4-loaf baking pan (each loaf measures

about 3 1/2 x 6 inches) or into five 3 1/4 x 5 3/4-inch greased loaf pans. Bake 40 to 50 minutes or until a toothpick inserted in center of cake comes out clean. Cool in pan 10 minutes. Transfer cakes to a wire rack with waxed paper underneath.

For glaze, combine sugar, butter, and water in a small saucepan over medium-high heat. Bring mixture to a boil. Reduce heat to medium. Stirring constantly, cook 2 to 3 minutes or until mixture begins to thicken. Remove from heat; stir in liqueur. Brush glaze over warm cakes. Let glaze harden. Store in an airtight container.
**Yield:** 4 cakes in decorative pan or 5 cakes in loaf pans

## GIFT BAG FOR CAKE

**You will need** one 17" square printed cotton napkin, thread, plastic wrap, and gold cord with tassel ends for tie.

**1.** (Unless otherwise indicated, use a 1/2" seam allowance.) Fold napkin in half with right sides together and edges even. For back seam, sew long edges together; press seam open. With seam at center back, press bag flat. For bottom seam, sew along one end of bag. For bottom corners, match bottom seam to each side fold. Sew across each corner 1" from end (**Fig. 1**).

**Fig. 1**

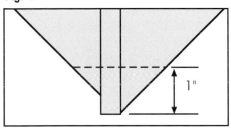

**2.** Turn bag right side out. Wrap cake with plastic wrap. Place cake inside bag. Use cord to tie bag closed.

## BRANDIED CHERRY HONEY SAUCE

    1   package (3 ounces) dried Bing
          cherries
  1/2   cup cherry brandy
    1   cup honey

In a small bowl, combine dried cherries and brandy; cover and let stand at room temperature overnight.

Stir honey into cherry mixture. Cover and store in refrigerator. Serve chilled or at room temperature with ice cream or cake.

**Yield:** about 1 1/2 cups sauce

Delightful Brandied Cherry Honey Sauce puts a crowning touch on cake or ice cream. We embellished a jar of the sauce with a sprig of flocked evergreen, a perky plaid bow, and a purchased gift tag mounted on green paper.

# GENERAL INSTRUCTIONS

## CROCHET

### Abbreviations:

| | |
|---|---|
| ch(s) | chain |
| dc | double crochet(s) |
| hdc | half double crochet(s) |
| mm | millimeters |
| Rnd(s) | Round(s) |
| sl st | slip stitch |
| sc | single crochet(s) |
| sp(s) | space(s) |
| st(s) | stitch(es) |
| tr | treble crochet(s) |
| YO | yarn over |

★ - work instructions following ★ as many **more** times as indicated in addition to the first time.

† **to** † - work all instructions from first † to second † **as many** times as specified.

() or [] - work enclosed instructions **as many** times as specified by the number immediately following **or** work all enclosed instructions in the stitch or space indicated **or** contains explanatory remarks.

Colon (:) - the number(s) given after a colon at the end of a row or round denote(s) the number of stitches you should have on that row or round.

**SINGLE CROCHET (sc):** To work a single crochet, insert hook in stitch or space indicated, YO and pull up a loop, YO and draw yarn through both loops on hook (**Fig. 1**).

**Fig. 1**

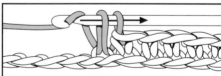

**DOUBLE CROCHET (dc):** To work a double crochet, YO, insert hook in stitch or space indicated, YO and pull up a loop (3 loops on hook), YO and draw yarn through 2 loops on hook (**Fig. 2**) (2 loops remain on hook), YO and draw yarn through remaining 2 loops on hook (**Fig. 3**).

**Fig. 2**

**Fig. 3**

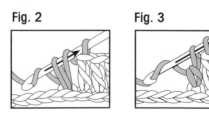

**HALF DOUBLE CROCHET (hdc):** YO, insert hook in stitch or space indicated, YO and pull up a loop (3 loops on hook), YO and draw yarn through all 3 loops on hook (**Fig. 4**).

**Fig. 4**

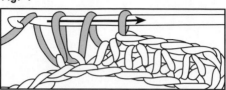

**SLIP STITCH (sl st):** This stitch is used to attach new yarn, to join work, or to move yarn across a group of stitches without adding height. Insert hook in stitch or space indicated, YO and draw yarn through stitch **and** loop on hook (**Fig. 5**).

**Fig. 5**

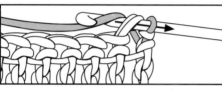

**TREBLE CROCHET (tr):** YO twice, insert hook in stitch or space indicated, YO and pull up a loop (4 loops on hook) (**Fig. 6**), (YO and draw yarn through 2 loops on hook) 3 times (**Fig. 7**).

**Fig. 6**

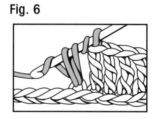

**Fig. 7**

## CROSS STITCH

**WORKING OVER TWO THREADS:** Use the "sewing" method, keeping stitching hand on right side of fabric and taking needle down and up with one stroke. To add support to stitches, place first Cross Stitch on fabric with stitch 1-2 beginning and ending where a vertical fabric thread crosses over a horizontal fabric thread (**Fig. 1**).

**Fig. 1**

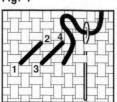

**COUNTED CROSS STITCH (X):** Work one Cross Stitch for each colored square on chart. For horizontal rows, work stitches in two journeys (**Fig. 2**). For vertical rows, complete each stitch as shown in **Fig. 3**. When working over two fabric threads, work Cross Stitch as shown in **Fig. 4**. When the chart shows a Backstitch crossing a colored square (**Fig. 5**), work the Cross Stitch first, then work the Backstitch over the Cross Stitch.

**Fig. 2**

**Fig. 3**

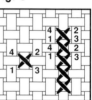

**Fig. 4**

**Fig. 5**

**HALF CROSS STITCH (½X):** This stitch is one journey of the Cross Stitch and is worked from lower left to upper right. **Fig. 6** shows two Half Cross Stitches, each worked over two fabric threads.

**Fig. 6**

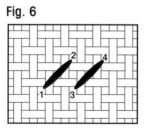

**QUARTER STITCH (¹/₄X):** Quarter Stitches are shown as triangular shapes of color in chart and color key. Come up at 1 (**Fig. 7**), then split fabric thread to take needle down at 2. When stitching over two threads, refer to **Fig. 8** to work Quarter Stitch.

Fig. 7

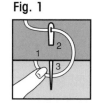
Fig. 8

**THREE-QUARTER STITCH (³/₄X):** Three-Quarter Stitches are shown as triangular shapes of color in chart and color key. Referring to **Fig. 9**, bring needle up at 1. Split fabric thread to go down at 2. To complete stitch, bring needle back up at 3 and go down at 4. When working over two fabric threads, refer to **Fig. 10**.

Fig. 9
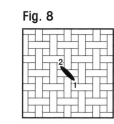

Fig. 10
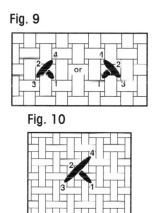

**BACKSTITCH (B'ST):** For outline or details, Backstitch (shown in chart and color key by colored straight lines) should be worked after the design has been completed (**Fig. 11**). When working over two threads, work Backstitch as shown in **Fig. 12**.

Fig. 11   Fig. 12
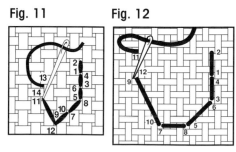

# EMBROIDERY STITCHES

## BLANKET STITCH
Bring needle up at 1; keeping thread below point of needle, go down at 2 and come up at 3 (**Fig. 1**). Continue working as shown in **Fig. 2**.

Fig. 1   Fig. 2
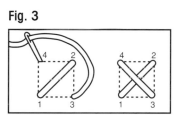

## CROSS STITCH
Bring needle up at 1 and go down at 2. Come up at 3 and go down at 4 (**Fig. 3**).

Fig. 3

## FRENCH KNOT
Bring needle up at 1. Wrap floss once around needle and insert needle at 2, holding floss with non-stitching fingers (**Fig. 4**). Tighten knot as close to fabric as possible while pulling needle back through fabric.

Fig. 4
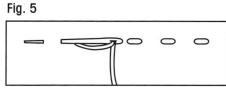

## RUNNING STITCH
Make a series of straight stitches with stitch length equal to the space between stitches (**Fig. 5**).

Fig. 5
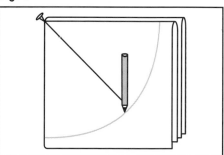

## STEM STITCH
Referring to **Fig. 6**, bring needle up at 1; keeping thread below stitching line, take needle down at 2 and bring needle up at 3. Take needle down at 4 and bring needle up at 5.

Fig. 6

## STRAIGHT STITCH
Bring needle up at 1 and go down at 2 (**Fig. 7**). Length of stitches may be varied as desired.

Fig. 7
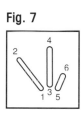

# CUTTING A FABRIC CIRCLE

1. Cut a square of fabric the size indicated in project instructions.
2. Matching right sides, fold fabric square in half from top to bottom and again from left to right.
3. Tie one end of string to a pencil. Measuring from pencil, insert a thumbtack through string at length indicated in project instructions. Insert thumbtack through folded corner of fabric. Holding tack in place and keeping string taut, mark cutting line (**Fig. 1**).

Fig. 1
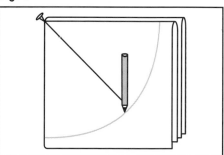

4. Cut along drawn line through all fabric layers.

## MAKING PATTERNS

**When pattern pieces are stacked or overlapped,** place tracing paper over pattern and follow a single colored line to trace pattern. Repeat to trace each pattern separately onto tracing paper.
**When entire pattern is shown,** place tracing paper over pattern and trace pattern. For a more durable pattern, use a permanent marker to trace pattern onto stencil plastic.
**When only half of pattern is shown (indicated by blue line on pattern),** fold tracing paper in half and match fold of paper to blue line of pattern. Trace pattern half; turn folded paper over and draw over traced lines on remaining side of paper. For a more durable pattern, use a permanent marker to trace pattern half onto stencil plastic. Turn stencil plastic over, align dashed lines, and trace pattern half again to form a whole pattern.

## MAKING APPLIQUÉS

**To prevent darker fabrics from showing through,** white or light-colored fabrics may need to be lined with fusible interfacing before applying fusible web.
**To make reverse appliqué pieces,** trace pattern onto tracing paper; turn traced pattern over and continue to follow all steps using reversed pattern.

1. Use a pencil to trace pattern onto paper side of web as many times as indicated in project instructions for a single fabric.
2. Follow manufacturer's instructions to fuse traced patterns to wrong side of fabrics. Do not remove paper backing.
3. Cut out appliqué pieces along traced lines. Remove paper backing.
4. Arrange appliqués web side down on project; overlapping as necessary. Appliqués can be temporarily held in place by touching appliqués with tip of iron. If appliqués are not in desired position, lift and reposition.
5. Fuse appliqués in place.

## MACHINE APPLIQUÉ

1. Pin or baste a piece of stabilizer slightly larger than design to wrong side of background fabric under design.
2. Set sewing machine for a medium width zigzag stitch. Beginning on a straight edge of appliqué if possible, position project under presser foot so that most of stitching will be on appliqué.

Take a stitch in fabric and bring bobbin thread to top. Holding both threads toward you, sew over threads for two or three stitches to secure. Stitch over all exposed raw edges of appliqué(s) and along detail lines as indicated in instructions.
3. When stitching is complete, remove stabilizer. Pull loose threads to wrong side of fabric; knot and trim ends.

## SEWING SHAPES

1. Center pattern on wrong side of one fabric piece and use fabric marking pen to draw around pattern. **Do not cut out**.
2. Place fabric pieces right sides together. Leaving an opening for turning, carefully sew **directly on drawn line** to join fabric pieces.
3. Leaving a $1/4$" seam allowance, cut out shape. Clip seam allowance at curves and corners. Turn shape right side out.

## BINDING

### MAKING BINDING
1. To determine length of binding strip needed, measure edges of item to be bound (**Fig. 1**). Add 12" to measurement.

**Fig. 1**

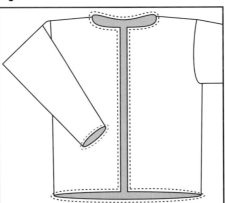

2. To give binding flexibility to fit around corners and curved edges, cut fabric strips on the bias. Cut bias strips the width indicated in project instructions and piece as necessary for determined length.

### ADDING SEWN BINDING
1. Matching wrong sides and raw edges, press binding strip in half lengthwise.
2. Press one end of binding strip diagonally (**Fig. 2**).

**Fig. 2**

3. Beginning with pressed end several inches from a corner, pin binding to right side of item along one edge.
4. When first corner is reached, mark $1/4$" from corner of item (**Fig. 3**).

**Fig. 3**

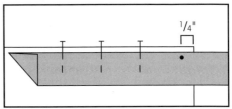

5. Using a $1/4$" seam allowance, sew binding to item, backstitching at beginning and when mark is reached (**Fig. 4**).

**Fig. 4**

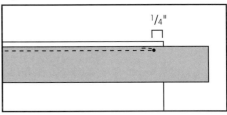

6. Fold binding up as shown in **Fig. 5**. Fold down and pin binding to adjacent side (**Fig. 6**). Mark $1/4$" from edge of item at next corner.

**Fig. 5**

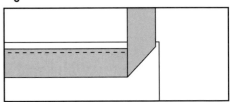

**Fig. 6**

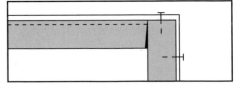

**7.** Backstitching at edge of binding, sew pinned binding to item (**Fig. 7**); backstitch when next mark is reached. Lift needle and clip thread.

**Fig. 7**

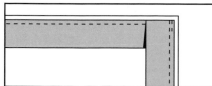

**8.** Repeat Steps 6 and 7 to continue sewing binding to item until binding overlaps beginning end by 2". Trim excess binding.
**9.** If binding a quilt, trim backing and batting even with edges of quilt top.
**10.** For a mitered corner, fold binding over to backing of item and pin pressed edge in place, covering stitching line (**Fig. 8**). Fold adjacent edge over to backing of item, forming a mitered corner (**Fig. 9**); pin in place. Repeat for each corner.

**Fig. 8**

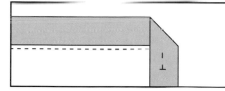

**Fig. 9**

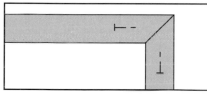

**11.** Hand sew binding to backing, taking care not to stitch through front of item.

## MAKING A BOW

**Note:** Loop sizes given in project instructions refer to the length of ribbon used to make one loop of bow.

**1.** Leaving one ribbon end free for desired length streamer, hold ribbon between index finger and thumb. Twisting ribbon to keep right side out, make a loop on each side of thumb (**Fig. 1**).

**Fig. 1**

**2.** Continue making loops on each side of thumb for desired number of loops. If center loop is desired, form half the number of bow loops, then loosely wrap ribbon around thumb as shown in **Fig. 2**; form remaining bow loops.

**Fig. 2**

**3.** To secure bow, tightly tie a length of ribbon or twist a length of wire around center of bow, threading length through center loop if necessary.

## WORKING WITH WAX

### MELTING WAX

**Caution:** Do not melt wax over an open flame or in a pan placed directly on burner.
**1.** Cover work area with newspaper.
**2.** Heat 1" of water in a saucepan to boiling. Add water as necessary.
**3.** Place wax in a large can. If pouring wax, pinch top rim of can to form a spout. If dipping candles, use a can 2" taller than height of candle to be dipped.
**4.** To melt wax, place can in boiling water, reduce heat to simmer. If desired, melt crayon pieces in wax for color. Use a craft stick to stir, if necessary.

### SETTING WICKS AND POURING WAX

**1.** Cut a length of wax-coated wick 1" longer than depth of candle container.
**2.** Using an oven mitt, carefully pour wax into container.
**3.** Allow wax to harden slightly and insert wick at center of candle. Allow wax to harden completely.

### DIPPING CANDLES

**1.** Holding candle by wick, carefully dip candle into wax. Remove from wax and allow to harden slightly. Repeat for additional coats of wax.
**2.** After final dipping, place candles away from heat and allow to harden completely.

## PAPER TWIST ROSES

**You will need** desired color of paper twist, tracing paper, pencil, and a hot glue gun.

**1.** For rose center, cut a 13" length of paper twist; untwist. Cut a 3" x 13" strip from untwisted paper. Fold one short edge of strip 1/4" to wrong side. Matching wrong sides, fold strip in half lengthwise.
**2.** Beginning with unfolded end and with long folded edge at top, roll about one quarter of strip tightly; glue to secure. Roll remainder of strip loosely, making small pleats in bottom edge and gluing to secure.
**3.** Trace rose petal pattern onto tracing paper. Use pattern to cut four to six petals from untwisted paper. Wrap side edges of each petal around a pencil to curl (**Fig. 1**).

**Fig. 1**      ROSE PETAL

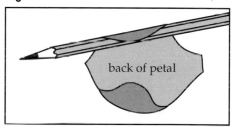

back of petal

**4.** Slightly overlapping petals, glue desired number of petals around base of rose center; allow to dry.

## MAKING A HANGER

Use needle to thread 8" of clear thread through top of ornament. Knot ends together 3" above ornament and trim ends.

# CREDITS

We want to extend a warm *thank you* to the generous people who allowed us to photograph our projects in their homes.

- *Country Spice* and *Yuletide Memories:* Charles and Peg Mills
- *Toyland Express:* Richard and Lange Cheek
- *Humble Holy Family:* Dennis and Tricia Hendrix
- *Snowman Frolic:* Tom and Robin Steves
- *Radiant White Christmas:* Dr. Jerry and Gwen Holton
- *Holly-Jolly Felt:* Mr. and Mrs. James M. Adams
- *A Festival of Wreaths:* William and Nancy Appleton, Charles and Peg Mills, Duncan and Nancy Porter
- *New England Holiday Brunch:* Duncan and Nancy Porter

A special thanks goes to the following businesses for permitting us to photograph projects on their premises.

- *Beribboned Elegance:* Hotze House Bed and Breakfast, 1619 Louisiana Street, Little Rock, Arkansas 72206 and The Empress of Little Rock Bed and Breakfast, 2120 Louisiana Street, Little Rock, Arkansas 72206
- *Ski Lodge Supper:* Pinnacle Vista Lodge, 7510 Highway 300, Little Rock, Arkansas 72212

We also want to recognize Mike and Jodie Davis, who allowed us to photograph a portion of the *Holiday Traditions* section in their home.

A special thanks is also extended to Monroe Salt Works of Monroe, Maine, for the use of dishes in *Ski Lodge Supper.*

We would like to recognize Viking Husqvarna Sewing Machine Company of Cleveland, Ohio, for providing the sewing machines used to make many of our projects.

To Magna IV Color Imaging of Little Rock, Arkansas, we say thank you for the superb color reproduction and excellent pre-press preparation.

Our sincere appreciation goes to photographers Ken West, Larry Pennington, Mark Mathews, Karen Shirey, and David Hale, Jr., of Peerless Photography, Little Rock, Arkansas; and Jerry R. Davis of Jerry Davis Photography, Little Rock, Arkansas, for their time, patience, and excellent work.

To the talented people who helped in the creation of the following projects and recipes in this book, we extend a special word of thanks.

- *Holly-Jolly Felt* collection, pages 80-87: Holly Witt for Banar Designs
- *Winter Warmer* design, page 113: Deborah Lambein
- *Fresh Apple and Orange Cake,* page 129: Etta Mae Spencer
- *Snowflake Mousse with Crimson Raspberry Sauce,* page 129: Becky Werle
- *Chicken-Rice Soup,* page 130: Aurora Huston
- *Strawberry Pretzel Salad,* page 130: Norma Siar
- *Cranberry Salad,* page 130: Gay Haller
- *Candied Apples,* page 131: Mamie Elizabeth Pulliam
- *Cheesy Spinach Casserole,* page 131: Linda Trimble
- *Mother's Chicken and Dressing,* page 131: Lucille Henry
- *Aunt Ruth's Cheese Grits,* page 132: Ruth Murphree
- *Cornish Game Hens,* page 132, and *Pumpkin-Eggnog Pie,* page 134: Roberta Aulwes
- *Refrigerator Yeast Rolls,* page 132: Leslie Loring Krebs
- *Glass Candy,* page 133, and *Spicy Cheese Crackers,* page 137: Jean Evans Pharr
- *Microwave Pecan Pralines,* page 133: Ellen Daniels
- *Peanut Butter Pie,* page 134: Lylln Craig
- *Italian Cream Cake,* page 134: Nelwyn Gray
- *Lemon Krumkake* and *Berlinerkranser,* page 135: Andrea Ahlen
- *Pumpkin Crème Brûlée,* page 135: Beth M. Knife
- *Double Chocolate Dreams,* page 139: Alan Caudle
- *Porcupine Candies,* page 148: Susan Warren Reeves

We are sincerely grateful to the people who assisted in making and testing the projects in this book: Arlene Allen, Debbie Anderson, Lisa Arey, Kandi Ashford, Linda Bassett, Vicky Bishop, JoAnn Bowling, Carolyn Breeding, Mike Cates, Alice Crowder, Melinda Galloway, Nelwyn Gray, Laura Holyfield, Catherine Hubmann, Karen Jackson, Mimi Jones, Ruby Solida, Helen Stanton, Margaret Taverner, Karen Tyler, and Janice Williams; and members of the Gardner Memorial United Methodist Church, North Little Rock, Arkansas: Elois Allain, Maxine Bramblett, Leon Dickey, Vina Lendermon, Fredda McBride, Carol Pittman, Edna Sikes, Betty Smith, Esther Starkey, and Thelma Starkey.